More Praise for

The Big Short

by Michael Lewis

"Lewis brilliantly takes us inside the subprime mortgage industry. . . . [He] has accessibly and expertly described a broken financial system that rewards bad decisions and fraudulent alchemy (turning garbage into gold), then shifts the inevitable losses to the strapped U.S. taxpayer." —Chuck Leddy, *Boston Globe*

"If you read only one book about the cause of the recent financial crisis, let it be Berkeley author Michael Lewis's *The Big Short* . . . [which] manages to give us the truest picture yet of what went wrong on Wall Street—and why." —Steven Pearlstein, *Washington Post*

"[A] rollicking narrative: a tale of beleaguered little guys betting against monster banks and fund managers, and, in the end, winning. . . . This is an assiduously reported and beautifully written book. There aren't many reasons to be happy about the global financial crisis, but here's one: that it brought Michael Lewis back to his roots, to produce what is probably the single best piece of financial journalism ever written." —Felix Salmon, Reuters blog / *Barnes & Noble Review*

"No one writes with more narrative panache about money and finance than Lewis. . . . [An] entertaining new book. . . . Lewis does a colorful job of introducing the lay reader to the Darwinian world of the bond market." —Michiko Kakutani, *New York Times*

"In *The Big Short* best-selling author Michael Lewis delivers fascinating tales of how a few professional investors foresaw the collapse of the subprime mortgage market and then pocketed millions from their big bets." —*USA Today*

"If you think you understand how and why our economy fell apart and haven't read *The Big Short*, you're wrong. The book is that important. Even more amazing, Lewis is such a good and entertaining writer that he's able to hold your attention while explaining what credit default swaps, collateralized debt obligation, and the mysteriously un-acronymized 'tranches' are and why they matter." —Bob Lewis, IS Survivor Publishing

"Lewis's book is as personal, entertaining, and startling as anything he's written . . . a chilling example of what happens when buyers fail to heed 'let the buyer beware.' " —Mark Lenz, *Daily Telegram* (Adrian, MI)

"Few works have shaped a legislative debate quite like Lewis's story about investors who made a killing by betting on the housing crash. . . . The book has created a kind of defining counternarrative of the economic collapse." —Marin Cogan, Politico.com

"Michael Lewis adds to his impressive collection of beautifully written books of nonfiction with a fascinating tale."
—G. Pascal Zachary, *San Francisco Chronicle*

"Best-selling author Michael Lewis creates a gem of a story . . . set in the late stages of the recent housing bubble, a period already chronicled in more than 100 nonfiction titles published in the past 18 months. But Lewis finds an ingenious new path. To treat his new book as another Wall Street exposé doesn't begin to do justice to the audacity of the story." —George Anders, *Forbes*

"The fastest-selling nonfiction book in America right now—an instant No. 1 on Amazon—is *The Big Short*, by the journalist Michael Lewis. An even better storyteller than Stieg Larsson."
—Frank Rich, *New York Times*

"Lewis turns the crisis into a true financial thriller that screams of Wall Street's greed, recklessness, deceit, incompetence and hubris. Readers from generalists through specialists will find this fast-paced, engaging account both illuminating and disturbing. Highly recommended." —*Library Journal*

"It is a testament to Lewis's writing skill that although everyone knows how things have turned out, *The Big Short* still crackles with tension and intrigue. A fine narrative about how the engines of greed, steered by the forces of amorality and stupidity, have driven us all off the cliff." —*Utah Daily Herald*

"It's the economy . . . the hows and whys behind its fall are the subjects of this humorous—yes, *humorous*—account." —*Booklist*

"In narrative, Lewis, as ever, doesn't disappoint: He gets inside the heads of his fascinating characters and vividly describes the complex financial structures they built and destroyed."
—Tim Fernholz, *American Prospect*

"Its narrative has the same seat-of-your-pants, almost breathless feel [as *Liar's Poker*]." —TJ, *Entertainment Weekly*

"The story of the crash is, overwhelmingly, a tale of failure. But Lewis managed to find quirky investors who minted fortunes by making unpopular, calculated bets on a financial meltdown. . . .

[He] constructs a story that is funny, incisive, profanity-laced and illuminating—full of difficult-to-like underdogs whose vindication and enrichment we end up cheering."

—*New York Times Book Review*

"Lewis is the rare writer who can tackle a subject arcane enough to make your eyes glaze over, and make it read like a thriller. . . . A fantastic read." —Michael Mechanic, *Mother Jones*

"Lewis does an extraordinary job elucidating the perils of shorting the very bonds that buoyed the American economy after September 11 and made a fortune for every firm on the Street. . . . His renowned eye for color is as sharp as ever." —Michael Osinki, *Bloomberg Businessweek*

"Lewis brings his gifts for narrative and his usual quest for value into the ultimate minefield: explaining how the American economy was collapsed by Wall Street's failure to distinguish wealth from value."

—Kevin Horrigan, *St. Louis Post-Dispatch*

"Lewis has a knack for illuminating abstraction via masterfully chosen human examples." —Anand Chokkavelu, *The Motley Fool*

"*The Big Short* is a rollicking read. . . . Somehow Michael has taken the bewildering events leading up to the financial crisis and found a breezy story to tell, one with a handful of vivid characters whose common virtue is the ability to smell a rat."

—Joel Achenbach, Achenblog, *Washington Post*

The Big Short

Also by Michael Lewis

Home Game

Liar's Poker

The Money Culture

Pacific Rift

Losers

The New New Thing

Next

Moneyball

Coach

The Blind Side

EDITED BY MICHAEL LEWIS

Panic

The Big Short

Inside the Doomsday Machine

Michael Lewis

W. W. NORTON & COMPANY

NEW YORK LONDON

Printed in the United States of America
First published as a Norton paperback 2011

For information about permission to reproduce selections from this book,
write to Permissions, W. W. Norton & Company, Inc.,
500 Fifth Avenue, New York, NY 10110

For information about special discounts for bulk purchases, please contact
W. W. Norton Special Sales at specialsales@wwnorton.com or 800-233-4830

Manufacturing by Courier Westford
Book design by Lovedog Studio
Production manager: Anna Oler

Library of Congress Cataloging-in-Publication Data

Lewis, Michael (Michael M.)
The big short : inside the doomsday machine / Michael Lewis.—1st ed.
p. cm.
ISBN 978-0-393-07223-5 (hardcover)
1. United States—Economic conditions—2001-2009. 2. Global Financial Crisis,
2008–2009. 3. Financial crises—United States—History—21st century. I. Title.
HC106.83.L5 2010
330.973—dc22

2010004804

ISBN 978-0-393-33882-9 pbk.

W. W. Norton & Company, Inc.
500 Fifth Avenue, New York, N.Y. 10110
www.wwnorton.com

W. W. Norton & Company Ltd.
Castle House, 75/76 Wells Street, London W1T 3QT

8 9 0

For
Michael Kinsley

To whom I still owe an article

The most difficult subjects can be explained to the most slow-witted man if he has not formed any idea of them already; but the simplest thing cannot be made clear to the most intelligent man if he is firmly persuaded that he knows already, without a shadow of doubt, what is laid before him.

—Leo Tolstoy, 1897

Contents

PROLOGUE

Poltergeist

The willingness of a Wall Street investment bank to pay me hundreds of thousands of dollars to dispense investment advice to grown-ups remains a mystery to me to this day. I was twenty-four years old, with no experience of, or particular interest in, guessing which stocks and bonds would rise and which would fall. Wall Street's essential function was to allocate capital: to decide who should get it and who should not. Believe me when I tell you that I hadn't the first clue. I'd never taken an accounting course, never run a business, never even had savings of my own to manage. I'd stumbled into a job at Salomon Brothers in 1985, and stumbled out, richer, in 1988, and even though I wrote a book about the experience, the whole thing still strikes me as totally preposterous—which is one reason the money was so easy to walk away from. I figured the situation was unsustainable. Sooner rather than later, someone was going to identify me, along with a lot of people more or less like me, as a fraud. Sooner rather than later would come a Great Reckoning, when Wall Street would wake up and hundreds, if not thousands, of young people like me, who had no business making huge bets with other people's money or persuading other people to make those bets, would be expelled from finance.

When I sat down to write my account of the experience—*Liar's Poker*, it was called—it was in the spirit of a young man who thought he was getting out while the getting was good. I was merely scribbling down a message and stuffing it into a bottle for those who passed through these parts in the far distant future. Unless some insider got all of this down on paper, I figured, no future human would believe that it had happened.

Up to that point, just about everything written about Wall Street had been about the stock market. The stock market had been, from the very beginning, where most of Wall Street lived. My book was mainly about the bond market, because Wall Street was now making even bigger money packaging and selling and shuffling around America's growing debts. This, too, I assumed was unsustainable. I thought that I was writing a period piece about the 1980s in America, when a great nation lost its financial mind. I expected readers of the future would be appalled that, back in 1986, the CEO of Salomon Brothers, John Gutfreund, was paid $3.1 *million* as he ran the business into the ground. I expected them to gape in wonder at the story of Howie Rubin, the Salomon mortgage bond trader, who had moved to Merrill Lynch and promptly lost $250 million. I expected them to be shocked that, once upon a time on Wall Street, the CEOs had only the vaguest idea of the complicated risks their bond traders were running.

And that's pretty much how I imagined it; what I never imagined is that the future reader might look back on any of this, or on my own peculiar experience, and say, "How quaint." How *innocent*. Not for a moment did I suspect that the financial 1980s would last for two full decades longer, or that the difference in degree between Wall Street and ordinary economic life would swell to a difference in kind. That a single bond trader might be paid $47 million a year and feel cheated. That the mortgage bond market invented on the Salomon Brothers trading floor, which seemed like such a good idea at the time, would lead to the most purely *financial* economic disaster in history. That exactly twenty years after Howie Rubin became a scandalous household name for losing $250 million, another mortgage bond trader named Howie, inside Morgan Stanley, would lose $9 *billion* on a single mortgage trade, and remain essentially unknown, without anyone beyond a small circle inside Morgan Stanley ever hearing about what he'd done, or why.

When I sat down to write my first book, I had no great agenda, apart from telling what I took to be a remarkable tale. If you'd gotten a few drinks in me and then asked what effect the book would have on the world, I might have said something like, "I hope that college students trying to decide what to do with their lives might read it and decide that it's silly to phony it up, and abandon their passions or even their faint interests, to become financiers." I hoped that some bright kid at Ohio State University who really wanted to be an oceanographer would read my book, spurn the offer from Goldman Sachs, and set out to sea.

Somehow that message was mainly lost. Six months after *Liar's Poker* was published, I was knee-deep in letters from students at Ohio State University who wanted to know if I had any other secrets to share about Wall Street. They'd read my book as a how-to manual.

In the two decades after I left, I waited for the end of Wall Street as I had known it. The outrageous bonuses, the endless parade of rogue traders, the scandal that sank Drexel Burnham, the scandal that destroyed John Gutfreund and finished off Salomon Brothers, the crisis following the collapse of my old boss John Meriwether's Long-Term Capital Management, the Internet bubble: Over and over again, the financial system was, in some narrow way, discredited. Yet the big Wall Street banks at the center of it just kept on growing, along with the sums of money that they doled out to twenty-six-year-olds to perform tasks of no obvious social utility. The rebellion by American youth against the money culture never happened. Why bother to overturn your parents' world when you can buy it and sell off the pieces?

At some point, I gave up waiting. There was no scandal or reversal, I assumed, sufficiently great to sink the system.

Then came Meredith Whitney, with news. Whitney was an obscure analyst of financial firms for an obscure financial firm, Oppenheimer and Co., who, on October 31, 2007, ceased to be obscure. On that day she predicted that Citigroup had so mismanaged its affairs that it would need to slash its dividend or go bust. It's never entirely clear on any given day what causes what inside the stock market, but it was pretty clear that, on October 31, Meredith Whitney caused the market in financial stocks to crash. By the end of the trading day, a woman whom basically no one had ever heard of, and who could have been dismissed as a nobody, had shaved 8 percent off the shares of Citigroup and $390 billion off the value of the U.S. stock market. Four days later, Citigroup CEO Chuck Prince resigned. Two weeks later, Citigroup slashed its dividend.

From that moment, Meredith Whitney became E. F. Hutton: When she spoke, people listened. Her message was clear: If you want to know what these Wall Street firms are really worth, take a cold, hard look at these crappy assets they're holding with borrowed money, and imagine what they'd fetch in a fire sale. The vast assemblages of highly paid people inside them were worth, in her view, nothing. All through 2008, she followed the bankers' and brokers' claims that they had put their problems behind them with this write-down or that capital raise with her own claim: *You're wrong. You're still not facing up to how badly you have mismanaged your business. You're still not acknowledging billions of dollars in losses on subprime mortgage bonds. The value of your securities is as illusory as the value of your people.* Rivals accused Whitney of being overrated; bloggers accused her of being lucky. What she was, mainly, was right. But it's true that she was, in part, guessing. There was no way she could have known what was going to happen to these Wall Street firms, or even the extent of their losses in the subprime mortgage market. The CEOs themselves didn't know. "Either that or they are all liars," she said, "but I assume they really just don't know."

Now, obviously, Meredith Whitney didn't sink Wall Street. She'd just expressed most clearly and most loudly a view that turned out to be far more seditious to the social order than, say, the many campaigns by various New York attorneys general against Wall Street corruption. If mere scandal could have destroyed the big Wall Street investment banks, they would have vanished long ago. This woman wasn't saying that Wall Street bankers were corrupt. She was saying that they were stupid. These people whose job it was to allocate capital apparently didn't even know how to manage their own.

I confess some part of me thought, *If only I'd stuck around, this is the sort of catastrophe I might have created*. The characters at the center of Citigroup's mess were the very same people I'd worked with at Salomon Brothers; a few of them had been in my Salomon Brothers training class. At some point I couldn't contain myself: I called Meredith Whitney. This was back in March 2008, just before the failure of Bear Stearns, when the outcome still hung in the balance. I thought, If she's right, this really could be the moment when the financial world gets put back into the box from which it escaped in the early 1980s. I was curious to see if she made sense, but also to know where this young woman who was crashing the stock market with her every utterance had come from.

She'd arrived on Wall Street in 1994, out of the Brown University Department of English. "I got to New York and I didn't even know research existed," she says. She'd wound up landing a job at Oppenheimer and Co. and then had the most incredible piece of luck: to be trained by a man who helped her to establish not merely a career but a worldview. His name, she said, was Steve Eisman. "After I made the

Citi call," she said, "one of the best things that happened was when Steve called and told me how proud he was of me." Having never heard of Steve Eisman, I didn't think anything of this.

But then I read the news that a little-known New York hedge fund manager named John Paulson had made $20 billion or so for his investors and nearly $4 billion for himself. This was more money than anyone had ever made so quickly on Wall Street. Moreover, he had done it by betting against the very subprime mortgage bonds now sinking Citigroup and every other big Wall Street investment bank. Wall Street investment banks are like Las Vegas casinos: They set the odds. The customer who plays zero-sum games against them may win from time to time but never systematically, and never so spectacularly that he bankrupts the casino. Yet John Paulson had been a Wall Street customer. Here was the mirror image of the same incompetence Meredith Whitney was making her name pointing out. The casino had misjudged, badly, the odds of its own game, and at least one person had noticed. I called Whitney again to ask her, as I was asking others, if she knew anyone who had anticipated the subprime mortgage cataclysm, thus setting himself up in advance to make a fortune from it. Who else had noticed, before the casino caught on, that the roulette wheel had become predictable? Who else inside the black box of modern finance had grasped the flaws of its machinery?

It was then late 2008. By then there was a long and growing list of pundits who claimed they predicted the catastrophe, but a far shorter list of people who actually did. Of those, even fewer had the nerve to bet on their vision. It's not easy to stand apart from mass hysteria —to believe that most of what's in the financial news is wrong, to believe that most important financial people are either lying or deluded—without being insane. Whitney rattled off a list with a half-dozen names on it, mainly investors she had personally advised. In the middle was John Paulson. At the top was Steve Eisman.

The Big Short

Chapter One

A Secret Origin Story

Eisman entered finance about the time I exited it. He'd grown up in New York City, gone to yeshiva schools, graduated from the University of Pennsylvania magna cum laude, and then with honors from Harvard Law School. In 1991 he was a thirty-year-old corporate lawyer wondering why he ever thought he'd enjoy being a lawyer. "I hated it," he says. "I hated being a lawyer. My parents worked as brokers at Oppenheimer securities. They managed to finagle me a job. It's not pretty but that's what happened."

Oppenheimer was among the last of the old-fashioned Wall Street partnerships and survived on the scraps left behind by Goldman Sachs and Morgan Stanley. It felt less like a corporation than a family business. Lillian and Elliot Eisman had been giving financial advice to individual investors on behalf of Oppenheimer since the early 1960s. (Lillian had created their brokerage business inside of Oppenheimer, and Elliot, who had started out as a criminal attorney, had joined her after being spooked once too often by midlevel Mafia clients.) Beloved and respected by colleagues and clients alike, they could hire whomever they pleased. Before rescuing their son from his legal career they'd installed his old nanny on the Oppenheimer trading floor. On his way to reporting to his mother and father, Eisman passed the woman who had once changed his diapers. Oppenheimer had a nepotism rule, however; if Lillian and Elliot wanted to hire their son, they had to pay his salary for the first year, while others determined if he was worth paying at all.

Eisman's parents, old-fashioned value investors at heart, had always told him that the best way to learn about Wall Street was to work as an equity analyst. He started in equity analysis, working for the people who shaped public opinion about public companies. Oppenheimer employed twenty-five or so analysts, most of whose analysis went ignored by the rest of Wall Street. "The only way to get paid as an analyst at Oppenheimer was being right and making enough noise about it that people noticed it," says Alice Schroeder, who covered insurance companies for Oppenheimer, moved to Morgan Stanley, and eventually wound up being Warren Buffett's official biographer. She added, "There was a counterculture element to Oppenheimer. The people at the big firms were all being paid to be consensus." Eisman turned out to have a special talent for making noise and breaking with consensus opinion. He started as a junior equity analyst, a helpmate, not expected to offer his own opinions. That changed in December 1991, less than a year into the new job. A subprime mortgage lender called Aames Financial went public, and no one at Oppenheimer particularly cared to express an opinion about it. One of Oppenheimer's bankers, who hoped to be hired by Aames, stomped around the research department looking for anyone who knew anything about the mortgage business. "I'm a junior analyst and I'm just trying to figure out which end is up," says Eisman, "but I told him that as a lawyer I'd worked on a deal for The Money Store." He was promptly appointed the lead analyst for Aames Financial. "What I didn't tell him was that my job had been to proofread the documents and that I hadn't understood a word of the fucking things."

Aames Financial, like The Money Store, belonged to a new category of firms extending loans to cash-strapped Americans, known euphemistically as "specialty finance." The category did not include Goldman Sachs or J.P. Morgan but did include many little-known companies involved one way or another in the early 1990s boom in subprime mortgage lending. Aames was the first subprime mortgage lender to go public. The second company for which Eisman was given sole responsibility was called Lomas Financial Corp. Lomas had just emerged from bankruptcy. "I put a sell rating on the thing because it was a piece of shit. I didn't know that you weren't supposed to put sell ratings on companies. I thought there were three boxes—buy, hold, sell—and you could pick the one you thought you should." He was pressured to be a bit more upbeat, but upbeat did not come naturally to Steve Eisman. He could fake upbeat, and sometimes did, but he was happier not bothering. "I could hear him shouting into his phone from down the hall," says a former colleague. "Joyfully engaged in bashing the stocks of the companies he covered. Whatever he's thinking, it comes out of his mouth." Eisman stuck to his sell rating on Lomas Financial, even after the Lomas Financial Corporation announced that investors needn't worry about its financial condition, as it had hedged its market risk. "The single greatest line I ever wrote as an analyst," says Eisman, "was after Lomas said they were hedged." He recited the line from memory: "'The Lomas Financial Corporation is a perfectly hedged financial institution: it loses money in every conceivable interest rate environment.' I enjoyed writing that sentence more than any sentence I ever wrote." A few months after he published that line, the Lomas Financial Corporation returned to bankruptcy.

Eisman quickly established himself as one of the few analysts at

Oppenheimer whose opinions might stir the markets. "It was like going back to school for me," he said. "I would learn about an industry and I would go and write a paper about it." Wall Street people came to view him as a genuine character. He dressed half-fastidiously, as if someone had gone to great trouble to buy him nice new clothes but not told him exactly how they should be worn. His short-cropped blond hair looked as if he had cut it himself. The focal point of his soft, expressive, not unkind face was his mouth, mainly because it was usually at least half open, even while he ate. It was as if he feared that he might not be able to express whatever thought had just flitted through his mind quickly enough before the next one came, and so kept the channel perpetually clear. His other features all arranged themselves, almost dutifully, around the incipient thought. It was the opposite of a poker face.

In his dealings with the outside world, a pattern emerged. The growing number of people who worked for Steve Eisman loved him, or were at least amused by him, and appreciated his willingness and ability to part with both his money and his knowledge. "He's a born teacher," says one woman who worked for him. "And he's fiercely protective of women." He identified with the little guy and the underdog without ever exactly being one himself. Important men who might have expected from Eisman some sign of deference or respect, on the other hand, often came away from encounters with him shocked and outraged. "A lot of people don't get Steve," Meredith Whitney had told me, "but the people who get him love him." One of the people who didn't get Steve was the head of a large U.S. brokerage firm, who listened to Eisman explain in front of several dozen investors at lunch why he, the brokerage firm head, didn't understand his own business, then watched him leave in the middle of the lunch and never return. ("I had to go to the bathroom," says Eisman. "I don't know why I never went back.") After the lunch, the guy had announced he'd never again agree to enter any room with Steve Eisman in it. The president of a large Japanese real estate firm was another. He'd sent Eisman his company's financial statements and then followed, with an interpreter, to solicit Eisman's investment. "You don't even own stock in your company," said Eisman, after the typically elaborate Japanese businessman introductions. The interpreter conferred with the CEO.

"In Japan it is not customary for management to own stock," he said at length.

Eisman noted that the guy's financial statements didn't actually disclose any of the really important details about the guy's company; but, rather than simply say that, he lifted the statement in the air, as if disposing of a turd. "This . . . this is toilet paper," he said. "Translate that."

"The Japanese guy takes off his glasses," recalled a witness to the strange encounter. "His lips are quavering. World War Three is about to break out. 'Toy-lay paper? Toy-lay paper?'"

A hedge fund manager who counted Eisman as a friend set out to explain him to me but quit a minute into it—after he'd described Eisman exposing various bigwigs as either liars or idiots—and started to laugh. "He's sort of a prick in a way, but he's smart and honest and fearless."

"Even on Wall Street people think he's rude and obnoxious and aggressive," says Eisman's wife, Valerie Feigen, who worked at J.P. Morgan before quitting to open the women's clothing store Edit New York, and to raise their children. "He has no interest in manners. Believe me, I've tried and I've tried and I've tried." After she'd brought him home for the first time, her mother had said, "Well, we can't use him but we can definitely auction him off at UJA."* Eisman had what amounted to a talent for offending people. "He's not tactically rude," his wife explains. "He's sincerely rude. He knows everyone thinks of him as a character but he doesn't think of himself that way. Steven lives inside his head."

* United Jewish Appeal.

When asked about the pattern of upset he leaves in his wake, Eisman simply looks puzzled, even a bit wounded. "I forget myself sometimes," he says with a shrug.

Here was the first of many theories about Eisman: He was simply so much more interested in whatever was rattling around his brain than he was in whoever happened to be standing in front of him that the one overwhelmed the other. This theory struck others who knew Eisman well as incomplete. His mother, Lillian, offered a second theory. "Steven actually has two personalities," she said carefully. One was that of the boy to whom she had given the brand-new bicycle he so desperately craved, only to have him pedal it into Central Park, lend it to a kid he'd never met, and watch it vanish into the distance. The other was that of the young man who set out to study the Talmud, not because he had the slightest interest in God but because he was curious about its internal contradictions. His mother had been appointed chairman of the Board of Jewish Education in New York City, and Eisman was combing the Talmud for inconsistencies. "Who else studies Talmud so that they can find the mistakes?" asks his mother. Later, after Eisman became seriously rich and had to think about how to give money away, he landed on an organization called Footsteps, devoted to helping Hasidic Jews flee their religion. He couldn't even give away his money without picking a fight.

By pretty much every account, Eisman was a curious character. And he'd walked onto Wall Street at the very beginning of a curious phase. The creation of the mortgage bond market, a decade earlier, had extended Wall Street into a place it had never before been: the debts of ordinary Americans. At first the new bond market machine concerned itself with the more solvent half of the American population. Now, with the extension of the mortgage bond market into the affairs of less creditworthy Americans, it found its fuel in the debts of the less solvent half.

The mortgage bond was different in important ways from old-fashioned corporate and government bonds. A mortgage bond wasn't a single giant loan for an explicit fixed term. A mortgage bond was a claim on the cash flows from a pool of thousands of individual home mortgages. These cash flows were always problematic, as the borrowers had the right to pay off any time they pleased. This was the single biggest reason that bond investors initially had been reluctant to invest in home mortgage loans: Mortgage borrowers typically repaid their loans only when interest rates fell, and they could refinance more cheaply, leaving the owner of a mortgage bond holding a pile of cash, to invest at lower interest rates. The investor in home loans didn't know how long his investment would last, only that he would get his money back when he least wanted it. To limit this uncertainty, the people I'd worked with at Salomon Brothers, who created the mortgage bond market, had come up with a clever solution. They took giant pools of home loans and carved up the payments made by homeowners into pieces, called tranches. The buyer of the first tranche was like the owner of the ground floor in a flood: He got hit with the first wave of mortgage prepayments. In exchange, he received a higher interest rate. The buyer of the second tranche—the second story of the skyscraper—took the next wave of prepayments and in exchange received the second highest interest rate, and so on. The investor in the top floor of the building received the lowest rate of interest but had the greatest assurance that his investment wouldn't end before he wanted it to.

The big fear of the 1980s mortgage bond investor was that he would be repaid too quickly, not that he would fail to be repaid at all. The pool of loans underlying the mortgage bond conformed to the standards, in their size and the credit quality of the borrowers, set by one of several government agencies: Freddie Mac, Fannie Mae, and Ginnie Mae. The loans carried, in effect, government guarantees; if the homeowners defaulted, the government paid off their debts. When Steve Eisman stumbled into this new, rapidly growing industry of specialty finance, the mortgage bond was about to be put to a new use: making loans that did not qualify for government guarantees. The purpose was to extend credit to less and less creditworthy homeowners, not so that they might buy a house but so that they could cash out whatever equity they had in the house they already owned.

The mortgage bonds created from subprime home loans extended the logic invented to address the problem of early repayment to cope with the problem of no repayment at all. The investor in the first floor, or tranche, would be exposed not to prepayments but to actual losses. He took the first losses until his investment was entirely wiped out, whereupon the losses hit the guy on the second floor. And so on.

In the early 1990s, just a pair of Wall Street analysts devoted their careers to understanding the effects of extending credit into places where that sun didn't often shine. Steve Eisman was one; the other was Sy Jacobs. Jacobs had gone through the same Salomon Brothers training program that I had, and now worked for a small investment bank called Alex Brown. "I sat through the Salomon training program and got to hear what this great new securitization model Lewie Ranieri was creating was going to do," he recalls. (Ranieri was the closest thing the mortgage bond market had to a founding father.) The implications of turning home mortgages into bonds were mind-bogglingly vast. One man's liability had always been another man's asset, but now more and more of the liabilities could be turned into bits of paper that you could sell to anyone. In short order, the Salomon Brothers trading floor gave birth to small markets in bonds funded by all sorts of strange stuff: credit card receivables, aircraft leases, auto loans, health club dues. To invent a new market was only a matter of finding a new asset to hock. The most obvious untapped asset in America was still the home. People with first mortgages had vast amounts of equity locked up in their houses; why shouldn't this untapped equity, too, be securitized? "The thinking in subprime," says Jacobs, "was there was this social stigma to being a second mortgage borrower and there really shouldn't be. If your credit rating was a little worse, you paid a lot more—and a lot more than you really should. If we can mass market the bonds, we can drive down the cost to borrowers. They can replace high interest rate credit card debt with lower interest rate mortgage debt. And it will become a self-fulfilling prophecy."

The growing interface between high finance and lower-middle-class America was assumed to be good for lower-middle-class America. This new efficiency in the capital markets would allow lower-middle-class Americans to pay lower and lower interest rates on their debts. In the early 1990s, the first subprime mortgage lenders—The Money Store, Greentree, Aames—sold shares to the public, so that they might grow faster. By the mid-1990s, dozens of small consumer lending companies were coming to market each year. The subprime lending industry was fragmented. Because the lenders sold many—though not all—of the loans they made to other investors, in the form of mortgage bonds, the industry was also fraught with moral hazard. "It was a fast-buck business," says Jacobs. "Any business where you can sell a product and make money without having to worry how the product performs is going to attract sleazy people. That was the seamy underbelly of the good idea. Eisman and I both believed in the big idea and we both met some really sleazy characters. That was our job: to figure out which of the characters were the right ones to pull off the big idea."

Subprime mortgage lending was still a trivial fraction of the U.S. credit markets—a few tens of billions in loans each year—but its existence made sense, even to Steve Eisman. "I thought it was partly a response to growing income inequality," he said. "The distribution of income in this country was skewed and becoming more skewed, and the result was that you have more subprime customers." Of course, Eisman was paid to see the sense in subprime lending: Oppenheimer quickly became one of the leading bankers to the new industry, in no small part because Eisman was one of its leading proponents. "I took a lot of subprime companies public," says Eisman. "And the story they liked to tell was that 'we're helping the consumer. Because we're taking him out of his high interest rate credit card debt and putting him into lower interest rate mortgage debt.' And I believed that story." Then something changed.

Vincent Daniel had grown up in Queens, without any of the perks Steve Eisman took for granted. And yet if you met them you might guess that it was Vinny who had grown up in high style on Park Avenue and Eisman who had been raised in the small duplex on Eighty-second Avenue. Eisman was brazen and grandiose and focused on the big kill. Vinny was careful and wary and interested in details. He was young and fit, with thick, dark hair and handsome features, but his appearance was overshadowed by his concerned expression—mouth ever poised to frown, eyebrows ever ready to rise. He had little to lose but still seemed perpetually worried that something important was about to be taken from him. His father had been murdered when he was a small boy—though no one ever talked about that—and his mother had found a job as a bookkeeper at a commodities trading firm. She'd raised Vinny and his brother alone. Maybe it was Queens, maybe it was what had happened to his father, or maybe it was just the way Vincent Daniel was wired, but he viewed his fellow man with the most intense suspicion. It was with the awe of a champion speaking of an even greater champion that Steve Eisman said, "Vinny is *dark*."

Eisman was an upper-middle-class kid who had been faintly surprised when he wound up at Penn instead of Yale. Vinny was a lower-middle-class kid whose mother was proud of him for getting into any college at all and prouder still when, in 1994, after Vinny graduated from SUNY–Binghamton, he'd gotten himself hired in Manhattan by Arthur Andersen, the accounting firm that would be destroyed a few years later, in the Enron scandal. "Growing up in Queens, you very quickly figure out where the money is," said Vinny. "It's in Manhattan." His first assignment in Manhattan, as a junior accountant, was to audit Salomon Brothers. He was instantly struck by the opacity of an investment bank's books. None of his fellow accountants was able to explain why the traders were doing what they were doing. "I didn't know what I was doing," said Vinny. "But the scary thing was, my managers didn't know anything either. I asked these basic questions—like, Why do they own this mortgage bond? Are they just betting on it, or is it part of some larger strategy? I thought I needed to know. It's really difficult to audit a company if you can't connect the dots."

He concluded that there was effectively no way for an accountant assigned to audit a giant Wall Street firm to figure out whether it was making money or losing money. They were giant black boxes, whose hidden gears were in constant motion. Several months into the audit, Vinny's manager grew tired of his questions. "He couldn't explain it to me. He said, 'Vinny, it's not your job. I hired you to do XYZ, do XYZ and shut your mouth.' I walked out of his office and said, 'I gotta get out of here.'"

Vinny went looking for another job. An old school friend of his worked at a place called Oppenheimer and Co. and was making good money. He handed Vinny's resume in to human resources, and it made its way to Steve Eisman, who turned out to be looking for someone to help him parse the increasingly arcane accounting used by subprime mortgage originators. "I can't add," says Eisman. "I think in stories. I need help with numbers." Vinny heard that Eisman could be difficult and was surprised that, when they met, Eisman seemed interested only in whether they'd be able to get along. "He seemed to be just looking for a good egg," says Vinny. They'd met twice when Eisman phoned him out of the blue. Vinny assumed he was about to be offered a job, but soon after they started to talk, Eisman received an emergency call on the other line and put Vinny on hold. Vinny sat waiting for fifteen minutes in silence, but Eisman never came back on the line.

Two months later, Eisman called him back. When could Vinny start?

Eisman didn't particularly recall why he had put Vinny on hold and never picked up again, any more than he recalled why he had gone to the bathroom in the middle of lunch with a big-time CEO and never returned. Vinny soon found his own explanation: When he'd picked up the other line, Eisman had been informed that his first child, a newborn son named Max, had died. Valerie, sick with the flu, had been awakened by a night nurse, who informed her that she, the night nurse, had rolled on top of the baby in her sleep and smothered him. A decade later, the people closest to Eisman would describe this as an event that changed his relationship to the world around him. "Steven always thought he had an angel on his shoulder," said Valerie. "Nothing bad ever happened to Steven. He was protected and he was safe. After Max, the angel on his shoulder was done. Anything can happen to anyone at any time." From that moment, she noticed many changes in her husband, large and small, and Eisman did not disagree. "From the point of view of the history of the universe, Max's death was not a big deal," said Eisman. "It was just my big deal."

At any rate, Vinny and Eisman never talked about what had happened. All Vinny knew was that the Eisman he went to work for was obviously not quite the same Eisman he'd met several months earlier. The Eisman Vinny had interviewed with was, by the standards of Wall Street analysts, honest. He was not completely uncooperative. Oppenheimer was among the leading bankers to the subprime mortgage industry. They never would have been given the banking business if Eisman, their noisiest analyst, had not been willing to say nice things about them. Much as he enjoyed bashing the less viable companies, he accepted that the subprime lending industry was a useful addition to the U.S. economy. His willingness to be rude about a few of these subprime originators was, in a way, useful. It lent credibility to his recommendations of the others.

Eisman was now about to become noticeably more negatively disposed, in ways that, from the point of view of his employer, were financially counterproductive. "It was like he'd smelled something," said Vinny. "And he needed my help figuring out what it was he'd smelled." Eisman wanted to write a report that more or less damned the entire industry, but he needed to be more careful than usual. "You can be positive and wrong on the sell side," says Vinny. "But if you're negative and wrong you get fired." Ammunition to cause trouble had just arrived a few months earlier from Moody's: The rating agency now possessed, and offered for sale, all sorts of new information about subprime mortgage loans. While the Moody's database did not allow you to examine individual loans, it offered a general picture of the pools of loans underlying individual mortgage bonds: how many were floating-rate, how many of the houses borrowed against were owner-occupied. Most importantly: how many were delinquent. "Here's this database," Eisman said simply. "Go into that room. Don't come out until you've figured out what it means." Vinny had the feeling Eisman already knew what it meant.

Vinny was otherwise on his own. "I'm twenty-six years old," he says, "and I haven't really understood what mortgage-backed securities really are." Eisman didn't know anything about them either—he was a stock market guy, and Oppenheimer didn't even have a bond department. Vinny had to teach himself. When he was done, he had an explanation for the unpleasant odor wafting from the subprime mortgage industry that Eisman had detected. These companies disclosed their ever-growing earnings, but not much else. One of the many items they failed to disclose was the delinquency rate of the home loans they were making. When Eisman had bugged them for these, they'd pretended that the fact was irrelevant, as they had sold all the loans off to people who packaged them into mortgage bonds: The risk was no longer theirs. This was untrue. All retained some small fraction of the loans they originated, and the companies were allowed to book as profit the expected future value of those loans. The accounting rules allowed them to assume the loans would be repaid, and not prematurely. This assumption became the engine of their doom.

What first caught Vinny's eye were the high prepayments coming in from a sector called "manufactured housing." ("It sounds better than 'mobile homes.'") Mobile homes were different from the wheel-less kind: Their value dropped, like cars', the moment they left the store. The mobile home buyer, unlike the ordinary home buyer, couldn't expect to refinance in two years and take money out. *Why were they prepaying so fast?* Vinny asked himself. "It made no sense to me. Then I saw that the reason the prepayments were so high is that they were involuntary." "Involuntary prepayment" sounds better than "default." Mobile home buyers were defaulting on their loans, their mobile homes were being repossessed, and the people who had lent them money were receiving fractions of the original loans. "Eventually I saw that all the subprime sectors were either being prepaid or going bad at an incredible rate," said Vinny. "I was just seeing stunningly high delinquency rates in these pools." The interest rate on the loans wasn't high enough to justify the risk of lending to this particular slice of the American population. It was as if the ordinary rules of finance had been suspended in response to a social problem. A thought crossed his mind: How do you make poor people feel wealthy when wages are stagnant? You give them cheap loans.

To sift every pool of subprime mortgage loans took him six months, but when he was done he came out of the room and gave Eisman the news. All these subprime lending companies were growing so rapidly, and using such goofy accounting, that they could mask the fact that they had no real earnings, just illusory, accounting-driven, ones. They had the essential feature of a Ponzi scheme: To maintain the fiction that they were profitable enterprises, they needed more and more capital to create more and more subprime loans. "I wasn't actually a hundred percent sure I was right," said Vinny, "but I go to Steve and say, 'This really doesn't look good.' That was all he needed to know. I think what he needed was evidence to downgrade the stock."

The report Eisman wrote trashed all of the subprime originators; one by one, he exposed the deceptions of a dozen companies. "Here is the difference," he said, "between the view of the world they are presenting to you and the actual numbers." The subprime companies did not appreciate his effort. "He created a shitstorm," said Vinny. "All these subprime companies were calling and hollering at him: *You're wrong. Your data's wrong.* And he just hollered back at them, 'It's YOUR fucking data!'" One of the reasons Eisman's report disturbed so many is that he'd failed to give the companies he'd insulted fair warning. He'd violated the Wall Street code. "Steve knew this was going to create a shitstorm," said Vinny. "And he wanted to create the shitstorm. And he didn't want to be talked out of it. And if he told them, he'd have had all these people trying to talk him out of it."

"We were never able to evaluate the loans before because we never had the data," said Eisman later. "My name was wedded to this industry. My entire reputation had been built on covering these stocks. If I was wrong, that would be the end of the career of Steve Eisman."

Eisman published his report in September 1997, in the middle of what appeared to be one of the greatest economic booms in U.S. history. Less than a year later, Russia defaulted and a hedge fund called Long-Term Capital Management went bankrupt. In the subsequent flight to safety, the early subprime lenders were denied capital and promptly went bankrupt en masse. Their failure was interpreted as an indictment of their accounting practices, which allowed them to record profits before they were realized. No one but Vinny, so far as Vinny could tell, ever really understood the crappiness of the loans they had made. "It made me feel good that there was such inefficiency to this market," he said. "Because if the market catches on to everything, I probably have the wrong job. You can't add anything by looking at this arcane stuff, so why bother? But I was the only guy I knew who was covering companies that were all going to go bust during the greatest economic boom we'll ever see in my lifetime. I saw how the sausage was made in the economy and it was really freaky."

That was the moment it first became clear that Eisman wasn't just a little cynical. He held a picture of the financial world in his head that was radically different from, and less flattering than, the financial world's self-portrait. A few years later, he quit his job and went to work for a giant hedge fund called Chilton Investment. He'd lost interest in telling other people where to put their money. He thought he might be able to remain interested if he managed money himself and bet on his own judgments. Having hired Eisman, Chilton Investment had second thoughts. "The whole thing about Steve," said a Chilton colleague, "was, 'Yeah, he's a really smart guy. But can he pick stocks?'" Chilton decided that he couldn't and relegated him to his old role of analyzing companies for the guy who actually made the investment decisions. Eisman hated it, but he did it, and in doing it he learned something that prepared him uniquely for the crisis that was about to occur. He learned what was really going on inside the market for consumer loans.

The year was now 2002. There were no public subprime lending companies left in America. There was, however, an ancient consumer lending giant called Household Finance Corporation. Created in the 1870s, it had long been a leader in the field. Eisman understood the company well, he thought, until he realized that he didn't. In early 2002 he got his hands on Household's new sales document offering home equity loans. The company's CEO, Bill Aldinger, had grown Household even as his competitors went bankrupt. Americans, digesting the Internet bust, seemed in no position to take on new debts, and yet Household was making loans at a faster pace than ever. A big source of its growth had been the second mortgage. The document offered a fifteen-year, fixed-rate loan, but it was bizarrely disguised as a thirty-year loan. It took the stream of payments the homeowner would make to Household over fifteen years, spread it hypothetically over thirty years, and asked: If you were making the same dollar payments over thirty years that you are in fact making over fifteen, what would your "effective rate" of interest be? It was a weird, dishonest sales pitch. The borrower was told he had an "effective interest rate of 7 percent" when he was in fact paying something like 12.5 percent. "It was blatant fraud," said Eisman. "They were tricking their customers."

It didn't take long for Eisman to find complaints from borrowers who had figured out what had just happened to them. He scoured small newspapers around the country. In the town of Bellingham, Washington—the last city of any size before you reach Canada—he found a reporter named John Stark, who wrote for the *Bellingham Herald*. Before Eisman called him out of the blue, Stark had written a small piece about four locals who thought they had been deceived by Household and found a plaintiff's attorney willing to sue the company and void the mortgage contracts. "I was skeptical at first," says Stark. "I thought, Here's another person who has borrowed too much money and hired a lawyer. I wasn't too sympathetic." When the piece was published, it drew a crowd: Hundreds of people in and around Bellingham had picked up the newspaper to discover that their 7 percent mortgage was in fact a 12.5 percent mortgage. "People were coming out of the woodwork," says Stark. "They were angry. A lot of them didn't realize what had happened to them."

Whatever Eisman was meant to be doing got pushed to one side. His job became a single-minded crusade against the Household Finance Corporation. He alerted newspaper reporters, he called up magazine writers, he became friendly with the Association of Community Organizations for Reform Now (ACORN), which must be the first time a guy from a Wall Street hedge fund exhibited such interest in an organization devoted to guarding the interests of the poor. He repeatedly pestered the office of the attorney general of the state of Washington. He was incredulous to learn that the attorney general had investigated Household and then been prevented, *by a state judge*, from releasing the results of his investigation. Eisman obtained a copy; its contents confirmed his worst suspicions. "I would say to the guy in the attorney general's office, 'Why aren't you arresting people?' He'd say, 'They're a powerful company. If they're gone, who would make subprime loans in the state of Washington?' I said, 'Believe me, there will be a train full of people coming to lend money.'"

Really, it was a federal issue. Household was peddling these deceptive mortgages all over the country. Yet the federal government failed to act. Instead, at the end of 2002, Household settled a class action suit out of court and agreed to pay a $484 million fine distributed to twelve states. The following year it sold itself, and its giant portfolio of subprime loans, for $15.5 billion to the British financial conglomerate the HSBC Group.

Eisman was genuinely shocked. "It never entered my mind that this could possibly happen," he said. "This wasn't just another company —this was the biggest company by far making subprime loans. And it was engaged in just blatant fraud. They should have taken the CEO out and hung him up by his fucking testicles. Instead they sold the company and the CEO made a hundred million dollars. And I thought, *Whoa! That one didn't end the way it should have.*" His pessimism toward high finance was becoming tinged with political ideas. "That's when I started to see the social implications," he said. "If you are going to start a regulatory regime from scratch, you'd design it to protect middle- and lower-middle-income people, because the opportunity for them to get ripped off was so high. Instead what we had was a regime where those were the people who were protected the least."

Eisman left work at noon every Wednesday so that he might be present at Midtown Comics when the new shipment of stories arrived. He knew more than any grown man should about the lives of various superheroes. He knew the Green Lantern oath by heart, for instance, and understood Batman's inner life better than the Caped Crusader himself. Before the death of his son, Eisman had read the adult versions of the comics he'd read as a child—*Spider-Man* was his favorite. Now he read only the darkest adult comics, and favored those that took familiar fairy tales and rearranged them without changing any of the facts, so that the story became less familiar, and something other than a fairy tale. "Telling a story that is consistent with everything that happened before," as he put it. "And yet the story is totally different. And it leads you to look at the earlier episodes differently." He preferred relations between Snow White and the dwarves to be a bit more fraught. Now a fairy tale was being reinvented before his eyes in the financial markets. "I started to look more closely at what a subprime mortgage loan was all about," he said. "A subprime auto loan is in some ways honest because it's at a fixed rate. They may be charging you high fees and ripping your heart out, but at least you know it. The subprime mortgage loan was a cheat. You're basically drawing someone in by telling them, 'You're going to pay off all your other loans—your credit card debt, your auto loans—by taking this one loan. And look at the low rate!' But that low rate isn't the real rate. It's a teaser rate."

Obsessing over Household, he attended a lunch organized by a big Wall Street firm. The guest speaker was Herb Sandler, the CEO of a giant savings and loan called Golden West Financial Corporation. "Someone asked him if he believed in the free checking model," recalls Eisman. "And he said, 'Turn off your tape recorders.' Everyone turned off their tape recorders. And he explained that they avoided free checking because it was really a tax on poor people—in the form of fines for overdrawing their checking accounts. And that banks that used it were really just banking on being able to rip off poor people even more than they could if they charged them for their checks."

Eisman asked, "Are any regulators interested in this?"

"No," said Sandler.

"That's when I decided the system was really, 'Fuck the poor.'"

In his youth, Eisman had been a strident Republican. He joined right-wing organizations, voted for Reagan twice, and even loved Robert Bork. It wasn't until he got to Wall Street, oddly, that his politics drifted left. He attributed his first baby steps back to the middle of the political spectrum to the end of the cold war. "I wasn't as right-wing because there wasn't as much to be right-wing about." By the time Household's CEO, Bill Aldinger, collected his $100 million, Eisman was on his way to becoming the financial market's first socialist. "When you're a conservative Republican, you never think people are making money by ripping other people off," he said. His mind was now fully open to the possibility. "I now realized there was an entire industry, called consumer finance, that basically existed to rip people off."

Denied the chance to manage money by his hedge fund employer, he quit and tried to start his own hedge fund. An outfit called FrontPoint Partners, soon to be wholly owned by Morgan Stanley, housed a collection of hedge funds. In early 2004, Morgan Stanley agreed to let Eisman set up a fund that focused exclusively on financial companies: Wall Street banks, home builders, mortgage originators, companies with big financial services divisions—General Electric (GE), for instance—and anyone else who touched American finance. Morgan Stanley took a cut of the fees off the top and provided him with office space, furniture, and support staff. The only thing they didn't supply him with was money. Eisman was expected to drum that up on his own. He flew all over the world and eventually met with hundreds of big-time investors. "Basically we tried to raise money, and didn't really do it," he says. "Everyone said, 'It's a pleasure to meet you. Let's see how you do.'"

By the spring of 2004 he was in a state. He hadn't raised money; he didn't know that he would; he didn't even know if he could. He certainly didn't believe that the world was fair, or that things always worked out for the best, or that he enjoyed some special protection from life's accidents. He was waking up at four in the morning, drenched in sweat. He was also in therapy. He was still Eisman, however, and so it wasn't conventional therapy. "Work group," it was called. A handful of professionals gathered with a trained psychotherapist to share their problems in a safe environment. Eisman would burst in late to these meetings, talk through whatever was bothering him, and then rush off before the others had a chance to tell him about *their* problems. After he'd done this a couple of times, the therapist said something to him about it, but he didn't appear to have heard her. So she took to calling Eisman's wife, whom she knew, to ask her to have a word with her husband. That didn't work either. "I always knew when he'd been to group," said Valerie, "because she'd call and say, 'He did it again!'"

Valerie was clearly weary of the rat race. She told Eisman that if this latest Wall Street venture didn't work out, they would leave New York for Rhode Island and open a bed-and-breakfast. Valerie had scouted places and spoke often about spending more time with the twins she'd given birth to, and even raising chickens. It was almost as hard for Eisman to imagine himself raising chickens as it was for people who knew him, but he'd agreed. "The idea of it was so unbelievably unappealing to him," says his wife, "that he started to work harder." Eisman traveled all over Europe and the United States searching for people willing to invest with him and found exactly one: an insurance company, which staked him to $50 million. It wasn't enough to create a sustainable equity fund, but it was a start.

Instead of money, Eisman attracted people, whose views of the world were as shaded as his own. Vinny, who had just coauthored a gloomy report called "A Home without Equity Is Just a Rental with Debt," came right away. Porter Collins, a two-time Olympic oarsman who had worked with Eisman at Chilton Investment and never really understood why the guy with the bright ideas wasn't given more authority, came along too. Danny Moses, who became Eisman's head trader, came third. Danny had worked as a salesman at Oppenheimer and Co. and had pungent memories of Eisman doing and saying all sorts of things that sell-side analysts seldom did. In the middle of one trading day, for instance, Eisman had walked to the podium at the center of the Oppenheimer trading floor, called for everyone's attention, announced that "the following eight stocks are going to zero," and then listed eight companies that indeed went bankrupt. Raised in Georgia, the son of a finance professor, Danny was less openly fatalistic than Vinny or Steve, but he nevertheless shared a general sense that bad things can and do happen, especially on Wall Street. When a Wall Street firm helped him to get into a trade that seemed perfect in every way, he asked the salesman, "I appreciate this, but I just want to know one thing: How are you going to fuck me?"

Heh-heh-heh, c'mon, we'd never do that, the trader started to say, but Danny, though perfectly polite, was insistent.

We both know that unadulterated good things like this trade don't just happen between little hedge funds and big Wall Street firms. I'll do it, but only after you explain to me how you are going to fuck me. And the salesman explained how he was going to fuck him. And Danny did the trade.

All of them enjoyed, immensely, the idea of running money with Steve Eisman. Working for Eisman, you never felt you were working *for* Eisman. He'd teach you but he wouldn't supervise you. Eisman also put a fine point on the absurdity they saw everywhere around them. "Steve's fun to take to any Wall Street meeting," said Vinny. "Because he'll say 'explain that to me' thirty different times. Or 'could you explain that more, in English?' Because once you do that, there's a few things you learn. For a start, you figure out if they even know what they're talking about. And a lot of times they don't!"

By early 2005 Eisman's little group shared a sense that a great many people working on Wall Street couldn't possibly understand what they were doing. The subprime mortgage machine was up and running again, as if it had never broken down in the first place. If the first act of subprime lending had been freaky, this second act was terrifying. Thirty billion dollars was a big year for subprime lending in the mid-1990s. In 2000 there had been $130 billion in subprime mortgage lending, and 55 billion dollars' worth of those loans had been repackaged as mortgage bonds. In 2005 there would be $625 billion in subprime mortgage loans, $507 billion of which found its way into mortgage bonds. *Half a trillion dollars in subprime mortgage–backed bonds in a single year.* Subprime lending was booming even as interest rates were rising—which made no sense at all. Even more shocking was that the terms of the loans were changing, in ways that increased the likelihood they would go bad. Back in 1996, 65 percent of subprime loans had been fixed-rate, meaning that typical subprime borrowers might be getting screwed, but at least they knew for sure how much they owed each month until they paid off the loan. By 2005, 75 percent of subprime loans were some form of floating-rate, usually fixed for the first two years.

The original cast of subprime financiers had been sunk by the small fraction of the loans they made that they had kept on their books. The market might have learned a simple lesson: Don't make loans to people who can't repay them. Instead it learned a complicated one: You can keep on making these loans, just don't keep them on your books. Make the loans, then sell them off to the fixed income departments of big Wall Street investment banks, which will in turn package them into bonds and sell them to investors. Long Beach Savings was the first existing bank to adopt what was called the "originate and sell" model. This proved such a hit—Wall Street would buy your loans, even if you would not!—that a new company, called B&C mortgage, was founded to do nothing but originate and sell. Lehman Brothers thought that was such a great idea that they bought B&C mortgage. By early 2005 all the big Wall Street investment banks were deep into the subprime game. Bear Stearns, Merrill Lynch, Goldman Sachs, and Morgan Stanley all had what they termed "shelves" for their subprime wares, with strange names like HEAT and SAIL and GSAMP, that made it a bit more difficult for the general audience to see that these subprime bonds were being underwritten by Wall Street's biggest names.

Eisman and his team had a from-the-ground-up understanding of both the U.S. housing market and Wall Street. They knew most of the subprime lenders—the guys on the ground making the loans. Many were the very same characters who had created the late 1990s debacle. Eisman was predisposed to suspect the worst of whatever Goldman Sachs might be doing with the debts of lower-middle-class Americans. "You have to understand," he says. "I did subprime first. I lived with the worst first. These guys lied to infinity. What I learned from that experience was that Wall Street didn't give a shit what it sold." What he couldn't understand was who was buying the bonds from this second wave of subprime mortgage lending. "The very first day, we said, 'There's going to come a time when we're going to make a fortune shorting this stuff. It's going to blow up. We just don't know how or when.'"

By "this stuff," Eisman meant the stocks of companies involved in subprime lending. Stock prices could do all sorts of crazy things: He didn't want to short them until the loans started going bad. To that end, Vinny kept a close eye on the behavior of the American subprime mortgage borrower. On the twenty-fifth of each month, the remittance reports arrived on his computer screen, and he scanned them for any upticks in delinquencies. "According to the things we were tracking," says Vinny, "the credit quality was still good. At least until the second half of 2005."

In the fog of the first eighteen months of running his own business, Eisman had an epiphany, an identifiable moment when he realized he'd been missing something obvious. Here he was, trying to figure out which stocks to pick, but the fate of the stocks depended increasingly on the bonds. As the subprime mortgage market grew, every financial company was, one way or another, exposed to it. "The fixed income world dwarfs the equity world," he said. "The equity world is like a fucking zit compared to the bond market." Just about every major Wall Street investment bank was effectively run by its bond departments. In most cases—Dick Fuld at Lehman Brothers, John Mack at Morgan Stanley, Jimmy Cayne at Bear Stearns—the CEO was a former bond guy. Ever since the 1980s, when the leading bond firm, Salomon Brothers, had made so much money that it looked as if it was in a different industry than the other firms, the bond market had been where the big money was made. "It was the golden rule," said Eisman. "The people who have the gold make the rules."

Most people didn't understand how what amounted to a two-decade boom in the bond market had overwhelmed everything else. Eisman certainly hadn't. Now he did. He needed to learn everything he could about the fixed income world. He had plans for the bond market. What he didn't know was that the bond market also had plans for him. It was about to create an Eisman-shaped hole.

CHAPTER TWO

In the Land of the Blind

Writing a check separates a commitment from a conversation.

—Warren Buffett

In early 2004 another stock market investor, Michael Burry, immersed himself for the first time in the bond market. He learned all he could about how money got borrowed and lent in America. He didn't talk to anyone about what became his new obsession; he just sat alone in his office, in San Jose, California, and read books and articles and financial filings. He wanted to know, especially, how subprime mortgage bonds worked. A giant number of individual loans got piled up into a tower. The top floors got their money back first and so got the highest ratings from Moody's and S&P and the lowest interest rate. The low floors got their money back last, suffered the first losses, and got the lowest ratings from Moody's and S&P. Because they were taking on more risk, the investors in the bottom floors received a higher rate of interest than investors in the top floors. Investors who bought mortgage bonds had to decide in which floor of the tower they wanted to invest, but Michael Burry wasn't thinking about buying mortgage bonds. He was wondering how he might short subprime mortgage bonds.

Every mortgage bond came with its own mind-numbingly tedious 130-page prospectus. If you read the fine print, you saw that each was its own little corporation. Burry spent the end of 2004 and early 2005 scanning hundreds and actually reading dozens of them, certain he was the only one apart from the lawyers who drafted them to do so—even though you could get them all for $100 a year from 10KWizard.com. As he explained in an e-mail:

> So you take something like NovaStar, which was an originate and sell subprime mortgage lender, an archetype at the time. The names [of the bonds] would be NHEL 2004-1, NHEL 2004-2, NHEL 2004-3, NHEL 2005-1, etc. NHEL 2004-1 would for instance contain loans from the first few months of 2004 and the last few months of 2003, and 2004-2 would have loans from the middle part, and 2004-3 would get the latter part of 2004. You could pull these prospectuses, and just quickly check the pulse of what was happening in the subprime mortgage portion of the originate-and-sell industry. And you'd see that 2/28 interest only ARM mortgages were only 5.85% of the pool in early 2004, but by late 2004 they were 17.48% of the pool, and by late summer 2005 25.34% of the pool. Yet average FICO [consumer credit] scores for the pool, percent of no-doc ["Liar"] loan to value measures and other indicators were pretty static. . . . The point is that these measures could stay roughly static, but the overall pool of mortgages being issued, packaged and sold off was worsening in quality, because for the same average FICO scores or the same average loan to value, you were getting a higher percentage of interest only mortgages.

As early as 2004, if you looked at the numbers, you could clearly see the decline in lending standards. In Burry's view, standards had not just fallen but hit bottom. The bottom even had a name: *the pay option negatively-amortizing adjustable-rate mortgage*. You, the home buyer, actually were given the option of paying nothing at all, and rolling whatever interest you owed the bank into a higher principal balance. It wasn't hard to see what sort of person might like to have such a loan: one with no income. What Burry couldn't understand was why a person who lent money would want to extend such a loan. "What you want to watch are the lenders, not the borrowers," he said. "The borrowers will always be willing to take a great deal for themselves. It's up to the lenders to show restraint, and when they lose it, watch out." By 2003 he knew that the borrowers had already lost it. By early 2005 he saw that lenders had, too.

A lot of hedge fund managers spent time chitchatting with their investors and treated their quarterly letters to them as a formality. Burry disliked talking to people face-to-face and thought of these letters as the single most important thing he did to let his investors know what he was up to. In his quarterly letters he coined a phrase to describe what he thought was happening: "the extension of credit by instrument." That is, a lot of people couldn't actually afford to pay their mortgages the old-fashioned way, and so the lenders were dreaming up new instruments to justify handing them new money. "It was a clear sign that lenders had lost it, constantly degrading their own standards to grow loan volumes," Burry said. He could see why they were doing this: They didn't keep the loans but sold them to Goldman Sachs and Morgan Stanley and Wells Fargo and the rest, which packaged them into bonds and sold them off. The end buyers of subprime mortgage, he assumed, were just "dumb money." He'd study up on them, too, but later.

He now had a tactical investment problem. The various floors, or tranches, of subprime mortgage bonds all had one thing in common: The bonds were impossible to sell short. To sell a stock or bond short, you needed to borrow it, and these tranches of mortgage bonds were tiny and impossible to find. You could buy them or not buy them, but you couldn't bet explicitly against them; the market for subprime mortgages simply had no place for people in it who took a dim view of them. You might know with certainty that the entire subprime mortgage bond market was doomed, but you could do nothing about it. You couldn't short houses. You could short the stocks of home building companies—Pulte Homes, say, or Toll Brothers—but that was expensive, indirect, and dangerous. Stock prices could rise for a lot longer than Burry could stay solvent.

A couple of years earlier, he'd discovered credit default swaps. A credit default swap was confusing mainly because it wasn't really a swap at all. It was an insurance policy, typically on a corporate bond, with semiannual premium payments and a fixed term. For instance, you might pay $200,000 a year to buy a ten-year credit default swap on $100 million in General Electric bonds. The most you could lose was $2 million: $200,000 a year for ten years. The most you could make was $100 million, if General Electric defaulted on its debt any time in the next ten years and bondholders recovered nothing. It was a zero-sum bet: If you made $100 million, the guy who had sold you the credit default swap lost $100 million. It was also an asymmetric bet, like laying down money on a number in roulette. The most you could lose were the chips you put on the table; but if your number came up you made thirty, forty, even fifty times your money. "Credit default swaps remedied the problem of open-ended risk for me," said Burry. "If I bought a credit default swap, my downside was defined and certain, and the upside was many multiples of it."

He was already in the market for corporate credit default swaps. In 2004 he began to buy insurance on companies he thought might suffer in a real estate downturn: mortgage lenders, mortgage insurers, and so on. This wasn't entirely satisfying. A real estate market meltdown might cause these companies to lose money; there was no guarantee that they would actually go bankrupt. He wanted a more direct tool for betting against subprime mortgage lending. On March 19, 2005, alone in his office with the door closed and the shades drawn, reading an abstruse textbook on credit derivatives, Michael Burry got an idea: credit default swaps on subprime mortgage bonds.

The idea hit him as he read a book about the evolution of the U.S. bond market and the creation, in the mid-1990s, at J.P. Morgan, of the first corporate credit default swaps. He came to a passage explaining why banks felt they needed credit default swaps at all. It wasn't immediately obvious—after all, the best way to avoid the risk of General Electric's defaulting on its debt was not to lend to General Electric in the first place. In the beginning, credit default swaps had been a tool for hedging: Some bank had loaned more than they wanted to General Electric because GE had asked for it, and they feared alienating a long-standing client; another bank changed its mind about the wisdom of lending to GE at all. Very quickly, however, the new derivatives became tools for speculation: A lot of people wanted to make bets on the likelihood of GE's defaulting. It struck Burry: Wall Street is bound to do the same thing with subprime mortgage bonds, too. Given what was happening in the real estate market—and given what subprime mortgage lenders were doing—a lot of smart people eventually were going to want to make side bets on subprime mortgage bonds. And the only way to do it would be to buy a credit default swap.

The credit default swap would solve the single biggest problem with Mike Burry's big idea: timing. The subprime mortgage loans being made in early 2005 were, he felt, almost certain to go bad. But as their interest rates were set artificially low, and didn't reset for two years, it would be two years before that happened. Subprime mortgages almost always bore floating interest rates, but most of them came with a fixed, two-year "teaser" rate. A mortgage created in early 2005 might have a two-year "fixed" rate of 6 percent that, in 2007, would jump to 11 percent and provoke a wave of defaults. The faint ticking sound of these loans would grow louder with time, until eventually a lot of people would suspect, as he suspected, that they were bombs. Once that happened, no one would be willing to sell insurance on subprime mortgage bonds. He needed to lay his chips on the table now and wait for the casino to wake up and change the odds of the game. A credit default swap on a thirty-year subprime mortgage bond was a bet designed to last for thirty years, in theory. He figured that it would take only three to pay it off.

The only problem was that there was no such thing as a credit default swap on a subprime mortgage bond, not that he could see. He'd need to prod the big Wall Street firms to create them. But which firms? If he was right and the housing market crashed, these firms in the middle of the market were sure to lose a lot of money. There was no point buying insurance from a bank that went out of business the minute the insurance became valuable. He didn't even bother calling Bear Stearns and Lehman Brothers, as they were more exposed to the mortgage bond market than the other firms. Goldman Sachs, Morgan Stanley, Deutsche Bank, Bank of America, UBS, Merrill Lynch, and Citigroup were, to his mind, the most likely to survive a crash. He called them all. Five of them had no idea what he was talking about; two came back and said that, while the market didn't exist, it might one day. Inside of three years, credit default swaps on subprime mortgage bonds would become a trillion-dollar market and precipitate hundreds of billions of dollars' worth of losses inside big Wall Street firms. Yet, when Michael Burry pestered the firms in the beginning of 2005, only Deutsche Bank and Goldman Sachs had any real interest in continuing the conversation. No one on Wall Street, as far as he could tell, saw what he was seeing.

He sensed that he was different from other people before he understood why. When he was two years old he'd developed a rare form of cancer, and the operation to remove the tumor had cost him his left eye. A boy with one eye sees the world differently than everyone else, but it didn't take long for Mike Burry to see his literal distinction in more figurative terms. Grown-ups were forever insisting that he should look other people in the eye, especially when he was talking to them. "It took all my energy to look someone in the eye," he said. "If I am looking at you, that's the one time I know I won't be listening to you." His left eye didn't line up with whomever he was trying to talk to; when he was in social situations trying to make chitchat, the person to whom he was speaking would steadily drift left. "I don't really know how to stop it," he said, "so people just keep moving left until they're standing way to my left, and I'm trying not to turn my head anymore. I end up facing right and looking left with my good eye, through my nose."

His glass eye, he assumed, was the reason that face-to-face interaction with other people almost always ended badly for him. He found it maddeningly difficult to read people's nonverbal signals; and their verbal signals he often took more literally than they meant them. When trying his best he was often at his worst. "My compliments tended not to come out right," he said. "I learned early that if you compliment somebody it'll come out wrong. *For your size, you look good. That's a really nice dress: It looks homemade.* The glass eye became his private explanation for why he hadn't really fit in with groups. The eye oozed and wept and required constant attention. It wasn't the sort of thing other kids ever allowed him to be unselfconscious about. They called him cross-eyed, even though he wasn't. Every year they begged him to pop his eye out of its socket—but when he complied, it became infected and disgusting and a cause of further ostracism.

In his glass eye he found the explanation for other traits peculiar to himself. His obsession with fairness, for example. When he noticed that pro basketball stars were far less likely to be called for traveling than lesser players, he didn't just holler at the refs. He stopped watching basketball altogether; the injustice of it killed his interest in the sport. Even though he was ferociously competitive, well built, physically brave, and a good athlete, he didn't care for team sports. The eye helped to explain this, as most team sports were ball sports, and a boy with poor depth perception and limited peripheral vision couldn't very well play ball sports. He tried hard at the less ball-centric positions in football, but his eye popped out if he hit someone too hard.

Again, it was hard for him to see where his physical limitations ended and his psychological ones began—he assumed the glass eye was at the bottom of both. He couldn't stand the unfairness of coaches who favored their own kids. Umpires who missed calls drove him to distraction. He preferred swimming, as it required virtually no social interaction. No teammates. No ambiguity. You just swam your time and you won or you lost.

After a while even he ceased to find it surprising that he spent most of his time alone. By his late twenties he thought of himself as the sort of person who didn't have friends. He'd gone through Santa Teresa High School in San Jose, UCLA, and Vanderbilt University School of Medicine and created not a single lasting bond. What friendships he did have were formed and nurtured in writing, by e-mail; the two people he considered to be true friends he had known for a combined twenty years but had met in person a grand total of eight times. "My nature is not to have friends," he said. "I'm happy in my own head." Somehow he'd married twice. His first wife was a woman of Korean descent who wound up living in a different city ("she often complained that I appeared to like the idea of a relationship more than living the actual relationship") and his second, to whom he was still married, was a Vietnamese-American woman he'd met on Match.com. In his Match.com profile, he described himself frankly as "a medical student with only one eye, an awkward social manner, and $145,000 in student loans." His obsession with personal honesty was a cousin to his obsession with fairness.

Obsessiveness—that was another trait he came to think of as

peculiar to himself. His mind had no temperate zone: He was either possessed by a subject or not interested in it at all. There was an obvious downside to this quality—he had more trouble than most faking interest in other people's concerns and hobbies, for instance—but an upside, too. Even as a small child he had a fantastic ability to focus and learn, with or without teachers. When it synced with his interests, school came easy for him—so easy that, as an undergraduate at UCLA, he could flip back and forth between English and economics and pick up enough premedical training on the side to get himself admitted to the best medical schools in the country. He attributed his unusual powers of concentration to his lack of interest in human interaction, and his lack of interest in human interaction . . . well, he was able to argue that basically everything that happened was caused, one way or the other, by his fake left eye.

This ability to work and to focus set him apart even from other medical students. In 1998, as a resident in neurology at Stanford Hospital, he mentioned to his superiors that, between fourteen-hour hospital shifts, he had stayed up two nights in a row taking apart and putting back together his personal computer in an attempt to make it run faster. His superiors sent him to a psychiatrist, who diagnosed Mike Burry as bipolar. He knew instantly he'd been misdiagnosed: How could you be bipolar if you were never depressed? Or, rather, if you were only depressed while doing your rounds and pretending to be interested in practicing, as opposed to studying, medicine? He'd become a doctor not because he enjoyed medicine but because he didn't find medical school terribly difficult. The actual practice of medicine, on the other hand, either bored or disgusted him. Of his first brush with gross anatomy: "One scene with people carrying legs over their shoulders to the sink to wash out the feces just turned my stomach, and I was done." Of his feeling about the patients: "I wanted to help people—but not really."

He was genuinely interested in computers, not for their own sake but for their service to a lifelong obsession: the inner workings of the stock market. Ever since grade school, when his father had shown him the stock tables at the back of the newspaper and told him that the stock market was a crooked place and never to be trusted, let alone invested in, the subject had fascinated him. Even as a kid he had wanted to impose logic on this world of numbers. He began to read about the market as a hobby. Pretty quickly he saw that there was no logic at all in the charts and graphs and waves and the endless chatter of many self-advertised market pros. Then along came the dot-com bubble and suddenly the entire stock market made no sense at all. "The late nineties almost forced me to identify myself as a value investor, because I thought what everybody else was doing was insane," he said. Formalized as an approach to financial markets during the Great Depression by Benjamin Graham, "value investing" required a tireless search for companies so unfashionable or misunderstood that they could be bought for less than their liquidation value. In its simplest form value investing was a formula, but it had morphed into other things—one of them was whatever Warren Buffett, Benjamin Graham's student, and the most famous value investor, happened to be doing with his money.

Burry did not think investing could be reduced to a formula or learned from any one role model. The more he studied Buffett, the less he thought Buffett could be copied; indeed, the lesson of Buffett was: To succeed in a spectacular fashion you had to be spectacularly unusual. "If you are going to be a great investor, you have to fit the style to who you are," Burry said. "At one point I recognized that Warren Buffett, though he had every advantage in learning from Ben Graham, did not copy Ben Graham, but rather set out on his own path, and ran money his way, by his own rules. . . . I also immediately internalized the idea that no school could teach someone how to be a great investor. If it were true, it'd be the most popular school in the world, with an impossibly high tuition. So it must not be true."

Investing was something you had to learn how to do on your own, in your own peculiar way. Burry had no real money to invest, but he nevertheless dragged his obsession along with him through high school, college, and medical school. He'd reached Stanford Hospital without ever taking a class in finance or accounting, let alone working for any Wall Street firm. He had maybe $40,000 in cash, against $145,000 in student loans. He had spent the previous four years working medical student hours. Nevertheless, he had found time to make himself a financial expert of sorts. "Time is a variable continuum," he wrote to one of his e-mail friends, one Sunday morning in 1999:

> An afternoon can fly by or it can take 5 hours. Like you probably do, I productively fill the gaps that most people leave as dead time. My drive to be productive probably cost me my first marriage and a few days ago almost cost me my fiancée. Before I went to college the military had this "we do more before 9am than most people do all day" and I used to think *and I do more than the military.* As you know there are some select people that just find a drive in certain activities that supersedes EVERYTHING else.

He wasn't bipolar. He was merely isolated and apart, without actually feeling lonely or deeply unhappy. He didn't regard himself as a tragedy; he thought, among other things, that his unusual personality enabled him to concentrate better than other people. All of it followed, in his mind, from the warping effects of his fake eye. "That's why I thought people thought I was different," he said. "That's why I thought I was different." Thinking himself different, he didn't find what happened to him when he collided with Wall Street nearly as bizarre as it was.

Late one night in November 1996, while on a cardiology rotation at St. Thomas Hospital, in Nashville, Tennessee, he logged on to a hospital computer and went to a message board called techstocks.com.

There he created a thread called value investing. Having read everything there was to read about investing, he decided to learn a bit more about "investing in the real world." A mania for Internet stocks gripped the market. A site for the Silicon Valley investor, circa 1996, was not a natural home for a sober-minded value investor. Still, many came, all with opinions. A few people grumbled about the very idea of a doctor having anything useful to say about investments, but over time he came to dominate the discussion. *Dr.* Mike Burry—as he always signed himself—sensed that other people on the thread were taking his advice and making money with it.

Once he figured out he had nothing more to learn from the crowd on his thread, he quit it to create what later would be called a blog but at the time was just a weird form of communication. He was working sixteen-hour shifts at the hospital, confining his blogging mainly to the hours between midnight and three in the morning. On his blog he posted his stock market trades and his arguments for making the trades. People found him. As a money manager at a big Philadelphia value fund said, "The first thing I wondered was, *When is he doing this?* The guy was a medical intern. I only saw the nonmedical part of his day, and it was simply awesome. He's showing people his trades. And people are following it in real time. He's doing value investing—in the middle of the dot-com bubble. He's buying value stocks, which is what we're doing. But we're losing money. We're losing clients. All of a sudden he goes on this tear. He's up fifty percent. It's uncanny. He's uncanny. And we're not the only ones watching it."

Mike Burry couldn't see exactly who was following his financial moves, but he could tell which domains they came from. In the beginning his readers came from EarthLink and AOL. Just random individuals. Pretty soon, however, they weren't. People were coming to his site from mutual funds like Fidelity and big Wall Street investment banks like Morgan Stanley. One day he lit into Vanguard's index funds and almost instantly received a cease and desist order from Vanguard's attorneys. Burry suspected that serious investors might even be acting on his blog posts, but he had no clear idea who they might be. "The market found him," says the Philadelphia mutual fund manager. "He was recognizing patterns no one else was seeing."

By the time Burry moved to Stanford Hospital in 1998 to take up his residency in neurology, the work he had done between midnight and three in the morning had made him a minor but meaningful hub in the land of value investing. By this time the craze for Internet stocks was completely out of control and had infected the Stanford University medical community. "The residents in particular, and some of the faculty, were captivated by the dot-com bubble," said Burry. "A decent minority of them were buying and discussing everything—Polycom, Corel, Razorfish, Pets.com, TIBCO, Microsoft, Dell, Intel are the ones I specifically remember, but areyoukiddingme-dot-com was how my brain filtered a lot of it. . . . I would just keep my mouth shut, because I didn't want anybody there knowing what I was doing on the side. I felt I could get in big trouble if the doctors there saw I wasn't one hundred and ten percent committed to medicine."

People who worry about seeming sufficiently committed to medicine probably aren't sufficiently committed to medicine. The deeper he got into his medical career, the more Burry felt constrained by his problems with other people in the flesh. He briefly tried to hide in pathology, where the people had the decency to be dead, but that didn't work. ("Dead people, dead parts. More dead people, more dead parts. I thought, I want something more cerebral.")

He'd moved back to San Jose, buried his father, remarried, and been misdiagnosed by experts as bipolar when he shut down his Web site and announced he was quitting neurology to become a money manager. The chairman of the Stanford Department of Neurology thought he'd lost his mind and told him to take a year to think it over, but he'd already thought it over. "I found it fascinating and seemingly true," he said, "that if I could run a portfolio well, then I could achieve success in life, and that it wouldn't matter what kind of person I was perceived to be, even though I felt I was a good person deep down." His $40,000 in assets against $145,000 in student loans posed the question of exactly what portfolio he would run. His father had died after another misdiagnosis: A doctor had failed to spot the cancer on an X-ray, and the family had received a small settlement. The father disapproved of the stock market, but the payout from his death funded his son into it. His mother was able to kick in $20,000 from her settlement, his three brothers kicked in $10,000 each of theirs. With that, Dr. Michael Burry opened Scion Capital. (As a boy he'd loved the book *The Scions of Shannara.*) He created a grandiose memo to lure people not related to him by blood. "The minimum net worth for investors should be $15 million," it said, which was interesting, as it excluded not only himself but basically everyone he'd ever known.

As he scrambled to find office space, buy furniture, and open a brokerage account, he received a pair of surprising phone calls. The first came from a big investment fund in New York City, Gotham Capital. Gotham was founded by a value investment guru named Joel Greenblatt. Burry had read Greenblatt's book *You Can Be a Stock Market Genius.* ("I hated the title but liked the book.") Greenblatt's people told him that they had been making money off his ideas for some time and wanted to continue to do so—might Mike Burry consider allowing Gotham to invest in his fund? "Joel Greenblatt himself called and said, 'I've been waiting for you to leave medicine.'" Gotham flew Burry and his wife to New York—and it was the first time Michael Burry had flown to New York or flown first-class—and put him up in a suite at the Intercontinental Hotel.

On his way to his meeting with Greenblatt, Burry was wracked with the anxiety that always plagued him before face-to-face encounters with people. He took some comfort in the fact that the Gotham people seemed to have read so much of what he had written. "If you read what I wrote first, and then meet me, the meeting goes fine," he said. "People who meet me who haven't read what I wrote—it almost never goes well. Even in high school it was like that—even with teachers." He was a walking blind taste test: You had to decide if you approved of him before you laid eyes on him. In this case he was at a serious disadvantage, as he had no clue how big-time money managers dressed. "He calls me the day before the meeting," says one of his e-mail friends, himself a professional money manager. "And he asks, 'What should I wear?' He didn't own a tie. He had one blue sports coat, for funerals." This was another quirk of Mike Burry's. In writing he presented himself formally, even a bit stuffily, but he dressed for the beach. Walking to Gotham's office, he panicked and ducked into a Tie Rack and bought a tie.

He arrived at the big New York money management firm as formally attired as he had ever been in his entire life to find its partners in t-shirts and sweatpants. The exchange went something like this.

"We'd like to give you a million dollars."

"Excuse me?"

"We want to buy a quarter of your new hedge fund. For a million dollars."

"You do?"

"Yes. We're offering a million dollars."

"After tax!"

Somehow Burry had it in his mind that one day he wanted to be worth a million dollars, after tax. At any rate, he'd just blurted that last bit out before he fully understood what they were after. And they gave it to him! At that moment, on the basis of what he'd written on his blog, he went from being an indebted medical student with a net worth of minus $105,000 to a millionaire with a few outstanding loans. Burry didn't know it, but it was the first time Joel Greenblatt had done such a thing. "He was just obviously this brilliant guy, and there aren't that many of them," says Greenblatt.

Shortly after that odd encounter, he had a call from the insurance holding company White Mountains. White Mountains was run by Jack Byrne, a member of Warren Buffett's inner circle, and they had spoken to Gotham Capital. "We didn't know you were selling part of your firm," they said—and Burry explained that he didn't realize it either until a few days earlier, when someone offered a million dollars, after tax, for it. It turned out that White Mountains, too, had been watching Michael Burry closely. "What intrigued us more than anything was that he was a neurology resident," says Kip Oberting, then at White Mountains. "When the hell was he doing this?" From White Mountains he extracted $600,000 for a smaller piece of his fund, plus a promise to send him $10 million to invest. "And yes," said Oberting, "he was the only person we found on the Internet and cold-called and gave him money."

In Dr. Mike Burry's first year in business, he grappled briefly with the social dimension of running money. "Generally you don't raise any money unless you have a good meeting with people," he said, "and generally I don't want to be around people. And people who are with me generally figure that out." He went to a conference thrown by Bank of America to introduce new fund managers to wealthy investors, and those who attended figured that out. He gave a talk in which he argued that the way they measured risk was completely idiotic. They measured risk by volatility: how much a stock or bond happened to have jumped around in the past few years. Real risk was not volatility; real risk was stupid investment decisions. "By and large," he later put it, "the wealthiest of the wealthy and their representatives have accepted that most managers are average, and the better ones are able to achieve average returns while exhibiting below-average volatility. By this logic a dollar selling for fifty cents one day, sixty cents the next day, and forty cents the next somehow becomes worth less than a dollar selling for fifty cents all three days. I would argue that the ability to buy at forty cents presents opportunity, not risk, and that the dollar is still worth a dollar." He was greeted by silence and ate lunch alone. He sat at one of the big round tables just watching the people at the other tables happily jabber away.

When he spoke to people in the flesh, he could never tell what had put them off, his message or his person. He'd made a close study of Warren Buffett, who had somehow managed to be both wildly popular and hugely successful. Buffett had had trouble with people, too, in his youth. He'd used a Dale Carnegie course to learn how to interact more profitably with his fellow human beings. Mike Burry came of age in a different money culture. The Internet had displaced Dale Carnegie. He didn't need to meet people. He could explain himself online and wait for investors to find him. He could write up his elaborate thoughts and wait for people to read them and wire him their money to handle. "Buffett was too popular for me," said Burry. "I won't ever be a kindly grandfather figure."

This method of attracting funds suited Mike Burry. More to the point, it worked. He'd started Scion Capital with a bit more than a million dollars—the money from his mother and brothers and his own million, after tax. In his first full year, 2001, the S&P 500 fell 11.88 percent. Scion was up 55 percent. The next year, the S&P 500 fell again, by 22.1 percent, and yet Scion was up again: 16 percent. The next year, 2003, the stock market finally turned around and rose 28.69 percent, but Mike Burry beat it again—his investments rose by 50 percent. By the end of 2004, Mike Burry was managing $600 million and turning money away. "If he'd run his fund to maximize the amount he had under management, he'd have been running many, many billions of dollars," says a New York hedge fund manager who watched Burry's performance with growing incredulity. "He designed Scion so it was bad for business but good for investing."

"While capital raising may be a popularity contest," Burry wrote to his investors, perhaps to reassure them that it didn't matter if they loved their money manager, or even knew him, "intelligent investment is quite the opposite."

Warren Buffett had an acerbic partner, Charlie Munger, who evidently cared a lot less than Buffett did about whether people liked him. Back in 1995, Munger had given a talk at Harvard Business School called "The Psychology of Human Misjudgment." If you wanted to predict how people would behave, Munger said, you only had to look at their incentives. FedEx couldn't get its night shift to finish on time; they tried everything to speed it up but nothing worked—until they stopped paying night shift workers by the hour and started to pay them by the shift. Xerox created a new, better machine only to have it sell less well than the inferior older ones—until they figured out the salesmen got a bigger commission for selling the older one. "Well, you can say, 'Everybody knows that,'" said Munger. "I think I've been in the top five percent of my age cohort all my life in understanding the power of incentives, and all my life I've underestimated it. And never a year passes but I get some surprise that pushes my limit a little farther."

Munger's remarks articulated a great deal of what Mike Burry, too, believed about markets and the people who comprised them. "I read that speech and I said, I agree with every single word of that," Burry said, adding, "Munger also has a fake eye." Burry had his own angle on this same subject, derived from the time he'd spent in medicine. Even in life or death situations, doctors, nurses, and patients all responded to bad incentives. In hospitals in which the reimbursement rates for appendectomies ran higher, for instance, the surgeons removed more appendixes. The evolution of eye surgery was another great example. In the 1990s, the ophthalmologists were building careers on performing cataract procedures. They'd take half an hour or less, and yet Medicare would reimburse them $1,700 a pop. In the late 1990s, Medicare slashed reimbursement levels to around $450 per procedure, and the incomes of the surgically minded ophthalmologists fell. Across America, ophthalmologists rediscovered an obscure and risky procedure called radial keratotomy, and there was a boom in surgery to correct small impairments of vision. The inadequately studied procedure was marketed as a cure for the suffering of contact lens wearers. "In reality," says Burry, "the incentive was to maintain their high, often one- to two-million-dollar incomes, and the justification followed. The industry rushed to come up with something less dangerous than radial keratotomy, and Lasik was eventually born."

Thus when Mike Burry went into business he made sure that he had the proper incentives. He disapproved of the typical hedge fund manager's deal. Taking 2 percent of assets off the top, as most did, meant the hedge fund manager got paid simply for amassing vast amounts of other people's money. Scion Capital charged investors only its actual expenses—which typically ran well below 1 percent of the assets. To make the first nickel for himself, he had to make investors' money grow. "Think about the genesis of Scion," says one of his early investors. "The guy has no money and he chooses to forgo a fee that any other hedge fund takes for granted. It was unheard of."

Right from the start, Scion Capital was madly, almost comically, successful. By the middle of 2005, over a period in which the broad stock market index had fallen by 6.84 percent, Burry's fund was up 242 percent and he was turning away investors. To his swelling audience, it didn't seem to matter whether the stock market rose or fell; Mike Burry found places to invest money shrewdly. He used no leverage and avoided shorting stocks. He was doing nothing more promising than buying common stocks and nothing more complicated than sitting in a room reading financial statements. For roughly $100 a year he became a subscriber to 10-K Wizard. Scion Capital's decision-making apparatus consisted of one guy in a room, with the door closed and the shades drawn, poring over publicly available information and data on 10-K Wizard. He went looking for court rulings, deal completions, or government regulatory changes—anything that might change the value of a company.

Often as not, he turned up what he called "ick" investments. In October 2001, he explained the concept in his letter to investors: "Ick investing means taking a special analytical interest in stocks that inspire a first reaction of 'ick.'"

The alarmingly named Avant! Corporation was a good example. He'd found it searching for the word "accepted" in news stories. He knew that, standing on the edge of the playing field, he needed to find unorthodox ways to tilt it to his advantage, and that usually meant finding unusual situations the world might not be fully aware of. "I wasn't searching for a news report of a scam or fraud per se," he said. "That would have been too backward-looking, and I was looking to get in front of something. I was looking for something happening in the courts that might lead to an investment thesis. An argument being accepted, a plea being accepted, a settlement being accepted by the court." A court had accepted a plea from a software company called the Avant! Corporation. Avant! had been accused of stealing from a competitor the software code that was the whole foundation of Avant!'s business. The company had $100 million in cash in the bank, was still generating $100 million a year of free cash flow—and had a market value of only $250 million! Michael Burry started digging; by the time he was done, he knew more about the Avant! Corporation than any man on earth. He was able to see that even if the executives went to jail (as they did) and the fines were paid (as they were), Avant! would be worth a lot more than the market then assumed. Most of its engineers were Chinese nationals on work visas, and thus trapped—there was no risk that anyone would quit before the lights were out. To make money on Avant!'s stock, however, he'd probably have to stomach short-term losses, as investors puked up shares in horrified response to negative publicity.

Burry bought his first shares of Avant! in June 2001 at $12 a share.

Avant!'s management then appeared on the cover of an issue of *BusinessWeek* under the headline "Does Crime Pay?" The stock plunged; Burry bought more. Avant!'s management went to jail. The stock fell some more. Mike Burry kept on buying it—all the way down to $2 a share. He became Avant!'s single largest shareholder; he pressed management for changes. "With [the former CEO's] criminal aura no longer a part of operating management," he wrote to the new bosses, "Avant! has a chance to demonstrate its concern for shareholders." In August, in another e-mail, he wrote, "Avant! still makes me feel I'm sleeping with the village slut. No matter how well my needs are met, I doubt I'll ever brag about it. The 'creep' factor is off the charts. I half think that if I pushed Avant! too hard I'd end up being terrorized by the Chinese mafia." Four months later, Avant! got taken over for $22 a share. "That was a classic Mike Burry trade," says one of his investors. "It goes up by ten times but first it goes down by half."

This isn't the sort of ride most investors enjoy, but it was, Burry thought, the essence of value investing. His job was to disagree loudly with popular sentiment. He couldn't do this if he was at the mercy of very short-term market moves, and so he didn't give his investors the ability to remove their money on short notice, as most hedge funds did. If you gave Scion your money to invest, you were stuck for at least a year. Burry also designed his fund to attract people who wanted to be long the stock market—who wanted to bet on stocks going up rather than stocks going down. "I am not a short at heart," he said. "I don't dig into companies looking to short them, generally. I want the upside to be much more than the downside, fundamentally." He also didn't like the idea of taking the risk of selling a stock short, as the risk was, theoretically, unlimited. It could only fall to zero, but it could rise to infinity.

Investing well was all about being paid the right price for risk. Increasingly, Burry felt that he wasn't. The problem wasn't confined to individual stocks. The Internet bubble had burst, and yet house prices in San Jose, the bubble's epicenter, were still rising. He investigated the stocks of home builders, and then the stocks of companies that insured home mortgages, like PMI. To one of his friends—a big-time East Coast professional investor—he wrote in May 2003 that the real estate bubble was being driven ever higher by the irrational behavior of mortgage lenders who were extending easy credit. "You just have to watch for the level at which even nearly unlimited or unprecedented credit can no longer drive the [housing] market higher," he wrote. "I am extremely bearish, and feel the consequences could very easily be a 50% drop in residential real estate in the U.S. . . . A large portion of current [housing] demand at current prices would disappear if only people became convinced that prices weren't rising. The collateral damage is likely to be orders of magnitude worse than anyone now considers."

When he set out to bet against the subprime mortgage bond market, in early 2005, the first big problem that he encountered was that the Wall Street investment banks that might sell him credit default swaps didn't share his sense of urgency. Mike Burry believed he had to place this bet *now,* before the U.S. housing market woke up and was restored to sanity. "I didn't expect fundamental deterioration in the underlying mortgage pools to hit critical levels for a couple years," he said—when the teaser rates would vanish and monthly payments would skyrocket. But he thought the market inevitably would see what he had seen and adjust. Someone on Wall Street would notice the fantastic increase in the riskiness of subprime mortgages and raise the price of insuring them accordingly. "It's going to blow up before I can get this trade on," he wrote in an e-mail.

As Burry lived his life by e-mail, he inadvertently kept a record of the birth of a new market from the point of view of its first retail customer. In retrospect, the amazing thing was just how quickly Wall

Street firms went from having no idea what Mike Burry was talking about when he called and asked them about credit default swaps on subprime mortgage bonds, to reshaping their business in a way that left the new derivative smack at the center. The original mortgage bond market had come into the world in much the same way, messily, coaxed into existence by the extreme interest of a small handful of people on the margins of high finance. But it had taken years for that market to mature; this new market would be up and running and trading tens of billions of dollars' worth of risk within a few months.

The first thing Mike Burry needed, if he was going to buy insurance on a big pile of subprime mortgage bonds, was to create some kind of standard, widely agreed-upon contract. Whoever sold him a credit default swap on a subprime mortgage bond would one day owe him a great deal of money. He suspected that dealers might try to get out of paying it to him. A contract would make it harder for them to do that, and easier for him to sell to one dealer what he had bought from another—and thus to shop around for prices. An organization called International Swaps and Derivatives Association (ISDA) had the task of formalizing the terms of new securities.* ISDA already had a set of rules in place to govern credit default swaps on corporate bonds, but insurance on corporate bonds was a relatively simple matter. There was this event, called a default, that either did or did not happen. The company missed an interest payment, you had to

* ISDA had been created back in 1985, by my bosses at Salomon Brothers, to deal with the immediate problem of an innovation called an interest rate swap. What seemed like a simple trade to the people doing it—I pay you a fixed rate of interest in exchange for your paying me a floating rate—wound up needing a blizzard of rules to govern it. Beneath the rules was the simple fear that the party on the other side of a Wall Street firm's interest rate swap might go bust and fail to pay off its bets. The interest rate swap, like the credit default swap, exposed Wall Street firms to other people's credit, and other people to the credit of Wall Street firms, in new ways.

settle. The insurance buyer might not collect the full 100 cents on the dollar—just as the bondholder might not lose 100 cents on the dollar, as the company's assets were worth something—but an independent judge could decide, in a way that was generally fair and satisfying, what the recovery would be. If the bondholders received 30 cents on the dollar—thus experiencing a loss of 70 cents—the guy who had bought the credit default swap got 70 cents.

Buying insurance on a pool of U.S. home mortgages was more complicated, because the pool didn't default all at once; rather, one homeowner at a time defaulted. The dealers—led by Deutsche Bank and Goldman Sachs—came up with a clever solution: the pay-as-you-go credit default swap. The buyer of the swap—the buyer of insurance—would be paid off not all at once, if and when the entire pool of mortgages went bust, but incrementally, as individual homeowners went into default.

The ISDA agreement took months of haggling among lawyers and traders from the big Wall Street firms, who would run the market. Burry's lawyer, Steve Druskin, was for some reason allowed to lurk on the phone calls—and even jump in from time to time and offer the Wall Street customer's point of view. Historically, a Wall Street firm worried over the creditworthiness of its customers; its customers often took it on faith that the casino would be able to pay off its winners. Mike Burry lacked faith. "I'm not making a bet against a bond," he said. "I'm making a bet against a system." He didn't want to buy flood insurance from Goldman Sachs only to find, when the flood came, Goldman Sachs washed away and unable to pay him off. As the value of the insurance contract changed—say, as floodwaters approached but before they actually destroyed the building—he wanted Goldman Sachs and Deutsche Bank to post collateral, to reflect the increase in value of what he owned.

On May 19, 2005—a month before the terms were finalized—Mike Burry did his first subprime mortgage deals. He bought $60 million in credit default swaps from Deutsche Bank—$10 million each on six different bonds. "The reference securities," these were called. You didn't buy insurance on the entire subprime mortgage bond market but on a particular bond, and Burry had devoted himself to finding exactly the right ones to bet against. He'd read dozens of prospectuses and scoured hundreds more, looking for the dodgiest pools of mortgages, and was still pretty certain even then (and dead certain later) that he was the only human being on earth who read them, apart from the lawyers who drafted them. In doing so, he likely also became the only investor to do the sort of old-fashioned bank credit analysis on the home loans that should have been done before they were made. He was the opposite of an old-fashioned banker, however. He was looking not for the best loans to make but the worst loans—so that he could bet against them.

He analyzed the relative importance of the loan-to-value ratios of the home loans, of second liens on the homes, of the location of the homes, of the absence of loan documentation and proof of income of the borrower, and a dozen or so other factors to determine the likelihood that a home loan made in America circa 2005 would go bad. Then he went looking for the bonds backed by the worst of the loans. It surprised him that Deutsche Bank didn't seem to care which bonds he picked to bet against. From their point of view, so far as he could tell, all subprime mortgage bonds were the same. The price of insurance was driven not by any independent analysis but by the ratings placed on the bond by the rating agencies, Moody's and Standard & Poor's.* If he wanted to buy insurance on the supposedly riskless

* The two major rating agencies employ slightly different terminology to convey the same idea. What Standard & Poor's denotes as AAA, for instance, Moody's denotes as Aaa, but both terms describe a bond judged to have the least risk of default. For simplicity's sake, the text will use only the S&P terms, and AAA will be called triple-A, and so forth.

In 2008, when the ratings of a giant pile of subprime-related bonds triple-A-rated tranche, he might pay 20 basis points (0.20 percent); on the riskier AA-rated tranches, he might pay 50 basis points (0.50 percent); and, on the even less safe triple-B-rated tranches, 200 basis points—that is, 2 percent. (A basis point is one-hundredth of one percentage point.) The triple-B-rated tranches—the ones that would be worth zero if the underlying mortgage pool experienced a loss of just 7 percent—were what he was after. He felt this to be a very conservative bet, which he was able, through analysis, to turn into even more of a sure thing. Anyone who even glanced at the prospectuses could see that there were many critical differences between one triple-B bond and the next—the percentage of interest-only loans contained in their underlying pool of mortgages, for example. He set out to cherry-pick the absolute worst ones, and was a bit worried that the investment banks would catch on to just how much he knew about specific mortgage bonds, and adjust their prices.

Once again they shocked and delighted him: Goldman Sachs e-mailed him a great long list of crappy mortgage bonds to choose from. "This was shocking to me, actually," he says. "They were all priced according to the lowest rating from one of the big three ratings agencies." He could pick from the list without alerting them to the depth of his knowledge. It was as if you could buy flood insurance on the house in the valley for the same price as flood insurance on the house on the mountaintop.

---

proved meaningless, their intended meanings were hotly disputed. Wall Street investors had long interpreted them to mean the odds of default. For instance, a bond rated triple-A historically had less than a 1-in-10,000 chance of defaulting in its first year of existence. A bond rated double-A—the next highest rating—stood less than a 1-in-1,000 chance of default, and a bond rated triple-B, less than a 1-in-500 chance of default. In 2008, the rating agencies would claim that they never intended for their ratings to be taken as such precise measurements. Ratings were merely the agencies' best guess at a rank ordering of risk.

The market made no sense, but that didn't stop other Wall Street firms from jumping into it, in part because Mike Burry was pestering them. For weeks he hounded Bank of America until they agreed to sell him $5 million in credit default swaps. Twenty minutes after they sent their e-mail confirming the trade, they received another back from Burry: "So can we do another?" In a few weeks Mike Burry bought several hundred million dollars in credit default swaps from half a dozen banks, in chunks of $5 million. None of the sellers appeared to care very much which bonds they were insuring. He found one mortgage pool that was 100 percent floating-rate negative-amortizing mortgages—where the borrowers could choose the option of not paying any interest at all and simply accumulate a bigger and bigger debt until, presumably, they defaulted on it. Goldman Sachs not only sold him insurance on the pool but sent him a little note congratulating him on being the first person, on Wall Street or off, ever to buy insurance on that particular item. "I'm educating the experts here," Burry crowed in an e-mail.

He wasn't wasting a lot of time worrying about why these supposedly shrewd investment bankers were willing to sell him insurance so cheaply. He was worried that others would catch on and the opportunity would vanish. "I would play dumb quite a bit," he said, "making it seem to them like I don't really know what I'm doing. 'How do you do this again?' 'Oh, where can I find that information?' Or, 'Really?'—when they tell me something really obvious." It was one of the fringe benefits of living for so many years essentially alienated from the world around him: He could easily believe that he was right and the world was wrong.

The more Wall Street firms jumped into the new business, the easier it became for him to place his bets. For the first few months he was able to short, at most, $10 million at a time. Then, in late June 2005, he had a call from someone at Goldman Sachs asking him if he'd like to increase his trade size to $100 million a pop. "What needs to be remembered here," he wrote the next day, after he'd done it, "is that this is $100 million. That's an insane amount of money. And it just gets thrown around like it's three digits instead of nine."

By the end of July he owned credit default swaps on $750 million in subprime mortgage bonds and was privately bragging about it. "I believe no other hedge fund on the planet has this sort of investment, nowhere near to this degree, relative to the size of the portfolio," he wrote to one of his investors, who had caught wind that his hedge fund manager had some newfangled strategy. Now he couldn't help but wonder who exactly was on the other side of his trades—what madman would be selling him so much insurance on bonds he had handpicked to explode? The credit default swap was a zero-sum game. If Mike Burry made $100 million when the subprime mortgage bonds he had handpicked defaulted, someone else must have lost $100 million. Goldman Sachs made it clear that the ultimate seller wasn't Goldman Sachs. Goldman Sachs was simply standing between insurance buyer and insurance seller and taking a cut.

The willingness of whoever this person was to sell him such vast amounts of cheap insurance gave Mike Burry another idea: to start a fund that did nothing but buy insurance on subprime mortgage bonds. In a $600 million fund that was meant to be picking stocks, his bet was already gargantuan; but if he could raise the money explicitly for this new purpose, he could do many billions more. In August he wrote a proposal for a fund he called Milton's Opus and sent it out to his investors. ("The first question was always, 'What's Milton's Opus?'" He'd say, "*Paradise Lost*," but that usually just raised another question.) Most of them still had no idea that their champion stock picker had become so diverted by these esoteric insurance contracts called credit default swaps. Many wanted nothing to do with it; a few wondered if this meant that he was already doing this sort of thing with their money.

Instead of raising more money to buy credit default swaps on subprime mortgage bonds, he wound up making it more difficult to keep the ones he already owned. His investors were happy to let him pick stocks on their behalf, but they almost universally doubted his ability to foresee big macroeconomic trends. And they certainly didn't see why he should have any special insight into the multi-trillion-dollar subprime mortgage bond market. Milton's Opus died a quick death.

In October 2005, in his letter to investors, Burry finally came completely clean and let them know that they owned at least a billion dollars in credit default swaps on subprime mortgage bonds. "Sometimes markets err big time," he wrote.

> Markets erred when they gave America Online the currency to buy Time Warner. They erred when they bet against George Soros and for the British pound. And they are erring right now by continuing to float along as if the most significant credit bubble history has ever seen does not exist. Opportunities are rare, and large opportunities on which one can put nearly unlimited capital to work at tremendous potential returns are even more rare. Selectively shorting the most problematic mortgage-backed securities in history today amounts to just such an opportunity.

In the second quarter of 2005, credit card delinquencies hit an all-time high—even though house prices had boomed. That is, even with this asset to borrow against, Americans were struggling more than ever to meet their obligations. The Federal Reserve had raised interest rates, but mortgage rates were still effectively falling—because Wall Street was finding ever more clever ways to enable people to borrow money. Burry now had more than a billion-dollar bet on the table and couldn't grow it much more unless he attracted a lot more money. So he just laid it out for his investors: The U.S. mortgage bond market was huge, bigger than the market for U.S. Treasury notes and bonds. The entire economy was premised on its stability, and its stability in turn depended on house prices continuing to rise. "It is ludicrous to believe that asset bubbles can only be recognized in hindsight," he wrote. "There are specific identifiers that are entirely recognizable during the bubble's inflation. One hallmark of mania is the rapid rise in the incidence and complexity of fraud. . . . The FBI reports mortgage-related fraud is up fivefold since 2000." Bad behavior was no longer on the fringes of an otherwise sound economy; it was its central feature. "The salient point about the modern vintage of housing-related fraud is its integral place within our nation's institutions," he added.

This wasn't all that different from what he'd been saying in his quarterly letters to his investors for the past two years. Back in July 2003, he'd written them a long essay on the causes and consequences of what he took to be a likely housing crash: "Alan Greenspan assures us that home prices are not prone to bubbles—or major deflations—on any national scale," he'd said. "This is ridiculous, of course. . . . In 1933, during the fourth year of the Great Depression, the United States found itself in the midst of a housing crisis that put housing starts at 10% of the level of 1925. Roughly half of all mortgage debt was in default. During the 1930s, housing prices collapsed nationwide by roughly 80%." He harped on the same theme again in January 2004, then again in January 2005: "Want to borrow $1,000,000 for just $25 a month? Quicken Loans has now introduced an interest only adjustable rate mortgage that gives borrowers six months with both zero payments and a 0.03% interest rate, no doubt in support of that wholesome slice of Americana—the home buyer with the short term cash flow problem."

When his investors learned that their money manager had actually put their money directly where his mouth had long been, they were not exactly pleased. As one investor put it, "Mike's the best stock picker anyone knows. And he's doing . . . what?" Some were upset that a guy they had hired to pick stocks had gone off to pick rotten mortgage bonds instead; some wondered, if credit default swaps were such a great deal, why Goldman Sachs would be selling them; some questioned the wisdom of trying to call the top of a seventy-year housing cycle; some didn't really understand exactly what a credit default swap was, or how it worked. "It has been my experience that apocalyptic forecasts on the U.S. financial markets are rarely realized within limited horizons," one investor wrote to Burry. "There have been legitimate apocalyptic cases to be made on U.S. financial markets during most of my career. They usually have not been realized." Burry replied that while it was true that he foresaw Armageddon, he wasn't betting on it. That was the beauty of credit default swaps: They enabled him to make a fortune if just a tiny fraction of these dubious pools of mortgages went bad.

Inadvertently, he'd opened up a debate with his own investors, which he counted among his least favorite activities. "I hated discussing ideas with investors," he said, "because I then become a Defender of the Idea, and that influences your thought process." Once you became an idea's defender you had a harder time changing your mind about it. He had no choice: Among the people who gave him money there was pretty obviously a built-in skepticism of so-called macro thinking. They could understand why this very bright guy rooting around in financial statements might stumble across a small company no one else was paying attention to. They couldn't see why he should have a deeper understanding of trends and global forces apparent to any American who flipped on a cable news program. "I have heard that White Mountains would rather I stick to my knitting," he wrote, testily, to his original backer, "though it is not clear to me that White Mountains has historically understood what my knitting really is." No one seemed able to see what was so plain to him: These credit default swaps were all part of his global search for value. "I don't take breaks in my search for value," he wrote to White Mountains. "There is no golf or other hobby to distract me. Seeing value is what I do."

When he'd started Scion, he'd told potential investors that, because he was in the business of making unfashionable bets, they should evaluate him over the long term—say, five years. Now he was being evaluated moment to moment. "Early on, people invested in me because of my letters," he said. "And then somehow after they invested, they stopped reading them." His fantastic success attracted lots of new investors, but they were less interested in the spirit of his enterprise than in how much money he could make them quickly. Every quarter, he told them how much he'd made or lost from his stock picks. Now he had to explain that they had to subtract from that number these . . . subprime mortgage bond insurance premiums. One of his New York investors called and said ominously, "You know a lot of people are talking about withdrawing funds from you."

As their funds were contractually stuck inside Scion Capital for some time, the investors' only recourse was to send him disturbed-sounding e-mails asking him to justify his new strategy. "People get hung up on the difference between +5% and –5% for a couple of years," Burry replied to one investor who had protested the new strategy. "When the real issue is: over 10 years who does 10% better annually? And I firmly believe that to achieve that advantage on an annual basis, I have to be able to look out past the next couple of years. . . . I have to be steadfast in the face of popular discontent if that's what the fundamentals tell me." In the five years since he had started, the S&P 500, against which he was measured, was down 6.84 percent. In the same period, he reminded his investors, Scion Capital was up 242 percent. He assumed he'd earned the rope to hang himself. He assumed wrong. "I'm building breathtaking sand castles," he wrote, "but nothing stops the tide from coming and coming and coming."

Oddly, as Mike Burry's investors grew restive, his Wall Street counterparties took a new and envious interest in what he was up to. In late

October 2005, a subprime trader at Goldman Sachs called to ask him why he was buying credit default swaps on such very specific tranches of subprime mortgage bonds. The trader let it slip that a number of hedge funds had been calling Goldman to ask "how to do the short housing trade that Scion is doing." Among those asking about it were people Burry had solicited for Milton's Opus—people who had initially expressed great interest. "These people by and large did not know anything about how to do the trade and expected Goldman to help them replicate it," Burry wrote in an e-mail to his CFO. "My suspicion is Goldman helped them, though they deny it." If nothing else, he now understood why he couldn't raise money for Milton's Opus. "If I describe it enough it sounds compelling, and people think they can do it for themselves," he wrote to an e-mail confidant. "If I don't describe it enough, it sounds scary and binary and I can't raise the capital." He had no talent for selling.

Now the subprime mortgage bond market appeared to be unraveling. Out of the blue, on November 4, Burry had an e-mail from the head subprime guy at Deutsche Bank, a fellow named Greg Lippmann. As it happened, Deutsche Bank had broken off relations with Mike Burry back in June, after Burry had been, in Deutsche Bank's view, overly aggressive in his demands for collateral. Now this guy calls and says he'd like to buy back the original six credit default swaps Scion had bought in May. As the $60 million represented a tiny slice of Burry's portfolio, and as he didn't want any more to do with Deutsche Bank than Deutsche Bank wanted to do with him, he sold them back, at a profit. Greg Lippmann wrote back hastily and ungrammatically, "Would you like to give us some other bonds that we can tell you what we will pay you."

Greg Lippmann of Deutsche Bank wanted to buy his billion dollars in credit default swaps! "Thank you for the look Greg," Burry replied. "We're good for now." He signed off, thinking, How strange. I haven't dealt with Deutsche Bank in five months. How does Greg Lippmann even know I own this giant pile of credit default swaps?

Three days later he heard from Goldman Sachs. His saleswoman, Veronica Grinstein, called him on her cell phone, which is what she did when she wanted to talk without being recorded. (Wall Street firms now recorded all calls made from their trading desks.) "I'd like a special favor," she asked. She, too, wanted to buy some of his credit default swaps. "Management is concerned," she said. They thought the traders had sold all this insurance without having any place they could go to buy it back. Could Mike Burry sell them $25 million of the stuff, at really generous prices, on the subprime mortgage bonds of his choosing? Just to placate Goldman management, you understand. Hanging up, he pinged Bank of America, on a hunch, to see if they would sell him more. They wouldn't. They, too, were looking to buy. Next came Morgan Stanley—again out of the blue. He hadn't done much business with Morgan Stanley, but evidently Morgan Stanley, too, wanted to buy whatever he had. He didn't know exactly why all these banks were suddenly so keen to buy insurance on subprime mortgage bonds, but there was one obvious reason: The loans suddenly were going bad at an alarming rate. Back in May, Mike Burry was betting on his theory of human behavior: The loans were structured to go bad. Now, in November, they were actually going bad.

The next morning, Burry opened the *Wall Street Journal* to find an article explaining how the new wave of adjustable-rate mortgages were defaulting, in their first nine months, at rates never before seen. Lower-middle-class America was tapped out. There was even a little chart to show readers who didn't have time to read the article. He thought, The cat's out of the bag. The world's about to change. Lenders will raise their standards; rating agencies will take a closer look; and no dealers in their right mind will sell insurance on subprime mortgage bonds at anything like the prices they've been selling it.

"I'm thinking the lightbulb is going to pop on and some smart credit officer is going to say, 'Get out of these trades,'" he said. Most Wall Street traders were about to lose a lot of money—with perhaps one exception. Mike Burry had just received another e-mail, from one of his own investors, that suggested that Deutsche Bank might have been influenced by his one-eyed view of the financial markets: "Greg Lippmann, the head [subprime mortgage] trader at Deutsche Bank[,] was in here the other day," it read. "He told us that he was short 1 billion dollars of this stuff and was going to make 'oceans' of money (or something to that effect.) His exuberance was a little scary."

CHAPTER THREE

"How Can a Guy Who Can't Speak English Lie?"

By the time Greg Lippmann turned up in the FrontPoint conference room, in February 2006, Steve Eisman knew enough about the bond market to be wary, and Vincent Daniel knew enough to have decided that no one in it could ever be trusted. An investor who went from the stock market to the bond market was like a small, furry creature raised on an island without predators removed to a pit full of pythons. It was possible to get ripped off by the big Wall Street firms in the stock market, but you really had to work at it. The entire market traded on screens, so you always had a clear view of the price of the stock of any given company. The stock market was not only transparent but heavily policed. You couldn't expect a Wall Street trader to share with you his every negative thought about public companies, but you could expect he wouldn't work very hard to sucker you with outright lies, or blatantly use inside information to trade against you, mainly because there was at least a chance he'd be caught if he did. The presence of millions of small investors had politicized the stock market. It had been legislated and regulated to at least seem fair.

The bond market, because it consisted mainly of big institutional investors, experienced no similarly populist political pressure. Even as it came to dwarf the stock market, the bond market eluded serious regulation. Bond salesmen could say and do anything without fear that they'd be reported to some authority. Bond traders could exploit inside information without worrying that they would be caught. Bond technicians could dream up ever more complicated securities without worrying too much about government regulation—one reason why so many derivatives had been derived, one way or another, from bonds. The bigger, more liquid end of the bond market—the market for U.S. Treasury bonds, for example—traded on screens, but in many cases the only way to determine if the price some bond trader had given you was even close to fair was to call around and hope to find some other bond trader making a market in that particular obscure security. The opacity and complexity of the bond market was, for big Wall Street firms, a huge advantage. The bond market customer lived in perpetual fear of what he didn't know. If Wall Street bond departments were increasingly the source of Wall Street profits, it was in part because of this: In the bond market it was still possible to make huge sums of money from the fear, and the ignorance, of customers.

And so it was no particular reflection on Greg Lippmann that, upon entering Steve Eisman's office, he collided with a wall of suspicion. "Moses could have walked in the door, and if he said he came from fixed income, Vinny wouldn't have trusted him," said Eisman.

Still, if a team of experts had set out to create a human being to maximize the likelihood that he would terrify a Wall Street customer, they might have designed something like Lippmann. He traded bonds for Deutsche Bank, but, like most people who traded bonds for Deutsche Bank—or for Credit Suisse or UBS or one of the other big foreign banks that had purchased a toehold in the U.S. financial markets—he was an American. Thin and tightly wound, he spoke too quickly for anyone to follow exactly what he was saying. He wore his hair slicked back, in the manner of Gordon Gekko, and the sideburns long, in the fashion of an 1820s Romantic composer or a 1970s porn star. He wore loud ties, and said outrageous things without the slightest apparent awareness of how they might sound if repeated unsympathetically. He peppered his conversation with cryptic references to how much money he made, for instance. People on Wall Street had long ago learned that their bonuses were the last thing they should talk about with people off Wall Street. "Let's say they paid me six million last year," Lippmann would say. "I'm not saying they did. It was less than that. I'm not saying how much less." Before you could protest—*But I never asked!*—he'd say, "The kind of year I had, no way they pay me less than four million." Now he had you thinking about it: *So the number is between $4 million and $6 million*. You could have started out talking about New York City Ballet, and you wound up playing Battleship. Lippmann kept giving you these coordinates, until you were almost forced to identify the location of the ship—exactly what just about everyone else on Wall Street hoped you'd never do.

In further violation of the code, Lippmann was quick to let people know that whatever he'd been paid by his employer was not anything like what he'd been worth. "Senior management's job is to pay people," he'd say. "If they fuck a hundred guys out of a hundred grand each, that's ten million more for them. They have four categories: happy, satisfied, dissatisfied, disgusted. If they hit happy, they've screwed up: They never want you happy. On the other hand, they don't want you so disgusted you quit. The sweet spot is somewhere between dissatisfied and disgusted." At some point in between 1986 and 2006 a memo had gone out on Wall Street, saying that if you wanted to keep on getting rich shuffling bits of paper around to no obvious social purpose, you had better camouflage your true nature. Greg Lippmann was incapable of disguising himself or his motives.

"I don't have any particular allegiance to Deutsche Bank," he'd say. "I just work there." This was not an unusual attitude. What was unusual was that Lippmann said it.

The least controversial thing to be said about Lippmann was that he was controversial. He wasn't just a good bond trader, he was a great bond trader. He wasn't cruel. He wasn't even rude, at least not intentionally. He simply evoked extreme feelings in others. A trader who worked near him for years referred to him as "the asshole known as Greg Lippmann." When asked why, he said, "He took everything too far."

"I love Greg," said one of his bosses at Deutsche Bank. "I have nothing bad to say about him except that he's a fucking whack job." But when you cleared away the controversy around Lippmann's persona you could see it was rooted in two simple complaints. The first was that he was transparently self-interested and self-promotional. The second was that he was excessively alert to the self-interest and self-promotion of others. He had an almost freakish ability to identify shadowy motives. If you had just donated $20 million to your alma mater, say, and were feeling the glow of selfless devotion to a cause greater than yourself, Lippmann would be the first to ask, "So you gave twenty million because that's the minimum to get your name on a building, right?"

Now this character turns up out of nowhere to sell Steve Eisman on what he claims is his own original brilliant idea for betting against the subprime mortgage bond market. He made his case with a long and involved forty-two-page presentation: Over the past three years housing prices had risen far more rapidly than they had over the previous thirty; housing prices had not yet fallen but they had ceased to rise; even so, the loans against them were now going sour in their first year at amazing rates—up from 1 percent to 4 percent. Who borrowed money to buy a house and defaulted inside of twelve months?

He went on for a bit, then showed Eisman this little chart that he'd created, and which he claimed was the reason he had become interested in the trade. It illustrated an astonishing fact: Since 2000, people whose homes had risen in value between 1 and 5 percent were nearly four times more likely to default on their home loans than people whose homes had risen in value more than 10 percent. Millions of Americans had no ability to repay their mortgages unless their houses rose dramatically in value, which enabled them to borrow even more.

That was the pitch in a nutshell: Home prices didn't even need to fall. They merely needed to stop rising at the unprecedented rates they had the previous few years for vast numbers of Americans to default on their home loans.

"Shorting Home Equity Mezzanine Tranches," Lippmann called his presentation. "Shorting Home Equity Mezzanine Tranches" was just a fancy way to describe Mike Burry's idea of betting against U.S. home loans: buying credit default swaps on the crappiest triple-B slices of subprime mortgage bonds. Lippmann himself described it more bluntly to a Deutsche Bank colleague who had seen the presentation and dubbed him "Chicken Little." "Fuck you," Lippmann had said. "I'm short your house."

The beauty of the credit default swap, or CDS, was that it solved the timing problem. Eisman no longer needed to guess exactly when the subprime mortgage market would crash. It also allowed him to make the bet without laying down cash up front, and put him in a position to win many times the sums he could possibly lose. Worst case: Insolvent Americans somehow paid off their subprime mortgage loans, and you were stuck paying an insurance premium of roughly 2 percent a year for as long as six years—the longest expected lifespan of the putatively thirty-year loans.

The alacrity with which subprime borrowers paid off their loans was yet another strange aspect of this booming market. It had to do with the structure of the loans, which were fixed for two or three years at an artificially low teaser rate before shooting up to the "go-to" floating rate. "They were making loans to lower-income people at a teaser rate when they knew they couldn't afford to pay the go-to rate," said Eisman. "They were doing it so that when the borrowers get to the end of the teaser rate period, they'd have to refinance, so the lenders can make more money off them." Thirty-year loans were thus designed to be repaid in a few years. At worst, if you bought credit default swaps on $100 million in subprime mortgage bonds you might wind up shelling out premium for six years—call it $12 million. At best: Losses on the loans rose from the current 4 percent to 8 percent, and you made $100 million. The bookies were offering you odds of somewhere between 6:1 and 10:1 when the odds of it working out felt more like 2:1. Anyone in the business of making smart bets couldn't not do it.

The argument stopper was Lippmann's one-man quantitative support team. His name was Eugene Xu, but to those who'd heard Lippmann's pitch, he was generally spoken of as "Lippmann's Chinese quant." Xu was an analyst employed by Deutsche Bank, but Lippmann gave everyone the idea he kept him tied up to his Bloomberg terminal like a pet. A real Chinese guy—not even Chinese American—who apparently spoke no English, just numbers. China had this national math competition, Lippmann told people, in which Eugene had finished second. *In all of China*. Eugene Xu was responsible for every piece of hard data in Lippmann's presentation. Once Eugene was introduced into the equation, no one bothered Lippmann about his math or his data. As Lippmann put it, "How can a guy who can't speak English lie?"

There was a lot more to it than that. Lippmann brimmed with fascinating details: the historical behavior of the American homeowner; the idiocy and corruption of the rating agencies, Moody's and S&P, who stuck a triple-B rating on subprime bonds that went bad when losses in the underlying pools of home loans reached just 8 percent;* the widespread fraud in the mortgage market; the folly of subprime mortgage investors, some large number of whom seemed to live in Düsseldorf, Germany. "Whenever we'd ask him who was buying this crap," said Vinny, "he always just said, 'Düsseldorf.'" It didn't matter whether Düsseldorf was buying actual cash subprime mortgage bonds or selling credit default swaps on those same mortgage bonds, as they amounted to one and the same thing: the long side of the bet.

Lippmann brimmed, also, with Lippmann. He hinted Eisman might get so rich from the trade he could buy the Los Angeles Dodgers. ("I'm not saying you're going to be able to buy the Dodgers.") Eisman might become so rich that movie stars would crave his body. ("I'm not saying you're going to date Jessica Simpson.") With one hand Lippmann presented the facts of the trade; with the other he tap-tap-tapped away, like a dowser probing for a well hidden deep in Eisman's character.

Keeping one eye on Greg Lippmann and the other on Steve Eisman, Vincent Daniel half expected the room to explode. Instead Steve Eisman found nothing even faintly objectionable about Greg Lippmann. *Great guy!* Eisman really only had a couple of questions. The first: Tell me again how the hell a credit default swap works? The second: Why are you asking me to bet against bonds your own firm is creating, and arranging for the rating agencies to mis-rate? "In my entire life I never saw a sell-side guy come in and say, 'Short my market,'" said Eisman. Lippmann wasn't even a bond salesman; he

* These losses turned not only on how many borrowers defaulted, but also on the cost of each default. After all, the lender held the collateral of the house. As a rule of thumb, in the event of default, the lender collected roughly 50 cents on the dollar. And so roughly 16 percent of the borrowers in a mortgage pool needed to default for the pool to experience losses of 8 percent.

was a bond trader who might be expected to be long these very same subprime mortgage bonds. "I didn't mistrust him," says Eisman. "I didn't understand him. Vinny was the one who was sure he was going to fuck us in some way."

Eisman had no trouble betting against subprime mortgages. Indeed, he could imagine very little that would give him so much pleasure as the thought of going to bed each night, possibly for the next six years, knowing he was short a financial market he had come to know and despise and was certain would one day explode. "When he walked in and said you can make money shorting subprime paper, it was like putting a naked supermodel in front of me," said Eisman. "What I couldn't understand was why he wanted me to do it." That question, as it turned out, was more interesting than even Eisman suspected.

The subprime mortgage market was generating half a trillion dollars' worth of new loans a year, but the circle of people redistributing the risk that the entire market would collapse was tiny. When the Goldman Sachs saleswoman called Mike Burry and told him that her firm would be happy to sell him credit default swaps in $100 million chunks, Burry guessed, rightly, that Goldman wasn't ultimately on the other side of his bets. Goldman would never be so stupid as to make huge naked bets that millions of insolvent Americans would repay their home loans. He didn't know who, or why, or how much, but he knew that some giant corporate entity with a triple-A rating was out there selling credit default swaps on subprime mortgage bonds. Only a triple-A-rated corporation could assume such risk, no money down, and no questions asked. Burry was right about this, too, but it would be three years before he knew it. The party on the other side of his bet against subprime mortgage bonds was the triple-A-rated insurance company AIG—American International Group, Inc. Or, rather, a unit of AIG called AIG FP.

AIG Financial Products was created in 1987 by refugees from Michael Milken's bond department at Drexel Burnham, led by a trader named Howard Sosin, who claimed to have a better model to trade and value interest rate swaps. Nineteen eighties financial innovation had all sorts of consequences, but one of them was a boom in the number of deals between big financial firms that required them to take each other's credit risks. Interest rate swaps—in which one party swaps a floating rate of interest for another party's fixed rate of interest—was one such innovation. Once upon a time, Chrysler issued a bond through Morgan Stanley, and the only people who wound up with credit risk were the investors who bought the Chrysler bond. Chrysler might sell its bonds and simultaneously enter into a ten-year interest rate swap transaction with Morgan Stanley—and just like that, Chrysler and Morgan Stanley were exposed to each other. If Chrysler went bankrupt, its bondholders obviously lost; depending on the nature of the swap, and the movement of interest rates, Morgan Stanley might lose, too. If Morgan Stanley went bust, Chrysler, along with anyone else who had done interest rate swaps with Morgan Stanley, stood to suffer. Financial risk had been created out of thin air, and it begged to be either honestly accounted for or disguised.

Enter Sosin, with his supposedly new and improved interest rate swap model—even though Drexel Burnham was not at the time a market leader in interest rate swaps. There was a natural role for a blue-chip corporation with the highest credit rating to stand in the middle of swaps and long-term options and the other risk-spawning innovations. The traits required of this corporation were that it not be a bank—and thus subject to bank regulation, and the need to reserve capital against risky assets—and that it be willing and able to bury exotic risks on its balance sheet. It needed to be able to insure $100 billion in subprime mortgage loans, for instance, without having to disclose to anyone what it had done. There was no real reason that company had to be AIG; it could have been any triple-A-rated entity with a huge balance sheet. Berkshire Hathaway, for instance, or General Electric. AIG just got there first.

In a financial system that was rapidly generating complicated risks, AIG FP became a huge swallower of those risks. In the early days it must have seemed as if it was being paid to insure events extremely unlikely to occur, as it was. Its success bred imitators: Zurich Re FP, Swiss Re FP, Credit Suisse FP, Gen Re FP. ("Re" stands for Reinsurance.) All of these places were central to what happened in the last two decades; without them, the new risks being created would have had no place to hide and would have remained in full view of bank regulators. All of these places, when the crisis came, would be washed away by the general nausea felt in the presence of complicated financial risks, but there was a moment when their existence seemed cartographically necessary to the financial world. AIG FP was the model for them all.

The division's first fifteen years were consistently, amazingly profitable—there wasn't the first hint that it might be running risks that would cause it to lose money, much less cripple its giant parent. In 1993, when Howard Sosin left, he took with him nearly $200 million, his share of what appeared to be a fantastic money machine. In 1998, AIG FP entered the new market for corporate credit default swaps: It sold insurance to banks against the risk of defaults by huge numbers of investment-grade public corporations. The credit default swap had just been invented by bankers at J.P. Morgan, who then went looking for a triple-A-rated company willing to sell them—and found AIG FP.* The market began innocently enough, by Wall Street standards.

Large numbers of investment-grade companies in different countries and different industries were indeed unlikely to default on their debt at the same time. The credit default swaps sold by AIG FP that

* The story of how and why they did this has been painstakingly told by *Financial Times* journalist Gillian Tett, in her book *Fool's Gold*.

insured pools of such loans proved to be a good business. By 2001, AIG FP, now being run by a fellow named Joe Cassano, could be counted on to generate $300 million a year, or 15 percent of AIG's profits.

But then, in the early 2000s, the financial markets performed this fantastic bait and switch, in two stages. Stage One was to apply a formula that had been dreamed up to cope with corporate credit risk to consumer credit risk. The banks that used AIG FP to insure piles of loans to IBM and GE now came to it to insure much messier piles, which included credit card debt, student loans, auto loans, prime mortgages, aircraft leases, and just about anything else that generated a cash flow. As there were many different sorts of loans, to different sorts of people, the logic that had applied to corporate loans seemed to apply to them, too: They were sufficiently diverse that they were unlikely all to go bad at once.

Stage Two, beginning at the end of 2004, was to replace the student loans and the auto loans and the rest with bigger piles consisting of nothing but U.S. subprime mortgage loans. "The problem," as one AIG FP trader put it, "is that something else came along that we thought was the same thing as what we'd been doing." The "consumer loan" piles that Wall Street firms, led by Goldman Sachs, asked AIG FP to insure went from being 2 percent subprime mortgages to being 95 percent subprime mortgages. In a matter of months, AIG FP, in effect, bought $50 billion in triple-B-rated subprime mortgage bonds by insuring them against default. And yet no one said anything about it—not AIG CEO Martin Sullivan, not the head of AIG FP, Joe Cassano, not the guy in AIG FP's Connecticut office in charge of selling his firm's credit default swap services to the big Wall Street firms, Al Frost. The deals, by all accounts, were simply rubber-stamped inside AIG FP, and then again by AIG brass. Everyone concerned apparently assumed they were being paid insurance premiums to take basically the same sort of risk they had been taking for nearly a decade. They weren't. They were now, in effect, the world's biggest owners of subprime mortgage bonds.

Greg Lippmann watched his counterparts at Goldman Sachs find and exploit someone else's willingness to sell huge amounts of cheap insurance on subprime mortgage bonds and pretty much instantly guessed the seller's identity. Word spread quickly in the small world of subprime mortgage bond creators and traders: AIG FP was now selling credit default swaps on triple-A-rated subprime bonds for a mere 0.12 percent a year. Twelve basis points! Lippmann didn't know exactly how Goldman Sachs had persuaded AIG FP to provide the same service to the booming market in subprime mortgage loans that it provided to the market for corporate loans. All he knew was that, in rapid succession, Goldman created a bunch of multibillion-dollar deals that transferred to AIG the responsibility for all future losses from $20 billion in triple-B-rated subprime mortgage bonds. It was incredible: In exchange for a few million bucks a year, this insurance company was taking the very real risk that $20 billion would simply go *poof*. The deals with Goldman had gone down in a matter of months and required the efforts of just a few geeks on a Goldman bond trading desk and a Goldman salesman named Andrew Davilman, who, for his services, soon would be promoted to managing director. The Goldman traders had booked profits of somewhere between $1.5 billion and $3 billion—even by bond market standards, a breathtaking sum.

In the process, Goldman Sachs created a security so opaque and complex that it would remain forever misunderstood by investors and rating agencies: the synthetic subprime mortgage bond–backed CDO, or collateralized debt obligation. Like the credit default swap, the CDO had been invented to redistribute the risk of corporate and government bond defaults and was now being rejiggered to disguise the risk of subprime mortgage loans. Its logic was exactly that of the original mortgage bonds. In a mortgage bond, you gathered thousands of loans and, assuming that it was extremely unlikely that they would all go bad together, created a tower of bonds, in which both risk and return diminished as you rose. In a CDO you gathered one hundred different *mortgage bonds*—usually, the riskiest, lower floors of the original tower—and used them to erect an entirely new tower of bonds. The innocent observer might reasonably ask, What's the point of using floors from one tower of debt simply to create another tower of debt? The short answer is, They are too near to the ground. More prone to flooding—the first to take losses—they bear a lower credit rating: triple-B. Triple-B-rated bonds were harder to sell than the triple-A-rated ones, on the safe, upper floors of the building.

The long answer was that there were huge sums of money to be made, if you could somehow get them re-rated as triple-A, thereby lowering their perceived risk, however dishonestly and artificially. This is what Goldman Sachs had cleverly done. Their—soon to be everyone's—nifty solution to the problem of selling the lower floors appears, in retrospect, almost magical. Having gathered 100 ground floors from 100 different subprime mortgage buildings (100 different triple-B-rated bonds), they persuaded the rating agencies that these weren't, as they might appear, all exactly the same things. They were another diversified portfolio of assets! This was absurd. The 100 buildings occupied the same floodplain; in the event of flood, the ground floors of all of them were equally exposed. But never mind: The rating agencies, who were paid fat fees by Goldman Sachs and other Wall Street firms for each deal they rated, pronounced 80 percent of the new tower of debt triple-A.

The CDO was, in effect, a credit laundering service for the residents of Lower Middle Class America. For Wall Street it was a machine that turned lead into gold.

Back in the 1980s, the original stated purpose of the mortgage-backed bond had been to redistribute the risk associated with home mortgage lending. Home mortgage loans could find their way to the bond market investors willing to pay the most for them. The interest rate paid by the homeowner would thus fall. The goal of the innovation, in short, was to make the financial markets more efficient. Now, somehow, the same innovative spirit was being put to the opposite purpose: to hide the risk by complicating it. The market was paying Goldman Sachs bond traders to make the market less efficient. With stagnant wages and booming consumption, the cash-strapped American masses had a virtually unlimited demand for loans but an uncertain ability to repay them. All they had going for them, from the point of view of Wall Street financial engineers, was that their financial fates could be misconstrued as uncorrelated. By assuming that one pile of subprime mortgage loans wasn't exposed to the same forces as another—that a subprime mortgage bond with loans heavily concentrated in Florida wasn't very much like a subprime mortgage bond more concentrated in California—the engineers created the illusion of security. AIG FP accepted the illusion as reality.

The people who worked on the relevant Goldman Sachs mortgage bond trading desk were all extremely intelligent. They'd all done amazingly well in school and had gone to Ivy League universities. But it didn't require any sort of genius to see the fortune to be had from the laundering of triple-B-rated bonds into triple-A-rated bonds. What demanded genius was finding $20 billion in triple-B-rated bonds to launder. In the original tower of loans—the original mortgage bond—only a single, thin floor got rated triple-B. A billion dollars of crappy home loans might yield just $20 million of the crappiest triple-B tranches. Put another way: To create a billion-dollar CDO composed solely of triple-B-rated subprime mortgage bonds, you needed to lend $50 billion in cash to actual human beings. That took time and effort. A credit default swap took neither.

There was more than one way to think about Mike Burry's purchase of a billion dollars in credit default swaps. The first was as a simple, even innocent, insurance contract. Burry made his semiannual premium payments and, in return, received protection against the default of a billion dollars' worth of bonds. He'd either be paid zero, if the triple-B-rated bonds he'd insured proved good, or a billion dollars, if those triple-B-rated bonds went bad. But of course Mike Burry didn't own any triple-B-rated subprime mortgage bonds, or anything like them. He had no property to "insure"; it was as if he had bought fire insurance on some slum with a history of burning down. To him, as to Steve Eisman, a credit default swap wasn't insurance at all but an outright speculative bet against the market—and this was the second way to think about it.

There was also a third, even more mind-bending, way to think of this new instrument: as a near-perfect replica of a subprime mortgage bond. The cash flows of Mike Burry's credit default swaps replicated the cash flows of the triple-B-rated subprime mortgage bond that he wagered against. The 2.5 percent a year in premium Mike Burry was paying mimicked the spread over LIBOR* that triple-B subprime mortgage bonds paid to an actual investor. The billion dollars whoever had sold Mike Burry his credit default swaps stood to lose, if the bonds went bad, replicated the potential losses of an actual bond owner.

On its surface, the booming market in side bets on subprime mortgage bonds seemed to be the financial equivalent of fantasy football: a benign, if silly, facsimile of investing. Alas, there was a difference between fantasy football and fantasy finance: When a fantasy football player drafts Peyton Manning to be on his team, he doesn't create a second Peyton Manning. When Mike Burry bought a credit default swap based on a Long Beach Savings subprime–backed bond,

* London Interbank Offered Rate—the interest rate at which banks will lend money to each other. Once thought more or less riskless, it is now, more or less, not.

he enabled Goldman Sachs to create another bond identical to the original in every respect but one: There were no actual home loans or home buyers. Only the gains and losses from the side bet on the bonds were real.

And so, to generate $1 billion in triple-B-rated subprime mortgage bonds, Goldman Sachs did not need to originate $50 billion in home loans. They needed simply to entice Mike Burry, or some other market pessimist, to pick 100 different triple-B bonds and buy $10 million in credit default swaps on each of them. Once they had this package (a "synthetic CDO," it was called, which was the term of art for a CDO composed of nothing but credit default swaps), they'd take it over to Moody's and Standard & Poor's. "The ratings agencies didn't really have their own CDO model," says one former Goldman CDO trader. "The banks would send over their own model to Moody's and say, 'How does this look?'" Somehow, roughly 80 percent of what had been risky triple-B-rated bonds now looked like triple-A-rated bonds. The other 20 percent, bearing lower credit ratings, generally were more difficult to sell, but they could, incredibly, simply be piled up in yet another heap and reprocessed yet again, into more triple-A bonds. The machine that turned 100 percent lead into an ore that was now 80 percent gold and 20 percent lead would accept the residual lead and turn 80 percent of that into gold, too.

The details were complicated, but the gist of this new money machine was not: It turned a lot of dicey loans into a pile of bonds, most of which were triple-A-rated, then it took the lowest-rated of the remaining bonds and turned most of those into triple-A CDOs. And then—because it could not extend home loans fast enough to create a sufficient number of lower-rated bonds—it used credit default swaps to replicate the very worst of the existing bonds, many times over. Goldman Sachs stood between Michael Burry and AIG. Michael Burry forked out 250 basis points (2.5 percent) to own credit default swaps on the very crappiest triple-B bonds, and AIG was paid a mere 12 basis points (0.12 percent) to sell credit default swaps on those very same bonds, filtered through a synthetic CDO, and pronounced triple-A-rated. There were a few other messy details*—some of the lead was sold off directly to German investors in Düsseldorf—but when the dust settled, Goldman Sachs had taken roughly 2 percent off the top, risk-free, and booked all the profit up front. There was no need on either side—long or short—for cash to change hands. Both sides could do a deal with Goldman Sachs by signing a piece of paper. The original home mortgage loans on whose fate both sides were betting played no other role. In a funny way, they existed only so that their fate might be gambled upon.

The market for "synthetics" removed any constraint on the size of risk associated with subprime mortgage lending. To make a billion-dollar bet, you no longer needed to accumulate a billion dol-

* Dear Reader: If you have followed the story this far, you deserve not only a gold star but an answer to a complicated question: If Mike Burry was the only one buying credit default swaps on subprime mortgage bonds, and he bought a billion dollars' worth of them, who took the other $19 billion or so on the short side of the trade with AIG? The answer is, first, Mike Burry soon was joined by others, including Goldman Sachs itself—and so Goldman was in the position of selling bonds to its customers created by its own traders, so they might bet against them. Secondly, there was a crude, messy, slow, but acceptable substitute for Mike Burry's credit default swaps: the actual cash bonds. According to a former Goldman derivatives trader, Goldman would buy the triple-A tranche of some CDO, pair it off with the credit default swaps AIG sold Goldman that insured the tranche (at a cost well below the yield on the tranche), declare the entire package risk-free, and hold it off its balance sheet. Of course, the whole thing wasn't risk-free: If AIG went bust, the insurance was worthless, and Goldman could lose everything. Today Goldman Sachs is, to put it mildly, unhelpful when asked to explain exactly what it did, and this lack of transparency extends to its own shareholders. "If a team of forensic accountants went over Goldman's books, they'd be shocked at just how good Goldman is at hiding things," says one former AIG FP employee, who helped to unravel the mess, and who was intimate with his Goldman counterparts.

lars' worth of actual mortgage loans. All you had to do was find someone else in the market willing to take the other side of the bet.

No wonder Goldman Sachs was suddenly so eager to sell Mike Burry credit default swaps in giant, $100 million chunks, or that the Goldman Sachs bond trader had been surprisingly indifferent to which subprime bonds Mike Burry bet against. The insurance Mike Burry bought was inserted into a synthetic CDO and passed along to AIG. The roughly $20 billion in credit default swaps sold by AIG to Goldman Sachs meant roughly $400 million in riskless profits for Goldman Sachs. *Each year*. The deals lasted as long as the underlying bonds, which had an expected life of about six years, which, when you did the math, implied a profit for the Goldman trader of $2.4 billion.

Wall Street's newest technique for squeezing profits out of the bond markets should have raised a few questions. Why were supposedly sophisticated traders at AIG FP doing this stuff? If credit default swaps were insurance, why weren't they regulated as insurance? Why, for example, wasn't AIG required to reserve capital against them? Why, for that matter, were Moody's and Standard & Poor's willing to bless 80 percent of a pool of dicey mortgage loans with the same triple-A rating they bestowed on the debts of the U.S. Treasury? Why didn't someone, anyone, inside Goldman Sachs stand up and say, "This is obscene. The rating agencies, the ultimate pricers of all these subprime mortgage loans, clearly do not understand the risk, and their idiocy is creating a recipe for catastrophe"? Apparently none of those questions popped into the minds of market insiders as quickly as another: How do I do what Goldman Sachs just did? Deutsche Bank, especially, felt something like shame that Goldman Sachs had been the first to find this particular pay dirt. Along with Goldman, Deutsche Bank was the leading market maker in abstruse mortgage derivatives. Düsseldorf was playing some kind of role in the new market. If there were stupid Germans standing ready to buy U.S.

subprime mortgage derivatives, Deutsche Bank should have been the first to find them.

None of this was of any obvious concern to Greg Lippmann. Lippmann did not run Deutsche Bank's CDO business—a fellow named Michael Lamont did. Lippmann was merely the trader responsible for buying and selling subprime mortgage bonds and, by extension, credit default swaps on subprime mortgage bonds. But with so few investors willing to make an outright bet against the subprime bond market, Lippmann's bosses asked Lippmann to take one for the team: in effect, to serve as a stand-in for Mike Burry, and to make an explicit bet against the market. If Lippmann would buy credit default swaps from Deutsche Bank's CDO department, they, too, might do these trades with AIG, before AIG woke up and stopped doing them. "Greg was forced to get short into the CDOs," says a former senior member of Deutsche Bank's CDO team. "I say forced, but you can't really force Greg to do anything." There was some pushing and pulling with the people who ran his firm's CDO operations, but Lippmann found himself uncomfortably short subprime mortgage bonds.

Lippmann had at least one good reason for not putting up a huge fight: There was a fantastically profitable market waiting to be created. Financial markets are a collection of arguments. The less transparent the market and the more complicated the securities, the more money the trading desks at big Wall Street firms can make from the argument. The constant argument over the value of the shares of some major publicly traded company has very little value, as both buyer and seller can see the fair price of the stock on the ticker, and the broker's commission has been driven down by competition. The argument over the value of credit default swaps on subprime mortgage bonds—a complex security whose value was derived from that of another complex security—could be a gold mine. The only other dealer making serious markets in credit default swaps was Goldman

Sachs, so there was, in the beginning, little price competition. Supply, thanks to AIG, was virtually unlimited. The problem was demand: investors who wanted to do Mike Burry's trade. Incredibly, at this critical juncture in financial history, after which so much changed so quickly, the only constraint in the subprime mortgage market was a shortage of people willing to bet against it.

To sell investors on the idea of betting against subprime mortgage bonds—on buying his pile of credit default swaps—Greg Lippmann needed a new and improved argument. Enter the Great Chinese Quant. Lippmann asked Eugene Xu to study the effect of home price appreciation on subprime mortgage loans. Eugene Xu went off and did whatever the second smartest man in China does, and at length returned with a chart illustrating default rates in various home price scenarios: home prices up, home prices flat, home prices down. Lippmann looked at it . . . and looked again. The numbers shocked even him. *They didn't need to collapse; they merely needed to stop rising so fast*. House prices were still rising, and yet default rates were approaching 4 percent; if they rose to just 7 percent, the lowest investment-grade bonds, rated triple-B-minus, went to zero. If they rose to 8 percent, the next lowest-rated bonds, rated triple-B, went to zero.

At that moment—in November 2005—Greg Lippmann realized that he didn't mind owning a pile of credit default swaps on subprime mortgage bonds. They weren't insurance; they were a gamble; and he liked the odds. He *wanted* to be short.

This was new. Greg Lippmann had traded bonds backed by various consumer loans—auto loans, credit card loans, home equity loans—since 1991, when he had graduated from the University of Pennsylvania and taken a job at Credit Suisse. He'd never before been able to sell them short, because they were impossible to borrow. The only choice he and every other asset-backed bond trader ever had to make was whether to like them or to love them. There was never any point in hating them. Now he could, and did. But hating them set him apart from the crowd—and that represented, for Greg Lippmann, a new career risk. As he put it to others, "If you're in a business where you can do only one thing and it doesn't work out, it's hard for your bosses to be mad at you." It was now possible to do more than one thing, but if he bet against subprime mortgage bonds and was proven wrong, his bosses would find it easy to be mad at him.

In the righteous spirit of a man bearing an inconvenient truth, Greg Lippmann, a copy of "Shorting Home Equity Mezzanine Tranches" tucked under his arm, launched himself at the institutional investing public. He may have begun his investigation of the subprime mortgage market in the spirit of a Wall Street salesman, searching less for the truth than for a persuasive-sounding pitch. Now, shockingly, he thought he had an ingenious plan to make customers rich. He'd charge them fat fees to get in and out of their credit default swaps, of course, but these would prove trivial compared to the fortunes they stood to make. He was no longer selling; he was dispensing favors. *Behold. A gift from me to you.*

Institutional investors didn't know what to make of him, at least not at first. "I think he has some kind of narcissistic personality disorder," said one money manager who heard Lippmann's pitch but did not do his trade. "He scared the shit out of us," said another. "He comes in and describes this brilliant trade. It makes total sense. To us the risk was, we do it, it works, then what? How do we get out? He controls the market; he may be the only one we can sell to. And he says, 'You have no way out of this swimming pool but through me, and when you ask for the towel I'm going to rip your eyeballs out.' He actually said that, that he was going to rip our eyeballs out. The guy was totally transparent."

They loved it, in a way, but decided they didn't want to experience the thrill of eyeball removal. "What worked against Greg," this fund manager said, "was that he was too candid."

Lippmann faced the usual objections any Wall Street bond customer voiced to any Wall Street bond salesmen—*If it's such a great trade, why are you offering it to me?*—but other, less usual ones, too. Buying credit default swaps meant paying insurance premiums for perhaps years as you waited for American homeowners to default. Bond market investors, like bond market traders, viscerally resisted any trade that they had to pay money to be in, and instinctively sought out trades that paid them just for showing up in the morning. (One big bond market investor christened his yacht *Positive Carry*.) Trades where you fork over 2 percent a year just to be in them were anathema. Other sorts of investors found other sorts of objections. "I can't explain credit default swaps to my investors" was a common response to Greg Lippmann's pitch. Or "I have a cousin who works at Moody's and he says this stuff [subprime mortgage bonds] is all good." Or "I talked to Bear Stearns and they said you were crazy." Lippmann spent twenty hours with one hedge fund guy and thought he had him sold, only to have the guy call his college roommate, who worked for some home builder, and change his mind.

But the most common response of all from investors who heard Lippmann's argument was, "I'm convinced. You're right. But it's not my job to short the subprime market."

"That's why the opportunity exists," Lippmann would reply. "It's nobody's job."

It wasn't Lippmann's, either. He was meant to be the toll booth, taking a little from buyers and sellers as they passed through his trading books. He was now in a different, more opinionated relationship to his market and his employer. Lippmann's short position may have been forced upon him, but by the end of 2005 he'd made it his own, and grown it to a billion dollars. Sixteen floors above him inside Deutsche Bank's Wall Street headquarters, several hundred highly paid employees bought subprime mortgage loans, packaged them into bonds, and sold them off. Another group packaged the most repellent, unsalable tranches of those bonds, and CDSs on the bonds, into CDOs. The bigger Lippmann's short position grew, the greater the implicit expression of contempt for these people and their industry—an industry quickly becoming Wall Street's most profitable business. The running cost, in premiums Lippmann paid, was tens of millions of dollars a year, and his losses looked even bigger. The buyer of a credit default swap agreed to pay premiums for the lifespan of the underlying mortgage bond. So long as the underlying bonds remained outstanding, both buyer and seller of credit default swaps were obliged to post collateral, in response to their price movements. Astonishingly, the prices of subprime mortgage bonds were rising. Within a few months, Lippmann's credit default swap position had to be marked down by $30 million. His superiors repeatedly asked him to explain why he was doing what he was doing. "A lot of people wondered if this was the best use of Greg's time and our money," said a senior Deutsche Bank official who watched the growing conflict.

Rather than cave to the pressure, Lippmann instead had an idea for making it vanish: kill the new market. AIG was very nearly the only buyer of triple-A-rated CDOs (that is, triple-B-rated subprime mortgage bonds repackaged into triple-A-rated CDOs). AIG was, ultimately, the party on the other side of the credit default swaps Mike Burry was buying. If AIG stopped buying bonds (or, more exactly, stopped insuring them against default), the entire subprime mortgage bond market might collapse, and Lippmann's credit default swaps would be worth a fortune. At the end of 2005, Lippmann flew to London to try to make that happen. He met with an AIG FP employee named Tom Fewings, who worked directly for AIG FP's head, Joe Cassano. Lippmann, who was forever adding data to his presentation, produced his latest version of "Shorting Home Equity Mezzanine Tranches" and walked Fewings through his argument. Fewings offered him no serious objections, and Lippmann left AIG's London office feeling as if Fewings had been converted to his cause. Sure enough, shortly after Lippmann's visit, AIG FP stopped selling credit default swaps. Even better: AIG FP hinted that they might actually like to *buy* some credit default swaps. In anticipation of selling them some, Lippmann accumulated more.

For a brief moment, Lippmann thought he'd changed the world, all by himself. He had walked into AIG FP and had shown them how Deutsche Bank, along with every other Wall Street firm, was playing them for fools, and they'd understood.

CHAPTER FOUR

How to Harvest a Migrant Worker

They hadn't. Not really. The first person inside AIG FP to awaken to the madness of his firm's behavior, and sound an alarm, was not Tom Fewings, who quickly forgot his meeting with Lippmann, but Gene Park. Park worked in AIG FP's Connecticut office and sat close enough to the credit default swap traders to have a general idea of what they were up to. In mid-2005 he read a front-page story in the *Wall Street Journal* about the mortgage lender New Century. He noted how high the company's dividend was and wondered if he should buy some of its stock for himself. As he dug into New Century, however, Park saw that they owned all these subprime mortgages—and he could see from their own statements that the quality of these loans was frighteningly poor. Soon after his private investigation of New Century, Park had a phone call from a penniless, jobless old college friend who had been offered several loans from banks to buy a house he couldn't afford. That's when the penny dropped for him: Park had noticed his colleague, Al Frost, announcing credit default swap deals with big Wall Street firms at a new clip. A year before, Frost might have done one billion-dollar deal each month; now he was doing twenty, all of them insuring putatively diversified piles of consumer loans. "We were doing every single deal with every single Wall Street firm, except Citigroup," says one trader. "Citigroup decided it liked the risk, and kept it on their books. We took all the rest." When traders asked Frost why Wall Street was suddenly so eager to do business with AIG, as one put it, "he would explain that they liked us because we could act quickly." Park put two and two together and guessed that the nature of these piles of consumer loans insured by AIG FP was changing, that they contained a lot more subprime mortgages than anyone knew, and that if U.S. homeowners began to default in sharply greater numbers, AIG didn't have anywhere near the capital required to cover the losses. When he brought this up at a meeting, his reward was to be hauled into a separate room by Joe Cassano, who screamed at him that he didn't know what he was talking about.

That Joe Cassano, the boss of AIG FP, was the son of a police officer and had been a political science major at Brooklyn College seems, in retrospect, far less relevant than his need for obedience and total control. He'd spent most of his career, first at Drexel Burnham and then at AIG FP, not as a bond trader but working in the back office. Across AIG FP the view of the boss was remarkably consistent: Cassano was a guy with a crude feel for financial risk but a real talent for bullying people who doubted him. "AIG FP became a dictatorship," says one London trader. "Joe would bully people around. He'd humiliate them and then try to make it up to them by giving them huge amounts of money."

"One day he got me on the phone and was pissed off about a trade that had lost money," says a Connecticut trader. "He said, *When you lose money it's my fucking money. Say it.* I said, 'What?'

"Say, 'Joe, it's your fucking money'! So I said, 'It's your fucking money, Joe.'"

"The culture changed," says a third trader. "The fear level was so high that when we had these morning meetings, you presented what you did not to upset him. And if you were critical of the organization, all hell would break loose." Says a fourth, "Joe always said, 'This is my company. You work for my company.' He'd see you with a bottle of water. He'd come over and say, 'That's my water.' Lunch was free, but Joe always made you feel he had bought it." And a fifth: "Under Joe, the debate and discussion that was common under Tom [Savage, the previous CEO] ceased. I would say [to Tom] what I'm saying to you. But with Joe as the audience." A sixth: "The way you dealt with Joe was to start everything by saying, 'You're right, Joe.'"

Even by the standards of Wall Street villains whose character flaws wind up being exaggerated to fit the crime, Cassano, in the retelling, became a cartoon monster. "One day he came in and saw that someone had left the weights on the Smith machine, in the gym," says a seventh source, in Connecticut. "He was literally walking around looking for people who looked buff, trying to find the guy who did it. He was screaming, 'Who left the fucking weight on the fucking Smith machine? Who left the fucking weight on the fucking Smith machine?'"

Oddly, Cassano was as likely to direct his anger at profitable traders as at unprofitable ones, for the anger was triggered not by financial loss but by the faintest whiff of insurrection. Even more oddly, his anger had no obvious effect on the recipient's paycheck; a trader might find himself routinely abused by his boss and yet delighted by his year-end bonus, determined by that same boss. One reason none of AIG FP's traders took a swing at Joe Cassano, before walking out the door, was that the money was simply too good. A man who valued loyalty and obedience above all other traits had no tool to command it except money. Money worked as a management tool, but only up to a point. If you were going to be on the other side of a trade from Goldman Sachs, you had better know what, exactly, Goldman Sachs was up to. AIG FP could attract extremely bright people who were perfectly capable of keeping up with their counterparts at Goldman Sachs. They were constrained, however, by a boss with an imperfect understanding of the nuances of his own business, and whose judgment was clouded by his insecurity.

Toward the end of 2005, Cassano promoted Al Frost, then went looking for someone to replace him as the ambassador to Wall Street's bond trading desks. The job, in effect, was to say "yes" every time some Wall Street trader asked him if he'd like to insure—and so, in effect, purchase—a billion-dollar pile of bonds backed by consumer loans. For a number of reasons, Gene Park was a likely candidate, and so he decided to examine these loans that AIG FP was insuring a bit more closely. The magnitude of the misunderstanding shocked him: These supposedly diversified piles of consumer loans now consisted almost entirely of U.S. subprime mortgages. Park conducted a private survey. He asked the people most directly involved in the decision to sell credit default swaps on consumer loans what percentage of those loans were subprime mortgages. He asked Gary Gorton, a Yale professor who had built the model that Cassano used to price the credit default swaps: Gorton guessed that the piles were no more than 10 percent subprime. He asked a risk analyst in London, who guessed 20 percent. "None of them knew it was 95 percent," says one trader. "And I'm sure that Cassano didn't, either." In retrospect, their ignorance seems incredible—but, then, an entire financial system was premised on their not knowing, and paying them for this talent.

By the time Joe Cassano invited Gene Park to London for the meeting in which he would be "promoted" to the job of creating even more of these ticking bombs, Park knew he wanted no part of it. If he was forced to take the job, he said, he'd quit. This, naturally, infuriated Joe Cassano, who accused Park of being lazy, of dreaming up reasons not to do the deals that would require complicated paperwork. Confronted with the new fact—that his company was effectively *long* $50 billion in triple-B subprime mortgage bonds, masquerading as triple-

A-rated diversified pools of consumer loans—Cassano at first sought to rationalize it. He clearly thought that any money he received for selling default insurance on highly rated bonds was free money. For the bonds to default, he now said, U.S. house prices had to fall, and Joe Cassano didn't believe house prices could ever fall everywhere in the country at once. After all, Moody's and S&P had both rated this stuff triple-A!

Cassano nevertheless agreed to meet with all the big Wall Street firms and discuss the logic of their deals—to investigate how a bunch of shaky loans could be transformed into triple-A-rated bonds. Together with Gene Park and a few others, he set out on a series of meetings with traders at Deutsche Bank, Goldman Sachs, and the rest, all of whom argued how unlikely it was for housing prices to fall all at once. "They all said the same thing," said one of the traders present. "They'd go back to historical real estate prices over sixty years and say they had never fallen nationally, all at once." (Two months after their meeting with Goldman Sachs, one of the AIG FP traders bumped into the Goldman guy who had made this argument and who now said, *Between you and me, you're right. These things are going to blow up.*) The AIG FP traders present were shocked by how little thought or analysis seemed to underpin the subprime mortgage machine: It was simply a bet that home prices would never fall. Once he understood this, and once he could construe it as his own idea, Joe Cassano changed his mind. By early 2006 he openly agreed with Gene Park: AIG FP shouldn't insure any more of these deals—though they would continue to insure the ones they had already insured.

At the time, this decision didn't really seem like all that big a deal for AIG FP. The division was generating almost $2 billion a year in profits. At the peak, the entire credit default swap business contributed only $180 million of that. Cassano had been upset with Park, and slow to change his mind, it seemed, mainly because Park had dared to contradict him.

The one Wall Street trader who had tried to persuade AIG FP to stop betting on the subprime mortgage bond market witnessed none of these internal politics. Greg Lippmann simply assumed that the force of his argument had won them over—until it didn't. He never understood why AIG FP changed its mind but left itself so exposed. It sold no more credit default swaps to Wall Street but did nothing to offset the 50 billion dollars' worth that it had already sold.

Even that, Lippmann thought, might cause the market to crash. If AIG FP refused to take the long side of the trade, he thought, no one would, and the subprime mortgage market would shut down. But—and here was the start of a great mystery—the market didn't so much as blink. Wall Street firms found new buyers of triple-A-rated subprime CDOs—new places to stuff the riskiest triple-B tranches of subprime mortgage bonds—though who these people were was not entirely clear for some time, even to Greg Lippmann.

The subprime mortgage machine roared on. The loans that were being made to actual human beings only grew crappier, but, bizarrely, the price of insuring them—the price of buying credit default swaps—fell. By April 2006 Lippmann's superiors at Deutsche Bank were asking him to defend his quixotic gamble. They wanted him to make money just by sitting in the middle of this new market, the way Goldman Sachs did, crossing buyers and sellers. They reached an agreement: Lippmann could keep his expensive short position as long as he could prove that, if he had to sell it, there'd be some other investor willing to take it off his hands on short notice. That is, he needed to foster a more active market in credit default swaps; if he wanted to keep his bet he had to find others to join him in it.

By the summer of 2006 Greg Lippmann had a new metaphor in his head: a tug-of-war. The entire subprime mortgage lending machine—including his own employer, Deutsche Bank—pulled on one end of the rope, while he, Greg Lippmann, hauled back on the other. He needed others to join him. They'd all pull together. His teammates would pay him a fee for being on his side, but they'd get rich, too.

Lippmann soon found that the people he most expected to see the ugly truth of the subprime mortgage market—the people who ran funds that specialized in mortgage bond trading—were the ones least likely to see anything but what they had been seeing for years. Here was a strange but true fact: The closer you were to the market, the harder it was to perceive its folly. Realizing this, Lippmann went looking for stock investors with a lot of exposure to falling home prices, or falling housing stock prices, and showed them his idea as a hedge. *Look, you're making a fortune as this stuff keeps going up. Why not spend a little to cover yourself in a collapse?* Greed hadn't worked, so he tried fear. He obtained a list of all the big stockholders in New Century, the big subprime lender. Prominent on the list was a hedge fund called FrontPoint Partners. He called the relevant Deutsche Bank salesman to set up a meeting. The salesman failed to notice that there was more than one hedge fund inside FrontPoint—it wasn't a single fund but a collection of independently managed hedge funds—and that the fund that was long New Century stock was a small group based on the West Coast.

When Greg Lippmann arrived in Steve Eisman's conference room in midtown Manhattan, Eisman surprised him by saying, "We're not the FrontPoint that is long New Century stock. We're the FrontPoint that is *short* New Century stock." Eisman was already betting against the shares of companies, such as New Century and IndyMac Bank, which originated subprime loans, along with companies that built the houses bought with the loans, such as Toll Brothers. These bets were not entirely satisfying because they weren't bets against the companies but market sentiment about the companies. Also, the bets were expensive to maintain. The companies paid high dividends, and their shares were often costly to borrow: New Century, for instance, paid a 20 percent dividend, and its shares cost 12 percent a year to borrow. For the pleasure of shorting 100 million dollars' worth of New Century's shares, Steve Eisman forked out $32 million a year.

In his search for stock market investors he might terrify with his Doomsday scenario, Lippmann had made a lucky strike: He had stumbled onto a stock market investor who held an even darker view of the subprime mortgage market than he did. Eisman knew more about that market, its characters, and its depravities than anyone Lippmann had ever spoken with. If anyone would make a dramatic bet against subprime, he thought, it was Eisman—and so he was puzzled when Eisman didn't do it. He was even more puzzled when, several months later, Eisman's new head trader, Danny Moses, and his research guy, Vinny Daniels, asked him to come back in to explain it all over again.

The problem with someone who is transparently self-interested is that the extent of his interests is never clear. Danny simply mistrusted Lippmann at first sight. "Fucking Lippmann," he called him, as in, "Fucking Lippmann never looks you in the eye when he talks to you. It bothers the shit out of me." Vinny could not believe that Deutsche Bank would let this guy loose to run around and torpedo their market unless it served the narrow interests of Deutsche Bank. To Danny and Vinny, Greg Lippmann was a walking embodiment of the bond market, which is to say he was put on earth to screw the customer.

Three times in as many months, Danny and Vinny called, and Lippmann returned—and that fact alone heightened their suspicion of him. He wasn't driving up from Wall Street to Midtown to promote world peace. So why was he here? Each time, Lippmann would talk a mile a minute, and Danny and Vinny would stare in wonder. Their meetings acquired the flavor of a postmodern literary puzzle: The story rang true even as the narrator seemed entirely unreliable. At some point during each of these sessions, Vinny would stop him to ask, "Greg, I'm trying to figure out why you are even here." This was a signal to bombard Lippmann with accusatory questions:

If it's such a great idea, why don't you quit Deutsche Bank and start a hedge fund and make a fortune for yourself?

It'd take me six months to set up a hedge fund. The world might wake up to this insanity next week. I have to play the hand I've been dealt.

If it's such a great idea, why are you giving it away to us?

I'm not giving away anything. The supply is infinite.

Yeah. But why bother even telling us?

I'll charge you getting in and getting out. I need to pay the electric bills.

It's zero-sum. Who's on the other side? Who's the idiot?

Düsseldorf. Stupid Germans. They take rating agencies seriously. They believe in the rules.

Why does Deutsche Bank allow you to trash a market that they sit at the center of?

I don't have any particular allegiance to Deutsche Bank . . . I just work there.

Bullshit. They pay you. How do we know the people running your CDO machine aren't just using your enthusiasm for shorting your own market to exploit us?

Have you met the people running our CDO machine?

At some point Danny and Vinny dropped even the pretense that they were seeking new information about credit default swaps and subprime mortgage bonds. They were just hoping the guy might slip up in some way that confirmed that he was indeed the lying Wall Street scumbag that they presumed him to be. "We're trying to figure out where we fit into this world," said Vinny. "I don't believe him that he needs us because he has too much of this stuff. So why is he doing this?" Lippmann, for his part, felt like a witness under interrogation: These guys were trying to *crack* him. A few months later, he'd pitch his idea to Phil Falcone, who ran a giant hedge fund called Harbinger Capital. Falcone would buy billions of dollars in credit default swaps virtually on the spot. Falcone knew one-tenth of what these guys knew about the subprime mortgage market, but Falcone trusted Lippmann and these guys did not. In their final meeting, Vinny finally put the matter bluntly. "Greg," he said. "Don't take this the wrong way. But I'm just trying to figure out how you're going to fuck me."

They never actually finished weighing the soul of Greg Lippmann. Rather, they were interrupted by two pieces of urgent news. The first came in May 2006: Standard & Poor's announced its plans to change the model used to rate subprime mortgage bonds. The model would change July 1, 2006, the announcement said, but all the subprime bonds issued before that date would be rated by the old, presumably less rigorous, model. Instantly, the creation of subprime bonds shot up dramatically. "They were stuffing the channel," said Vinny. "Getting as much shit out so that it could be rated by the old model." The fear of new and better ratings suggested that even the big Wall Street firms knew that the bonds they'd been creating had been overrated.

The other piece of news concerned home prices. Eisman spoke often to a housing market analyst at Credit Suisse named Ivy Zelman. The simple measure of sanity in housing prices, Zelman argued, was the ratio of median home price to income. Historically, in the United States, it ran around 3:1; by late 2004, it had risen nationally, to 4:1. "All these people were saying it was nearly as high in some other countries," says Zelman. "But the problem wasn't just that it was four to one. In Los Angeles it was *ten to one* and in Miami, eight-point-five to one. And then you coupled that with the buyers. They weren't real buyers. They were speculators."* The number of For Sale signs began rising in mid-2005 and never stopped. In the summer of 2006, the Case-Shiller index of house prices peaked, and house prices across the country began to fall. For the entire year they would fall, nationally, by 2 percent.

Either piece of news—rising ratings standards or falling house prices—should have disrupted the subprime bond market and caused the price of insuring the bonds to rise. Instead, the price of insuring the bonds fell. Insurance on the crappiest triple-B tranche of a subprime mortgage bond now cost less than 2 percent a year. "We finally just did a trade with Lippmann," says Eisman. "Then we tried to figure out what we'd done."

The minute they'd done their first trade, they joined Greg Lippmann's long and growing e-mail list. Right up until the collapse, Lippmann would pepper them with agitprop about the housing market, and his own ideas of which subprime mortgage bonds his customers should bet against. "Any time Lippmann would offer us paper, Vinny and I would look at each other and say no," said Danny Moses. They'd take Lippmann's advice, but only up to a point. They still hadn't gotten around to trusting anyone inside a Wall Street bond department; anyway, it was their job, not Lippmann's, to evaluate the individual bonds.

Michael Burry focused, abstractly, on the structure of the loans, and

* Zelman alienated her Wall Street employer with her pessimism, and finally quit and set up her own consulting firm. "It wasn't that hard in hindsight to see it," she says. "It was very hard to know when it would stop." Zelman spoke occasionally with Eisman, and always left these conversations feeling better about her views, and worse about the world. "You needed the occasional assurance that you weren't nuts," she says.

bet on pools with high concentrations of the types that he believed were designed to fail. Eisman and his partners focused concretely on the people doing the borrowing and the lending. The subprime market tapped a segment of the American public that did not typically have anything to do with Wall Street: the tranche between the fifth and the twenty-ninth percentile in their credit ratings. That is, the lenders were making loans to people who were less creditworthy than 71 percent of the population. Which of these poor Americans were likely to jump which way with their finances? How much did their home prices need to fall for their loans to blow up? Which mortgage originators were the most corrupt? Which Wall Street firms were creating the most dishonest mortgage bonds? What kind of people, in which parts of the country, exhibited the highest degree of financial irresponsibility? The default rate in Georgia was five times higher than that in Florida, even though the two states had the same unemployment rate. Why? Indiana had a 25 percent default rate; California, only 5 percent, even though Californians were, on the face of it, far less fiscally responsible. Why? Vinny and Danny flew down to Miami, where they wandered around empty neighborhoods built with subprime loans, and saw with their own eyes how bad things were. "They'd call me and say, 'Oh my God, this is a calamity here,'" recalls Eisman.

In short, they performed the sort of nitty-gritty credit analysis on the mortgage loans that should have been done before the loans were made in the first place. Then they went hunting for crooks and fools. "The first time I realized how bad it was," said Eisman, "was when I said to Lippmann, 'Send me a list of the 2006 deals with high no-doc loans." Eisman, predisposed to suspect fraud in the market, wanted to bet against Americans who had been lent money without having been required to show evidence of income or employment. "I figured Lippmann was going to send me deals that had twenty percent no docs. He sent us a list and none of them had less than fifty percent."

They called Wall Street trading desks and asked for menus of subprime mortgage bonds, so they might find the most rotten ones and buy the smartest insurance. The juiciest shorts—the bonds ultimately backed by the mortgages most likely to default—had several characteristics. First, the underlying loans were heavily concentrated in what Wall Street people were now calling the sand states: California, Florida, Nevada, and Arizona. House prices in the sand states had risen fastest during the boom and so would likely crash fastest in a bust—and when they did, those low California default rates would soar. Second, the loans would have been made by the more dubious mortgage lenders. Long Beach Savings, wholly owned by Washington Mutual, was a prime example of financial incontinence. Long Beach Savings had been the first to embrace the originate and sell model and now was moving money out the door to new home buyers as fast as it could, few questions asked. Third, the pools would have a higher than average number of low-doc or no-doc loans—that is, loans more likely to be fraudulent. Long Beach Savings, it appeared to Eisman and his partners, specialized in asking homeowners with bad credit and no proof of income to accept floating-rate mortgages. No money down, interest payments deferred upon request. The housing blogs of southern California teemed with stories of financial abuses made possible by these so-called thirty-year payment option ARMs, or adjustable-rate mortgages. In Bakersfield, California, a Mexican strawberry picker with an income of $14,000 and no English was lent every penny he needed to buy a house for $724,000.

The more they examined the individual bonds, the more they came to see patterns in the loans that could be exploited for profit. The new taste for lending huge sums of money to poor immigrants, for instance. One day Eisman's housekeeper, a South American woman, came to him and told him that she was planning to buy a townhouse in Queens. "The price was absurd, and they were giving her a no money down option adjustable-rate mortgage," says Eisman, who talked her into taking out a conventional fixed-rate mortgage. Next, the baby nurse he'd hired back in 2003 to take care of his new twin daughters phoned him. "She was this lovely woman from Jamaica," he says. "She says she and her sister own six townhouses in Queens. I said, 'Corinne, how did that happen?'" It happened because after they bought the first one, and its value rose, the lenders came and suggested they refinance and take out $250,000—which they used to buy another. Then the price of that one rose, too, and they repeated the experiment. "By the time they were done they owned five of them, the market was falling, and they couldn't make any of the payments."

The sudden ability of his baby nurse to obtain loans was no accident: Like pretty much everything else that was happening between subprime mortgage borrowers and lenders, it followed from the defects of the models used to evaluate subprime mortgage bonds by the two major rating agencies, Moody's and Standard & Poor's.

The big Wall Street firms—Bear Stearns, Lehman Brothers, Goldman Sachs, Citigroup, and others—had the same goal as any manufacturing business: to pay as little as possible for raw material (home loans) and charge as much as possible for their end product (mortgage bonds). The price of the end product was driven by the ratings assigned to it by the models used by Moody's and S&P. The inner workings of these models were, officially, a secret: Moody's and S&P claimed they were impossible to game. But everyone on Wall Street knew that the people who ran the models were ripe for exploitation. "Guys who can't get a job on Wall Street get a job at Moody's," as one Goldman Sachs trader-turned-hedge fund manager put it. Inside the rating agency there was another hierarchy, even less flattering to the subprime mortgage bond raters. "At the ratings agencies the corporate credit people are the least bad," says a quant who engineered mortgage bonds for Morgan Stanley. "Next are the prime mortgage people. Then you have the asset-backed people, who are basically like brain-dead."* Wall Street bond trading desks, staffed by people making seven figures a year, set out to coax from the brain-dead guys making high five figures the highest possible ratings for the worst possible loans. They performed the task with Ivy League thoroughness and efficiency. They quickly figured out, for instance, that the people at Moody's and S&P didn't actually evaluate the individual home loans, or so much as look at them. All they and their models saw, and evaluated, were the general characteristics of loan pools.

Their handling of FICO scores was one example. FICO scores—so called because they were invented, in the 1950s, by a company called the Fair Isaac Corporation—purported to measure the creditworthiness of individual borrowers. The highest possible FICO score was 850; the lowest was 300; the U.S. median was 723. FICO scores were simplistic. They didn't account for a borrower's income, for instance. They could also be rigged. A would-be borrower could raise his FICO score by taking out a credit card loan and immediately paying it back. But never mind: The problem with FICO scores was overshadowed by the way they were misused by the rating agencies. Moody's and S&P asked the loan packagers not for a list of the FICO scores of all the borrowers but for the *average* FICO score of the pool. To meet the rating agencies' standards—to maximize the percentage of triple-A-rated bonds created from any given pool of loans—the average FICO score of the borrowers in the pool needed to be around 615. There was more than one way to arrive at that average number. And therein lay a huge opportunity. A pool of loans composed of borrowers all of whom had a FICO score of 615 was far less likely to suffer huge losses than a pool of loans composed of borrowers half of whom had FICO scores of 550 and half of whom had FICO scores of 680. A person

* Confusingly, subprime mortgage bonds are classified not as mortgage bonds but, along with bonds backed by credit card loans, auto loans, and other, wackier collateral, as "asset-backed securities."

with a FICO score of 550 was virtually certain to default and should never have been lent money in the first place. But the hole in the rating agencies' models enabled the loan to be made, as long as a borrower with a FICO score of 680 could be found to offset the deadbeat, and keep the average at 615.

Where to find the borrowers with high FICO scores? Here the Wall Street bond trading desks exploited another blind spot in the rating agencies' models. Apparently the agencies didn't grasp the difference between a "thin-file" FICO score and a "thick-file" FICO score. A thin-file FICO score implied, as it sounds, a short credit history. The file was thin because the borrower hadn't done much borrowing. Immigrants who had never failed to repay a debt, because they had never been given a loan, often had surprisingly high thin-file FICO scores. Thus a Jamaican baby nurse or Mexican strawberry picker with an income of $14,000 looking to borrow three-quarters of a million dollars, when filtered through the models at Moody's and S&P, became suddenly more useful, from a credit-rigging point of view. They might actually improve the perceived quality of the pool of loans and increase the percentage that could be declared triple-A. The Mexican harvested strawberries; Wall Street harvested his FICO score.

The models used by the rating agencies were riddled with these sorts of opportunities. The trick was finding them before others did—finding, for example, that both Moody's and S&P favored floating-rate mortgages with low teaser rates over fixed-rate ones. Or that they didn't care if a loan had been made in a booming real estate market or a quiet one. Or that they were seemingly oblivious to the fraud implicit in no-doc loans. Or that they were blind to the presence of "silent seconds"—second mortgages that left the homeowner with no equity in his home and thus no financial incentive not to hand the keys to the bank and walk away from it. Every time some smart Wall Street mortgage bond packager discovered another example of the rating agencies' idiocy or neglect, he had himself an edge in the marketplace: Crappier pools of loans were cheaper to buy than less crappy pools. Barbell-shaped loan pools, with lots of very low and very high FICO scores in them, were a bargain compared to pools clustered around the 615 average—at least until the rest of Wall Street caught on to the hole in the brains of the rating agencies and bid up their prices. Before that happened, the Wall Street firm enjoyed a perverse monopoly. They'd phone up an originator and say, "Don't tell anybody, but if you bring me a pool of loans teeming with high thin-file FICO scores I'll pay you more for it than anyone else." The more egregious the rating agencies' mistakes, the bigger the opportunity for the Wall Street trading desks.

In the late summer of 2006 Eisman and his partners knew none of this. All they knew was that Wall Street investment banks apparently employed people to do nothing but game the rating agencies' models. In a rational market, the bonds backed by pools of weaker loans would have been priced lower than the bonds backed by stronger loans. Subprime mortgage bonds all were priced by the ratings bestowed on them by Moody's. The triple-A tranches all traded at one price, the triple-B tranches all traded at another, even though there were important differences from one triple-B tranche to another. As the bonds were all priced off the Moody's rating, the most overpriced bonds were the bonds that had been most ineptly rated. And the bonds that had been most ineptly rated were the bonds that Wall Street firms had tricked the rating agencies into rating most ineptly. "I cannot fucking believe this is allowed," said Eisman. "I must have said that one thousand times."

Eisman didn't know exactly how the rating agencies had been gamed. He had to learn. Thus began his team's months-long quest to find the most overrated bonds in a market composed of overrated bonds. A month or so into it, after they bought their first credit default swaps on subprime mortgage bonds from Lippmann, Vincent Daniel and Danny Moses flew to Orlando for what amounted to a subprime mortgage bond conference. It had an opaque title—ABS East—but it was, in effect, a trade show for a narrow industry: the guys who originated subprime mortgages, the Wall Street firms that packaged and sold subprime mortgages, fund managers who invested in nothing but subprime mortgage–backed bonds, the agencies that rated subprime mortgage bonds, the lawyers who did whatever the lawyers did. Daniel and Moses thought they were paying a courtesy call on a cottage industry, but the cottage was a castle. "There were so many people being fed by this industry," said Daniel. "That's when we realized that the fixed income departments of the brokerage firms were built on this."

That's also when they made their first face-to-face contact with the rating agencies. Greg Lippmann's people set it up for them, on the condition they not mention that they were betting against, and not for, subprime mortgage bonds. "Our whole purpose," said Moses, "was supposed to be, 'We're here to buy these securities.' People were supposed to think, 'Oh, they're looking to buy paper because it's getting to attractive levels.'" In a little room inside the Orlando Ritz-Carlton hotel, they met with both Moody's and S&P. Vinny and Danny already suspected that the subprime market had subcontracted its credit analysis to people who weren't even doing the credit analysis. Nothing they learned that day allayed their suspicion. The S&P people were cagey, but the woman from Moody's was surprisingly frank. She told them, for instance, that even though she was responsible for evaluating subprime mortgage bonds, she wasn't allowed by her bosses simply to downgrade the ones she thought deserved to be downgraded. She submitted a list of the bonds she wished to downgrade to her superiors and received back a list of what she was permitted to downgrade. "She said she'd submit a list of a hundred bonds and get back a list with twenty-five bonds on it, with no explanation of why," said Danny.

Vinny, the analyst, asked most of the questions, but Danny attended with growing interest. "Vinny has a tell," said Moses. "When he gets excited he puts his hand over his mouth and leans his elbow on the table and says, 'Let me ask you a question about this . . .' When I saw the hand to face I knew Vinny was on to something."

> *Here's what I don't understand*, said Vinny, hand on chin. *You have two bonds that seem identical. How is one of them triple-A and the other not?*
>
> *I'm not the one who makes those decisions*, said the woman from Moody's, but she was clearly uneasy.
>
> *Here's another thing I don't understand*, said Vinny. *How could you rate any portion of a bond made up exclusively of subprime mortgages triple-A?*
>
> *That's a very good question.*
>
> Bingo.

"She was great," said Moses. "Because she didn't know what we were up to."

They called Eisman from Orlando and said, However corrupt you think this industry is, it's worse. "Orlando wasn't even the varsity conference," said Daniel. "Orlando was the JV conference. The varsity met in Vegas. We told Steve, 'You have to go to Vegas. Just to see this.'" They really thought that they had a secret. Through the summer and early fall of 2006, they behaved as if they had stumbled upon a fantastic treasure map, albeit with a few hazy directions. Eisman was now arriving home at night in a better mood than his wife had seen him in a very long time. "I was happy," says Valerie. "I thought, 'Thank God there's a place to put all this enthusiastic misery.' He'd say, 'I found this thing. It's a gold mine. And nobody else knows about it.'"

CHAPTER FIVE

Accidental Capitalists

The thing Eisman had found was indeed a gold mine, but it wasn't true that no one knew about it. By the fall of 2006 Greg Lippmann had made his case to maybe 250 big investors privately, and to hundreds more at Deutsche Bank sales conferences or on Deutsche Bank conference calls. By the end of 2006, according to the PerTrac Hedge Fund Database Study, there were 13,675 hedge funds reporting results, and thousands of other types of institutional investors allowed to invest in credit default swaps. Lippmann's pitch, in one form or another, reached many of them. Yet only one hundred or so dabbled in the new market for credit default swaps on subprime mortgage bonds. Most bought this insurance on subprime mortgages not as an outright bet against them but as a hedge against their implicit bet *on* them—their portfolios of U.S. real estate–related stocks or bonds. A smaller group used credit default swaps to make what often turned out to be spectacularly disastrous gambles on the relative value of subprime mortgage bonds—buying one subprime mortgage bond while simultaneously selling another. They would bet, for instance, that bonds with large numbers of loans made in California would underperform bonds with very little of California in them. Or that the upper triple-A-rated floor of some subprime mortgage bond would outperform the lower, triple-B-rated, floor. Or that bonds issued by Lehman Brothers or Goldman Sachs (both notorious for packaging America's worst home loans) would underperform bonds packaged by J.P. Morgan or Wells Fargo (which actually seemed to care a bit about which loans it packaged into bonds).

A smaller number of people—more than ten, fewer than twenty—made a straightforward bet against the entire multi-trillion-dollar subprime mortgage market and, by extension, the global financial system. In and of itself it was a remarkable fact: The catastrophe was foreseeable, yet only a handful noticed. Among them: a Minneapolis hedge fund called Whitebox, a Boston hedge fund called The Baupost Group, a San Francisco hedge fund called Passport Capital, a Westchester, New York, hedge fund called Elm Ridge, and a gaggle of New York City hedge funds: Elliott Associates, Cedar Hill Capital Partners, QVT Financial, and Philip Falcone's Harbinger Capital Partners. What most of these investors had in common was that they had heard, directly or indirectly, Greg Lippmann's argument. In Dallas, Texas, a former Bear Stearns bond salesman named Kyle Bass set up a hedge fund called Hayman Capital in mid-2006 and soon thereafter bought credit default swaps on subprime mortgage bonds. Bass had heard the idea from Alan Fournier of Pennant Capital, in New Jersey—who in turn had heard it from Lippmann. A rich American real estate investor named Jeff Greene went off and bought several billion dollars' worth of credit default swaps on subprime mortgage bonds for himself after hearing about it from the New York hedge fund manager John Paulson. Paulson, too, had heard Greg Lippmann's pitch—and, as he built a massive position in credit default swaps, used Lippmann as his sounding board. A proprietary trader at Goldman Sachs in London, informed that this trader at Deutsche Bank in New York was making a powerful argument, flew across the Atlantic to meet with Lippmann and went home owning a billion dollars' worth of credit default swaps on subprime mortgage bonds. A Greek hedge fund investor named Theo Phanos heard Lippmann pitch his idea at a Deutsche Bank conference in Phoenix, Arizona, and immediately placed his own bet. If you mapped the spread of the idea, as you might a virus, most of the lines pointed back to Lippmann. He was Patient Zero. Only one carrier of the disease could claim, plausibly, to have infected him. But Mike Burry was holed up in his office in San Jose, California, and wasn't talking to anyone.

This small world of investors who made big bets against subprime mortgage bonds itself contained an even smaller world: people for whom the trade became an obsession. A tiny handful of investors perceived what was happening not just to the financial system but to the larger society it was meant to serve, and made investments against that system that were so large, in relation to their capital, that they effectively gave up being conventional money managers and became something else. John Paulson had by far the most money to play with, and so was the most obvious example. Nine months after Mike Burry failed to raise a fund to do nothing but buy credit default swaps on subprime mortgage bonds, Paulson succeeded, by presenting it to investors not as a catastrophe almost certain to happen but as a cheap hedge against the remote possibility of catastrophe. Paulson was fifteen years older than Burry, and far better known on Wall Street, but he was still, in some ways, a Wall Street outsider. "I called Goldman Sachs to ask them about Paulson," said one rich man whom Paulson had solicited for funds in mid-2006. "They told me he was a third-rate hedge fund guy who didn't know what he was talking about." Paulson raised several billion dollars from investors who regarded his fund as an insurance policy on their portfolios of real estate–related stocks and bonds. What prepared him to see what was happening in the mortgage bond market, Paulson said, was a career of searching for overvalued bonds to bet against. "I loved the concept of shorting a bond because your downside was limited," he told me. "It's an asymmetrical bet." He was shocked how much easier and cheaper it was to buy a credit default swap than it was to sell short an actual cash bond—even though they represented exactly the same bet. "I did half a billion. They said, 'Would you like to do a billion?' And I said, 'Why am I pussyfooting around?' It took two or three days to place twenty-five billion." Paulson had never encountered a market in which an investor could sell short 25 billion dollars' worth of a stock or bond without causing its price to move, even crash. "And we could have done fifty billion, if we'd wanted to."

Even as late as the summer of 2006, as home prices began to fall, it took a certain kind of person to see the ugly facts and react to them—to discern, in the profile of the beautiful young lady, the face of an old witch. Each of these people told you something about the state of the financial system, in the same way that people who survive a plane crash told you something about the accident, and also about the nature of people who survive accidents. All of them were, almost by definition, odd. But they were not all odd in the same way. John Paulson was oddly interested in betting against dodgy loans, and oddly persuasive in talking others into doing it with him. Mike Burry was odd in his desire to remain insulated from public opinion, and even direct human contact, and to focus instead on hard data and the incentives that guide future human financial behavior. Steve Eisman was odd in his conviction that the leveraging of middle-class America was a corrupt and corrupting event, and that the subprime mortgage market in particular was an engine of exploitation and, ultimately, destruction. Each filled a hole; each supplied a missing insight, an attitude to risk which, if more prevalent, might have prevented the catastrophe. But there was at least one gaping hole no big-time professional investor filled. It was filled, instead, by Charlie Ledley.

Charlie Ledley—curiously uncertain Charlie Ledley—was odd

in his belief that the best way to make money on Wall Street was to seek out whatever it was that Wall Street believed was least likely to happen, and bet on its happening. Charlie and his partners had done this often enough, and had had enough success, to know that the markets were predisposed to underestimating the likelihood of dramatic change. Even so, in September 2006, as he paged through the document sent to him by a friend, a presentation about shorting subprime mortgage bonds by some guy at Deutsche Bank named Greg Lippmann, Ledley's first thought was, *This is just too good to be true.* He'd never traded a mortgage bond, knew essentially nothing about real estate, was bewildered by the jargon of the bond market, and wasn't even sure Deutsche Bank or anyone else would allow him to buy credit default swaps on subprime mortgage bonds—since this was a market for institutional investors, and he and his two partners, Ben Hockett and Jamie Mai, weren't anyone's idea of an institution. "But I just looked at it and said, 'How can this even be possible?'" He then sent the idea to his partners along with the question, *Why isn't someone smarter than us doing this?*

Every new business is inherently implausible, but Jamie Mai and Charlie Ledley's idea, in early 2003, for a money management firm bordered on the absurd: a pair of thirty-year-old men with a Schwab account containing $110,000 occupy a shed in the back of a friend's house in Berkeley, California, and dub themselves Cornwall Capital Management. Neither of them had any reason to believe he had any talent for investing. Both had worked briefly for the New York private equity firm Golub Associates as grunts chained to their desks, but neither had made actual investment decisions. Jamie Mai was tall and strikingly handsome and so, almost by definition, had the air of a man in charge—until he opened his mouth and betrayed his lack of confidence in everything from tomorrow's sunrise to the future of the human race. Jamie had a habit of stopping himself midsentence and stammering—"uh, uh, uh"—as if he was somehow unsettled by his own thought. Charlie Ledley was even worse: He had the pallor of a mortician and the manner of a man bent on putting off, for as long as possible, definite action. Asked a simple question, he'd stare mutely into space, nodding and blinking like an actor who has forgotten his lines, so that when he finally opened his mouth the sound that emerged caused you to jolt in your chair. *It speaks!*

Both were viewed by contemporaries as sweet-natured, disorganized, inquisitive, bright but lacking obvious direction—the kind of guys who might turn up at their fifteenth high school reunions with surprising facial hair and a complicated life story. Charlie left Amherst College after his freshman year to volunteer for Bill Clinton's first presidential campaign, and, though he eventually returned, he remained far more interested in his own idealism than in making money. Jamie's first job out of Duke University had been delivering sailboats to rich people up and down the East Coast. ("That's when it became clear to me that—uh, uh, uh—I was going to have to adopt some profession.") At the age of twenty-eight, he'd taken an eighteen-month "sabbatical," traveling around the world with his girlfriend. He'd come to Berkeley not looking for fertile soil in which to grow money but because the girlfriend wanted to move there. Charlie didn't even really want to be in Berkeley; he'd grown up in Manhattan and turned into a pumpkin when he got to the other side of a bridge or tunnel. He'd moved to Berkeley because the idea of running money together, and the $110,000, had been Jamie's. The garage in which Charlie now slept was Jamie's, too.

Instead of money or plausibility, what they had was an idea about financial markets. Or, rather, a pair of related ideas. Their stint in the private equity business—in which firms buy and sell entire companies over the counter—led them to believe that private stock markets might be more efficient than public ones. "In private transactions," said Charlie, "you usually have an advisor on both sides that's sophisticated. You don't have people who just fundamentally don't know what something's worth. In public markets you have people focused on quarterly earnings rather than the business franchise. You have people doing things for all sorts of insane reasons." They believed, further, that public financial markets lacked investors with an interest in the big picture. U.S. stock market guys made decisions within the U.S. stock market; Japanese bond market guys made decisions within the Japanese bond market; and so on. "There are actually people who do nothing but invest in European mid-cap health care debt," said Charlie. "I don't think the problem is specific to finance. I think that parochialism is common to modern intellectual life. There is no attempt to integrate." The financial markets paid a lot of people extremely well for narrow expertise and a few people, poorly, for the big, global views you needed to have if you were to allocate capital across markets.

In early 2003 Cornwall Capital had just opened for business, which meant Jamie and Charlie spent even more hours of their day than before sitting in the Berkeley garage—Charlie's bedroom—shooting the shit about the market. Cornwall Capital, they decided, would not merely search for market inefficiency but search for it globally, in every market: stocks, bonds, currencies, commodities. To these two not so simple ambitions they soon added a third, even less simple, one, when they stumbled upon their first big opportunity, a credit card company called Capital One Financial.

Capital One was a rare example of a company that seemed to have found a smart way to lend money to Americans with weak credit scores. Its business was credit cards, not home loans, but it dealt with the same socioeconomic class of people whose home loan borrowing would end in catastrophe just a few years later. Through the 1990s and into the 2000s, the company claimed, and the market believed, that it possessed better tools than other companies for analyzing the creditworthiness of subprime credit card users and for pricing the risk of lending to them. It had weathered a bad stretch for its industry, in the late 1990s, during which several of its competitors collapsed. Then, in July 2002, its stock crashed—falling 60 percent in two days, after Capital One's management voluntarily disclosed that they were in a dispute about how much capital they needed to reserve against potential subprime losses with their two government regulators, the Office of Thrift Supervision and the Federal Reserve.

Suddenly the market feared that Capital One wasn't actually smarter than everyone else in their industry about making loans but simply better at hiding their losses. The regulators had discovered fraud, the market suspected, and were about to punish Capital One. Circumstantial evidence organized itself into what seemed like a damning case. For instance, the SEC announced that it was investigating the company's CFO, who had just resigned, for selling his shares in the company two months before the company announced its dispute with regulators and its share price collapsed.

Over the next six months, the company continued to make money at impressive rates. It claimed that it had done nothing wrong, that the regulators were being capricious, and announced no special losses on its $20 billion portfolio of subprime loans. Its stock price remained depressed. Charlie and Jamie studied the matter, which is to say they went to industry conferences, and called up all sorts of people they didn't know and bugged them for information: short sellers, former Capital One employees, management consultants who had advised the company, competitors, and even government regulators. "What became clear," said Charlie, "was that there was a limited amount of information out there and we had the same information as everyone else." They decided that Capital One probably did have better tools for making subprime loans. That left only one question: Was it run by crooks?

It wasn't a question two thirty-something would-be professional investors in Berkeley, California, with $110,000 in a Schwab account should feel it was their business to answer. But they did. They went hunting for people who had gone to college with Capital One's CEO, Richard Fairbank, and collected character references. Jamie paged through the Capital One 10-K filing in search of someone inside the company he might plausibly ask to meet. "If we had asked to meet with the CEO, we wouldn't have gotten to see him," explained Charlie. Finally they came upon a lower-ranking guy named Peter Schnall, who happened to be the vice-president in charge of the subprime portfolio. "I got the impression they were like, 'Who calls and asks for Peter Schnall?'" said Charlie. "Because when we asked to talk to him they were like, 'Why not?'" They introduced themselves gravely as Cornwall Capital Management but refrained from mentioning what, exactly, Cornwall Capital Management was. "It's funny," says Jamie. "People don't feel comfortable asking how much money you have, and so you don't have to tell them."

They asked Schnall if they might visit him, to ask a few questions before they made an investment. "All we really wanted to do," said Charlie, "was to see if he seemed like a crook." They found him totally persuasive. Interestingly, he was buying stock in his own company. They left thinking that Capital One's dispute with its regulators was trivial and that the company was basically honest. "We concluded that maybe they were crooks," said Jamie, "but probably not."

What happened next led them, almost by accident, to the unusual approach to financial markets that would soon make them rich. In the six months following the news of its troubles with the Federal Reserve and the Office of Thrift Supervision, Capital One's stock traded in a narrow band around $30 a share. That stability obviously masked a deep uncertainty. Thirty dollars a share was clearly not the "right" price for Capital One. The company was either a fraud, in which case the stock was probably worth zero, or the company was as honest as it appeared to Charlie and Jamie, in which case the stock was worth around $60 a share. Jamie Mai had just read *You Can Be a Stock Market Genius*, the book by Joel Greenblatt, the same fellow who had staked Mike Burry to his hedge fund. Toward the end of his book Greenblatt described how he'd made a lot of money using a derivative security, called a LEAP (for Long-term Equity AnticiPation Security), which conveyed to its buyer the right to buy a stock at a fixed price for a certain amount of time. There were times, Greenblatt explained, when it made more sense to buy options on a stock than the stock itself. This, in Greenblatt's world of value investors, counted as heresy. Old-fashioned value investors shunned options because options presumed an ability to time price movements in undervalued stocks. Greenblatt's simple point: When the value of a stock so obviously turned on some upcoming event whose date was known (a merger date, for instance, or a court date), the value investor could in good conscience employ options to express his views. It gave Jamie an idea: Buy a long-term option to buy the stock of Capital One. "It was kind of like, Wow, we have a view: This common stock looks interesting. But, Holy shit, look at the prices of these options!"

The right to buy Capital One's shares for $40 at any time in the next two and a half years cost a bit more than $3. That made no sense. Capital One's problems with regulators would be resolved, or not, in the next few months. When they were, the stock would either collapse to zero or jump to $60. Looking into it a bit, Jamie found that the model used by Wall Street to price LEAPs, the Black-Scholes option pricing model, made some strange assumptions. For instance, it assumed a normal, bell-shaped distribution for future stock prices. If Capital One was trading at $30 a share, the model assumed that, over the next two years, the stock was more likely to get to $35 a share than to $40, and more likely to get to $40 a share than to $45, and so on. This assumption made sense only to those who knew nothing about the company. In this case the model was totally missing the point: When Capital One stock moved, as it surely would, it was more likely to move by a lot than by a little.

Cornwall Capital Management quickly bought 8,000 LEAPs. Their potential losses were limited to the $26,000 they paid for their option to buy the stock. Their potential gains were theoretically unlimited. Soon after Cornwall Capital laid their chips on the table, Capital One was vindicated by its regulators, its stock price shot up, and Cornwall Capital's $26,000 option position was worth $526,000. "We were pretty fired up," says Charlie.

"We couldn't believe people would sell us these long-term options so cheaply," said Jamie. "We went looking for more long-dated options."

It instantly became a fantastically profitable strategy: Start with what appeared to be a cheap option to buy or sell some Korean stock, or pork belly, or third-world currency—really anything with a price that seemed poised for some dramatic change—and then work backward to the thing the option allowed you to buy or sell. The options suited the two men's personalities: They never had to be sure of anything. Both were predisposed to feel that people, and by extension markets, were too certain about inherently uncertain things. Both sensed that people, and by extension markets, had difficulty attaching the appropriate probabilities to highly improbable events. Both had trouble generating conviction of their own but no trouble at all reacting to what they viewed as the false conviction of others. Each time they came upon a tantalizing long shot, one of them set to work on making the case for it, in an elaborate presentation, complete with PowerPoint slides. They didn't actually have anyone to whom they might give a presentation. They created them only to hear how plausible they sounded when pitched to each other. They entered markets only because they thought something dramatic might be about to happen in them, on which they could make a small bet with long odds that might pay off in a big way. They didn't know the first thing about Korean stocks or third world currencies, but they didn't really need to. If they found what appeared to be a cheap bet on the price movements of any security, they could then hire an expert to help them sort out the details. "That has been a pattern of ours," said Jamie Mai. "To rely on the work of smart people who know more than we do."

They followed their success with Capital One with a similar success, in a distressed European cable television company called United Pan-European Cable. This time, since they had more money, they bought $500,000 in call options, struck at a price far from the market. When UPC rallied, they turned a quick $5 million profit. "We're now getting really, really excited," says Jamie. Next they bet on a company that delivered oxygen tanks directly to sick people in their homes. That $200,000 bet quickly turned into $3 million. "We're now three for three," said Charlie. "We think it's hilarious. For the first time I could see myself doing this for a really long time."

They had stumbled either upon a serious flaw in modern financial markets or into a great gambling run. Characteristically, they were not sure which it was. As Charlie pointed out, "It's really hard to know when you're lucky and when you're smart." They reckoned that by the time they had a statistically valid track record they'd be dead, or close to it, and so they didn't spend a lot of time worrying about whether they'd been lucky, or smart. Either way, they knew they didn't know as much as they should, especially about financial options. They hired a PhD student from the statistics department at the University of California at Berkeley to help them, but he quit after they asked him to study the market for pork belly futures. "It turned out that he was a vegetarian," said Jamie. "He had a problem with capitalism in general, but the pork bellies pushed him over the edge." They were left to grapple on their own with a lot of complicated financial theory. "We spent a lot of time building Black-Scholes models ourselves, and seeing what happened when you changed various assumptions in them," said Jamie. What struck them powerfully was how cheaply the models allowed a person to speculate on situations that were likely to end in one of two dramatic ways. If, in the next year, a stock was going to be worth nothing or $100 a share, it was silly for anyone to sell a year-long option to buy the stock at $50 a share for $3. Yet the market often did something just like that. The model used by Wall Street to price trillions of dollars' worth of derivatives thought of the financial world as an orderly, continuous process. But the world was not continuous; it changed discontinuously, and often by accident.

Event-driven investing: That was the name they either coined or stole for what they were doing. That made it sound a lot less fun than it was. One day Charlie found himself intrigued by the market for ethanol futures. He didn't know much about ethanol, but he could see that it enjoyed a U.S. government subsidy of 50 cents a gallon, and so was supposed to trade at a 50-cent-a-gallon premium to gasoline, and always had. In early 2005, when he became interested, it traded, briefly, at a 50-cent *discount* to gas. He didn't know why and never found out; instead, Charlie bought two rail cars' worth of ethanol futures, and made headlines in *Ethanol Today*, a magazine of whose existence he was previously unaware. To the intense irritation of Cornwall's broker, they wound up having to accept rail cars filled with ethanol in some stockyard in Chicago—to make a sum of money that struck the broker as absurdly small. "The administrative complexity of what we were doing was out of proportion to our assets," said Charlie. "People who were our size didn't trade across asset classes."

"We were doing the sort of things that might cause your investors to yell at you," said Jamie, "but we didn't get yelled at by investors because we didn't have any investors."

They actually thought about handing their winnings over to some certified, qualified, sanitized, honest-to-God professional investor to run the money for them. They raced around New York for several weeks, interviewing hedge fund managers. "They all sounded great when you listened to them," said Jamie, "but then you'd look at their numbers and they were always flat." They decided to keep on investing their money themselves. Two years after they'd opened for business, they were running $12 million of their own and had moved themselves and their world headquarters from the Berkeley shed to an office in Manhattan—a floor of the Greenwich Village studio of the artist Julian Schnabel.

They'd also moved their account, from Schwab to Bear Stearns. They longed for a relationship with some big Wall Street trading firm and mentioned the desire to their accountant. "He said he knew Ace Greenberg and he could introduce us to him, and so we said great," said Charlie. The former chairman and CEO of Bear Stearns, and a Wall Street legend, Greenberg still kept an office at the firm and acted as a broker for a handful of presumably special investors. When Cornwall Capital moved their assets to Bear Stearns, sure enough, their brokerage statements soon came back with Ace Greenberg's name on top.

Like most of what befell them in the financial markets, their first brush with a big Wall Street firm was delightfully weird but ultimately inexplicable. Just like that, without ever having laid eyes on Ace Greenberg, they were his customers. "We were like, 'So how is it that Ace Greenberg is our broker?'" said Charlie. "I mean, we were nobody. And we'd never actually met Ace Greenberg." The mystery grew with their every attempt to speak with Greenberg. They had what they assumed was his phone number, but when they called it someone other than Greenberg answered. "It was totally bizarre," said Charlie. "Occasionally, Ace Greenberg himself would pick up the phone. But all he'd say was, 'Hold on.' Then a secretary would come on the line and take our order."

At length they talked their way into a face-to-face encounter with the Wall Street legend. The encounter was so brief, however, that they could not honestly say whether they had met Ace Greenberg, or an actor playing Ace Greenberg. "We were ushered in for thirty seconds—literally thirty seconds—and then unceremoniously ushered out," says Jamie. Ace Greenberg was still their broker. They just never spoke to him.

"The whole Ace Greenberg thing still doesn't make sense to us," says Charlie.

The man to whom they now referred as "the actor who plays Ace Greenberg" failed to resolve what they viewed as their biggest problem. They were small private investors. The Wall Street firms were largely a mystery to them. "I've never actually, like, been on the inside of a bank," said Charlie. "I can only imagine what's going on inside by imagining it through someone else's eyes." To do the sort of trades they wanted to do, they needed to be mistaken by the big Wall Street firms for investors who knew their way around a big Wall Street firm. "As a private investor you are a second-class citizen," said Jamie. "The prices you get are worse, the service is worse, everything is worse."

The thought had gained force with the help of Jamie's new neighbor in Berkeley, Ben Hockett. Hockett, also in his early thirties, had spent nine years selling and then trading derivatives for Deutsche Bank in Tokyo. Like Jamie and Charlie, he had the tangy, sweet-smelling aroma of the dropout about him. "When I started I was single and twenty-two," he said. "Now I have a wife and a baby and a dog. I'm sick of the business. I don't like who I am when I get home from work. I didn't want my kid to grow up with that as a dad. I thought, *I gotta get out of here.*" When he went in to quit, his Deutsche Bank bosses insisted that he list his grievances. "I told them I don't like going into an office. I don't like wearing a suit. And I don't like living in a big city. And they said, 'Fine.'" They told him he could wear whatever he wanted to wear, live wherever he wanted to live, and work wherever he wanted to work—and do it all while remaining employed by Deutsche Bank.

Ben moved from Tokyo to the San Francisco Bay area, along with

$100 million of Deutsche Bank's money, which he traded from the comfort of his new home in Berkeley Hills. He suspected, not unreasonably, that he might be the only person in Berkeley looking for arbitrage opportunities in the market for credit derivatives. The existence just down the street of a guy roaming the globe in his mind looking to buy long-term options on financial drama caught him by surprise. Ben and Jamie took to walking their dogs together. Jamie pumped Ben for information about how big Wall Street firms and esoteric financial markets worked, and finally prodded him to quit his real job and join Cornwall Capital. "After three years in a room by myself, I thought it would be nice to work with people," said Ben. He quit Deutsche Bank to join the happy hunt for accident and disaster, and pretty quickly found himself working alone again. Charlie moved back to Manhattan as soon as he could afford the ticket, and, when his relationship with his girlfriend ended, Jamie eagerly followed.

Theirs was a union of the weirdly like-minded. Ben shared Charlie and Jamie's view that people, and markets, tended to underestimate the probability of extreme change, but he took his thinking a step further. Charlie and Jamie were interested chiefly in the probabilities of disasters in financial markets. Ben walked around with some very tiny fraction of his mind alert to the probabilities of disasters in real life. People underestimated these, too, he believed, because they didn't want to think about them. There was a tendency, in markets and life, for people to respond to the possibility of extreme events in one of two ways: flight or fight. "Fight is, 'I'm going to get my guns,'" he said. "Flight is, 'We're all doomed so I can't do anything about it.'" Charlie and Jamie were flight types. When he'd mention to them the possibility that global warming might cause sea levels to rise by twenty feet, for instance, they'd just shrug and say, "I can't do anything about it, so why worry about it?" Or: "If that happens I don't want to be alive anyway."

"They're two single guys in Manhattan," said Ben. "They're both like, 'And if we can't live in Manhattan, we don't want to live at all.'" He was surprised that Charlie and Jamie, both now so alive to the possibility of dramatic change in the financial markets, were less alert and responsive to the possibilities outside those markets. "I'm trying to prepare myself and my children for an environment that is unpredictable," Ben said.

Charlie and Jamie preferred Ben to keep his apocalyptic talk to himself. It made people uncomfortable. There was no reason anyone needed to know, for example, that Ben had bought a small farm in the country, north of San Francisco, in a remote place without road access, planted with fruit and vegetables sufficient to feed his family, on the off chance of the end of the world as we know it. It was hard for Ben to keep his worldview to himself, however, especially since it was the first cousin of their investment strategy: The possibility of accident and disaster was just never very far from their conversations. One day on the phone with Ben, Charlie said, *You hate taking even remote risks, but you live in a house on top of a mountain that's on a fault line, in a housing market that's at an all-time high*. "He just said, 'I gotta go,' and hung up," recalled Charlie. "We had trouble getting hold of him for, like, two months."

"I got off the phone," said Ben, "and I realized, *I have to sell my house. Right now*." His house was worth a million dollars and maybe more yet would rent for no more than $2,500 a month. "It was trading more than thirty times gross rental," said Ben. "The rule of thumb is that you buy at ten and sell at twenty." In October 2005 he moved his family into a rental unit, away from the fault.

Ben thought of Charlie and Jamie less as professional money managers than as dilettantes or, as he put it, "a couple of smart guys just punting around in the markets." But their strategy of buying cheap tickets to some hoped-for financial drama resonated with him. It was hardly foolproof; indeed, it was almost certain to fail more often than it succeeded. Sometimes the hoped-for drama never occurred;

sometimes they actually didn't know what they were doing. Once, Charlie found what he thought was a strange price discrepancy in the market for gasoline futures, and quickly bought one gas contract, sold another, and made what he took to be a riskless profit—only to discover, as Jamie put it, "one was unleaded gasoline and the other was, like, diesel." Another time, the premise was right but the conclusion was wrong. "One day Ben calls me and says, 'Dude, I think there's going to be a coup in Thailand,'" said Jamie. There'd been nothing in the newspapers about a coup in Thailand; this was a genuine scoop. "I said, 'C'mon, Ben, you're crazy, there's not going to be a coup. Anyway, how would you even know? You're in Berkeley!'" Ben swore he had talked to a guy he used to work with in Singapore, who had his finger on the pulse in Thailand. He was so insistent that they went into the Thai currency market and bought what appeared to be stunningly cheap three-month puts (options to sell) on the Thai baht. One week later, the Thai military overthrew the elected prime minister. The Thai baht didn't budge. "We predicted a coup, and we lost money," said Jamie.

The losses, by design, were no big deal; the losses were part of the plan. They had more losers than winners, but their losses, the cost of the options, had been trivial compared to their gains. There was a possible explanation for their success, which Charlie and Jamie had only intuited but which Ben, who had priced options for a big Wall Street firm, came ready to explain: Financial options were systematically mispriced. The market often underestimated the likelihood of extreme moves in prices. The options market also tended to presuppose that the distant future would look more like the present than it usually did. Finally, the price of an option was a function of the volatility of the underlying stock or currency or commodity, and the options market tended to rely on the recent past to determine how volatile a stock or currency or commodity might be. When IBM stock was trading at $34 a share and had been hopping around madly for the past year, an option to buy it for $35 a share anytime soon was seldom underpriced. When gold had been trading around $650 an ounce for the past two years, an option to buy it for $2,000 an ounce anytime during the next ten years might well be badly underpriced. The longer-term the option, the sillier the results generated by the Black-Scholes option pricing model, and the greater the opportunity for people who didn't use it.

Oddly, it was Ben, the least personally conventional of the three, who had the Potemkin-village effect of making Cornwall Capital appear to outsiders to be a conventional institutional money manager. He knew his way around Wall Street trading floors and so also knew the extent to which Charlie and Jamie were being penalized for being perceived by the big Wall Street firms as a not terribly serious investor or, as Ben put it, "a garage band hedge fund." The longest options available to individual investors on public exchanges were LEAPs, which were two-and-a-half-year options on common stocks. *You know*, Ben said to Charlie and Jamie, *if you established yourself as a serious institutional investor, you could phone up Lehman Brothers or Morgan Stanley and buy eight-year options on whatever you wanted. Would you like that?*

They would! They wanted badly to be able to deal directly with the source of what they viewed as the most underpriced options: the most sophisticated, quantitative trading desks at Goldman Sachs, Deutsche Bank, Bear Stearns, and the rest. *The hunting license*, they called it. The hunting license had a name: an ISDA. They were the same agreements, dreamed up by the International Swaps and Derivatives Association, that Mike Burry secured before he bought his first credit default swaps. If you got your ISDA, you could in theory trade with the big Wall Street firms, if not as an equal then at least as a grown-up. The trouble was that, despite their success running money, they still didn't have much of it. Worse, what they had was their own.

Inside Wall Street they were classified, at best, as "high net worth individuals." Rich people. Rich people received a better class of service from Wall Street than middle-class people, but they were still second-class citizens compared to institutional money managers. More to the point, rich people were typically not invited to buy and sell esoteric securities, such as credit default swaps, not traded on open exchanges. Securities that were, increasingly, the beating heart of Wall Street.

By early 2006, Cornwall Capital had grown its stash to almost $30 million, but even that, to the desks inside the Wall Street firms that sold credit default swaps, was a risibly small sum. "We called Goldman Sachs," said Jamie, "and it was just immediately clear they didn't want our business. Lehman Brothers just laughed at us. There was this impenetrable fortress you had either to scale or dig underneath." "J.P. Morgan actually fired us as a customer," said Charlie. "They said we were too much trouble." And they were! In possession of childish sums of money, they wanted to be treated as grown-ups. "We wanted to buy options on platinum from Deutsche Bank," said Charlie, "and they were like, 'Sorry we can't do this with you.'" Wall Street made you pay for managing your own money rather than paying someone on Wall Street to do it for you. "No one was going to take us," said Jamie. "We called around and it was one hundred million bucks, minimum, to be credible."

By the time they called UBS, the big Swiss bank, they knew enough not to answer when the guy on the other end of the line asked them how much money they had. "We learned to spin that one," said Jamie. As a result, UBS took a bit longer than the others to turn them down. "They were, like, 'How much do you short?'" recalled Charlie. "And we said not very much. So they ask, 'How often do you trade?' We say, not very often. And there was this long silence. Then, 'Let me talk to my boss.' And we never heard back from them."

They had no better luck with Morgan Stanley or Merrill Lynch and the rest. "They would say, 'Show us your marketing materials,'" said Charlie, "and we would say, 'Uh, we don't have those.' They'd say, 'Okay, then show us your offering documents.' We didn't have any offering documents because it wasn't other people's money. So they'd say, 'Okay, then just show us your money.' We'd say, 'Um, we don't exactly have enough of that, either.' They'd say, 'Okay, then just show us your resumes.'" If Charlie and Jamie had any connection to the world of money management—former employment, say—it might have lent some credibility to their application, but they didn't. "It always ended with them sort of asking, 'So what *do you* have?'"

Chutzpah. Plus $30 million with which they were willing and able to do anything they wanted to do. Plus a former derivatives trader with an apocalyptic streak who knew how these big Wall Street firms worked. "Jamie and Charlie had been asking for an ISDA for two years, but they really just didn't know how to ask," said Ben. "They didn't even know the term 'ISDA.'"

Charlie never completely understood how Ben did it, but he somehow persuaded Deutsche Bank, which required an investor to control $2 billion to be treated as an institution, to accept Cornwall Capital on their "institutional platform." Ben claimed that it was really only a matter of knowing the right people to call, and the language in which to address their concerns. Before they knew it, a team from Deutsche Bank agreed to pay a call on Cornwall Capital to determine if they were worthy of the distinction: Deutsche Bank institutional customer. "Ben gives good bank," said Charlie.

Deutsche Bank had a program it called KYC (Know Your Customer), which, while it didn't involve anything so radical as actually knowing their customers, did require them to meet their customers, in person, at least once. Hearing that they were to be on the receiving end of KYC, it occurred to Charlie and Jamie, for the first time, that working out of Julian Schnabel's studio in the wrong part of Greenwich Village might raise more questions than it answered. "We had an appearance problem," said Jamie delicately. From upstairs wafted the smell of fresh paint; from downstairs, the site of the lone toilet, came the sounds of a sweatshop. "Before they came," said Charlie, "I remember thinking, *If anyone has to go to the bathroom, we're in trouble.*" Cornwall Capital's own little space inside the larger space was charmingly unfinancial—a dark room in the back with red brick walls that opened onto a small, junglelike garden in which it was easier to imagine a seduction scene than the purchase of a credit default swap. "There was an awkward moment or two, due to the fact that our offices had a tailor working downstairs, and they could hear her," said Jamie. But no one from Deutsche Bank had to go to the bathroom, and Cornwall Capital Management got its ISDA.

This agreement, in its fine print, turned out to be long on Cornwall Capital's duties to Deutsche Bank and short on Deutsche Bank's duties to Cornwall Capital. If Cornwall Capital made a bet with Deutsche Bank and it wound up "in the money," Deutsche Bank was not required to post collateral. Cornwall would just have to hope that Deutsche Bank could make good on its debts. If, on the other hand, the trade went against Cornwall Capital, they were required to post the amount they were down, daily. At the time, Charlie and Jamie and Ben didn't worry much about this provision, or similar provisions in the ISDA they landed with Bear Stearns. They were happy just to be allowed to buy credit default swaps from Greg Lippmann.

Now what? They were young men in a hurry—they couldn't believe the trade existed and didn't know how much longer it would—but they spent several weeks arguing among themselves about it. Lippmann's sales pitch was as alien to them as it was intriguing. Cornwall Capital had never bought or sold a mortgage bond, but they could see that a credit default swap was really just a financial option: You paid a small premium, and, if enough subprime borrowers defaulted on their mortgages, you got rich. In this case, however, they were being offered a cheap ticket to a drama that looked virtually certain to happen.

They created another presentation to give to themselves. "We're looking at the trade," said Charlie, "and we're thinking, like, this is too good to be true. Why the hell should I be able to buy CDSs on the triple-Bs [credit default swaps on the triple-B tranche of subprime mortgage bonds] at these levels? Who in their right mind is saying, 'Wow, I think I'll take two hundred basis points to take this risk?' It just seems like a ridiculously low price. It doesn't make sense." It was now early October 2006. A few months earlier, in June, national home prices, for the first time, had begun to fall. In five weeks, on November 29, the index of subprime mortgage bonds, called the ABX, would post its first interest-rate shortfall. The borrowers were failing to make interest payments sufficient to pay off the riskiest subprime bonds. The underlying mortgage loans were already going sour, and yet the prices of the bonds backed by the loans hadn't budged. "That was the part that was so weird," said Charlie. "They'd already started going bad. We just kept asking, 'Who the hell is taking the other side of this trade?' And the answer that kept coming back to us was, 'It's the CDOs.'" Which of course just raised another question: Who, or what, was a CDO?

Typically when they entered a new market—because they'd found some potential accident waiting to happen that seemed worth betting on—they found an expert to serve as a jungle guide. This market was so removed from their experience that it took them longer than usual to find help. "I had a vague idea what an ABS [asset-backed security] was," said Charlie. "But I had no idea what a CDO was." Eventually they figured out that language served a different purpose inside the bond market than it did in the outside world. Bond market terminology was designed less to convey meaning than to bewilder outsiders. Overpriced bonds were not "expensive"; overpriced bonds were "rich," which almost made them sound like something you should buy. The floors of subprime mortgage bonds were not called floors—or anything else that might lead the bond buyer to form any sort of concrete image in his mind—but tranches. The bottom tranche—the risky ground floor—was not called the ground floor but the mezzanine, or the mezz, which made it sound less like a dangerous investment and more like a highly prized seat in a domed stadium. A CDO composed of nothing but the riskiest, mezzanine layer of subprime mortgages was not called a subprime-backed CDO but a "structured finance CDO." "There was so much confusion about the different terms," said Charlie. "In the course of trying to figure it out, we realize that there's a reason why it doesn't quite make sense to us. It's because it doesn't quite make sense."

The subprime mortgage market had a special talent for obscuring what needed to be clarified. A bond backed entirely by subprime mortgages, for example, wasn't called a subprime mortgage bond. It was called an ABS, or asset-backed security. When Charlie asked Deutsche Bank exactly what assets secured an asset-backed security, he was handed lists of abbreviations and more acronyms—RMBS, HELs, HELOCs, Alt-A—along with categories of credit he did not know existed ("midprime"). RMBS stood for residential mortgage–backed security. HEL stood for home equity loan. HELOC stood for home equity line of credit. Alt-A was just what they called crappy mortgage loans for which they hadn't even bothered to acquire the proper documents—to verify the borrower's income, say. "A" was the designation attached to the most creditworthy borrowers; Alt-A, which stood for "Alternative A-paper," meant an alternative to the most creditworthy, which of course sounds a lot more fishy once it is put that way. As a rule, any loan that had been turned into an acronym or abbreviation could more clearly be called a "subprime loan," but the bond market didn't want to be clear. "Midprime" was a kind of triumph of language over truth. Some crafty bond market person had gazed upon the subprime mortgage sprawl, as an ambitious real estate developer might gaze upon Oakland, and found an opportunity to rebrand some of the turf. On Oakland's fringe there was a neighborhood, masquerading as an entirely separate town, called Rockridge. Simply by refusing to be called Oakland, Rockridge enjoyed higher property values. Inside the subprime mortgage market there was now a similar neighborhood known as midprime. Midprime was subprime—and yet somehow, ineffably, not. "It took me a while to figure out that all of this stuff inside the bonds was pretty much exactly the same thing," said Charlie. "The Wall Street firms just got the ratings agencies to accept different names for it so they could make it seem like a diversified pool of assets."

Charlie, Jamie, and Ben entered the subprime mortgage market assuming they wanted to do what Mike Burry and Steve Eisman had already done, and find the very worst subprime bonds to lay bets against. They quickly got up to speed on FICO scores and loan-to-value ratios and silent seconds and the special madness of California and Florida, and the shockingly optimistic structure of the bonds themselves: The triple-B-minus tranche, the bottom floor of the building, required just 7 percent losses in the underlying pool to be worth zero. But then they wound up doing something quite different from—and, ultimately, more profitable than—what everyone else who bet against the subprime mortgage market was doing: They bet against the upper floors—the double-A tranches—of the CDOs.

After the fact, they'd realize they'd had two advantages. The first was that they had stumbled into the market very late, just before its collapse, and after a handful of other money managers. "One of the reasons we could move so fast," said Charlie, "is that we were seeing a lot of compelling analysis that we didn't have to create from scratch." The other advantage was their quixotic approach to financial markets: They were consciously looking for long shots. They were combing the markets for bets whose true odds were 10:1, priced as if the odds were 100:1. "We were looking for nonrecourse leverage," said Charlie. "Leverage means to magnify the effect. You have a crowbar, you take a little bit of pressure, you turn it into a lot of pressure. We were looking to get ourselves into a position where small changes in states of the world created huge changes in values."

Enter the CDO. They may not have known what a CDO was, but their minds were prepared for it, because a small change in the state of the world created a huge change in the value of a CDO. A CDO, in their view, was essentially just a pile of triple-B-rated mortgage bonds. Wall Street firms had conspired with the rating agencies to represent the pile as a diversified collection of assets, but anyone with eyes could see that if one triple-B subprime mortgage went bad, most would go bad, as they were all vulnerable to the same economic forces. Subprime mortgage loans in Florida would default for the same reasons, and at the same time, as subprime mortgage loans in California. And yet fully 80 percent of the CDO composed of nothing but triple-B bonds was rated higher than triple-B: triple-A, double-A, or A. To wipe out any triple-B bond—the ground floor of the building—all that was needed was a 7 percent loss in the underlying pool of home loans. That same 7 percent loss would thus wipe out, entirely, any CDO made up of triple-B bonds, no matter what rating was assigned it. "It took us weeks to really grasp it because it was so weird," said Charlie. "But the more we looked at what a CDO really was, the more we were like, *Holy shit, that's just fucking crazy. That's fraud.* Maybe you can't prove it in a court of law. But it's fraud."

It was also a stunning opportunity: The market appeared to believe its own lie. It charged a lot less for insurance on a putatively safe double-A-rated slice of a CDO than it did for insurance on the openly risky triple-B-rated bonds. Why pay 2 percent a year to bet directly against triple-B-rated bonds when they could pay 0.5 percent a year to make effectively the same bet against the double-A-rated slice of the CDO? If they paid four times less to make what was effectively the same bet against triple-B-rated subprime mortgage bonds, they could afford to make four times more of it.

They called around big Wall Street firms to see if anyone could dissuade them from buying credit default swaps on the double-A tranche of CDOs. "It really looked just too good to be true," said Jamie. "And when something looks too good to be true, we try to find out why." A fellow at Deutsche Bank named Rich Rizzo, who worked for Greg Lippmann, gave it a shot. The ISDA agreement that standardized CDSs on CDOs (a different agreement than the ISDA agreement that had standardized CDSs on mortgage bonds) had only been created a few months before, in June 2006, Rizzo explained. No one had as yet bought credit default swaps on the double-A piece of a CDO, which meant there wasn't likely to be a liquid market for them. Without a liquid market, they were not assured of being able to sell them when they wanted to, or to obtain a fair price.

"The other thing he said," recalled Charlie, "was that [things] will never get so bad that CDOs will go bad."

Cornwall Capital disagreed. They didn't know for sure that subprime loans would default in sufficient numbers to cause the CDOs to collapse. All they knew was that Deutsche Bank didn't know, either, and neither did anybody else. There might be some "right" price for insuring the first losses on pools of bonds backed by pools of dubious loans, but it wasn't one-half of 1 percent.

Of course, if you are going to gamble on a CDO, it helps to know what, exactly, is inside a CDO, and they still didn't. The sheer difficulty they had obtaining the information suggested that most investors were simply skipping this stage of their due diligence. Each CDO contained pieces of a hundred different mortgage bonds—which in turn held thousands of different loans. It was impossible, or nearly so, to find out which pieces, or which loans. Even the rating agencies, who they at first assumed would be the most informed source, hadn't a clue. "I called S&P and asked if they could tell me what was in a CDO," said Charlie. "And they said, 'Oh yeah, we're working on that.'" Moody's and S&P were piling up these triple-B bonds, assuming they were diversified, and bestowing ratings on them—without ever knowing what was behind the bonds! There had been hundreds of CDO deals—400 billion dollars' worth of the things had been created in just the past three years—and yet none, as far as they could tell, had been properly vetted. Charlie located a reliable source for the contents of a CDO, a data company called Intex, but Intex wouldn't return his phone calls, and he gathered they didn't have much interest in talking to small investors. At length he found a Web site, run by Lehman Brothers, called LehmanLive.*

LehmanLive didn't tell you exactly what was in a CDO, either, but it did offer a crude picture of its salient characteristics: what year the bonds behind it had been created, for instance, and how many of those bonds were backed chiefly by subprime loans. Projecting data onto the red brick wall of Julian Schnabel's studio, Charlie and Jamie went searching for two specific traits: CDOs that contained the highest percentage of bonds backed entirely by recent subprime mortgage loans, and CDOs that contained the highest percentage of other CDOs. Here was another bizarre fact about CDOs: Often they simply repackaged tranches of other CDOs, presumably those tranches their Wall Street creators had found difficult to sell. Even more amazing was their circularity: CDO "A" would contain a piece of CDO "B"; CDO "B" would contain a piece of CDO "C"; and CDO "C" would contain a piece of CDO "A"! Looking for bad bonds inside a CDO was like fishing for crap in a Port-O-Let: The question wasn't whether you'd catch some but how quickly you'd be satisfied you'd caught enough. Their very names were disingenuous, and told you nothing about their contents, their creators, or their managers: Carina, Gemstone, Octans III, Glacier Funding. "They all had these random names," said Jamie. "A lot of them for some reason we never figured out were named for mountains in the Adirondacks."

* Even now, after the death of Lehman Brothers, LehmanLive remains the ghostly go-to source for the contents of many CDOs.

They made a hasty list of what they hoped was the worst crap and called up several brokers. It had been hard for them to wriggle free of the brokers who covered rich people and to get into the arms of brokers who covered big, stock market–investing institutions. It was hard all over again to escape the big-time stock market brokers and win acceptance from the people inside the subprime mortgage bond market. "A lot of people when we called them said, 'Hey, why don't you guys buy some stocks!'" said Charlie. Bear Stearns couldn't believe that these young guys with no money wanted to buy not just credit default swaps but a credit default swap so esoteric that no one else had bought it. "I remember laughing at them," said the Bear Stearns credit default swap salesman who took their first inquiry.

At Deutsche Bank they were passed off to a twenty-three-year-old bond salesman who had never had a customer of his own. "The reason I got to know Ben and Charlie," says this young man, "was that no one else at Deutsche Bank would deal with them. They had, like, twenty-five million bucks, which for Deutsche Bank was not really significant. No one wanted to pick up their calls. People were making fun of their name—they'd say, like, 'Oh, it's Cornhole Capital calling again.'" Still, Deutsche Bank proved, once again, the most willing to deal with them. On October 16, 2006, they bought from Greg Lippmann's trading desk $7.5 million in credit default swaps on the double-A tranche of a CDO named, for no apparent reason, Pine Mountain. Four days later, Bear Stearns sold them $50 million more. "They knew Ace somehow," said the Bear Stearns credit default swap salesman. "So we wound up dealing with them."

Charlie and Jamie continued to call everyone they could think of who was even remotely connected to this new market, in hopes of finding someone who could explain what appeared to them to be its sheer madness. A month later they finally found, and hired, their market expert—a fellow named David Burt. It was a measure of how much money people were making in the bond market that the magazine *Institutional Investor* was about to create a hot list of people who worked in it, called The 20 Rising Stars of Fixed Income. It was a measure of how much money people were making in the subprime mortgage market that David Burt made the list. Burt had worked for the $1 trillion bond fund BlackRock, owned, in part, by Merrill Lynch, evaluating subprime mortgage credit. His job was to identify for BlackRock the bonds that were going to go bad before they went bad. Now he had quit in hopes of raising his own fund to invest in subprime mortgage bonds, and, to make ends meet, he was willing to rent his expertise for $50,000 a month to these oddballs at Cornwall Capital. Burt had the most sensational information, and models to analyze that information—he could tell you, for example, what would happen to mortgage loans, zip code by zip code, in various house price scenarios. He could then take that information and tell you what was likely to happen to specific mortgage bonds. The best way to use this information, he thought, was to buy what appeared to be the sounder mortgage bonds and simultaneously sell the unsound ones.

The insider's artful complexity didn't much interest Cornwall Capital. Spending a lot of time trying to pick the best subprime mortgage bonds was silly, if you suspected that the entire market was about to blow up. They handed Burt the list of CDOs they had bet against and asked him what he thought. "We always looked for someone to explain to us why we didn't know what we were doing," said Jamie. "He couldn't." What Burt could tell them was that they were probably the first people ever to buy a credit default swap on the double-A tranche of a CDO. Not reassuring. They assumed there was a lot about the CDO market they didn't understand; they had selected the CDOs they had bet against inside of a day, and assumed they could do a craftier job of it. "We were already throwing darts," said Jamie. "We said, 'Let's throw darts a little better.'"

The analysis Burt gave them a few weeks later surprised them as much as it did him: They'd picked beautifully. "He said, like, 'Wow, you guys did great. There are a lot of really crappy bonds in these CDOs,'" said Charlie. They didn't realize yet that the bonds inside their CDOs were actually credit default swaps on the bonds, and so their CDOs weren't ordinary CDOs but synthetic CDOs, or that the bonds on which the swaps were based had been handpicked by Mike Burry and Steve Eisman and others betting against the market. In many ways, they were still innocents.

The challenge, as always, was to play the role of market generalist without also playing the role of fool at the poker table. By January 2007, in their tiny $30 million fund, they owned $110 million in credit default swaps on the double-A tranche of asset-backed CDOs. The people who had sold them the swaps still didn't know what to make of them. "They were putting on bets that were multiples of the capital they had," said the young Deutsche Bank broker. "And they were doing it in CDSs on CDOs, which probably, like, three or four guys in the whole bank could speak intelligently about." Charlie and Jamie and Ben sort of understood what they had done, but sort of didn't. "We're kind of obsessed about this trade," said Charlie. "And we've exhausted our network of people to talk to about it. And we still can't totally figure out who is on the other side. We kept trying to find people who could explain to us why we were wrong. We just kept wondering if we were crazy. There was this overwhelming feeling of, *Are we going out of our minds*?"

It's just weeks before the market will turn, and the crisis will commence, but they don't know that. They suspect that this empty theater into which they've stumbled is preparing to stage the most fantastic financial drama they'll ever see, but they don't know that, either. All they know is that there is a lot they don't know. On the phone one day, their Bear Stearns credit default swap salesman mentioned that the big annual subprime conference would be held five days hence, in Las Vegas. Every big cheese in the subprime mortgage market would be there, with a name tag, and wandering around The Venetian hotel.

Bear Stearns was planning a special outing for its customers, at a Vegas firing range, where they could learn to shoot everything from a Glock to an Uzi. "My parents were New York City liberals," said Charlie. "I wasn't even allowed to have, like, a toy gun." Off he flew, with Ben, to Las Vegas, to shoot with Bear Stearns, and to see if they could find anyone to explain to them why they were wrong to bet against the subprime mortgage market.

CHAPTER SIX

Spider-Man at The Venetian

Golfing with Eisman wasn't like golfing with other Wall Street people. The round usually began with a collective discomfort on the first tee, after Eisman turned up wearing something that violated the Wall Street golfer's notion of propriety. On January 28, 2007, he arrived at the swanky Bali Hai Golf Club in Las Vegas dressed in gym shorts, t-shirt, and sneakers. Strangers noticed; Vinny and Danny squirmed. "C'mon, Steve," Danny pleaded with a man who, technically, was his boss, "there's an etiquette here. You at least have to wear a collared shirt." Eisman took the cart to the clubhouse and bought a hoodie. The hoodie covered up his t-shirt and made him look a lot like a guy who had just bought a hoodie to cover up his t-shirt. In hoodie, gym shorts, and sneakers, Eisman approached his first shot. Like every other swing of the Eisman club, this was less a conclusive event than a suggestion. Displeased with where the ball had landed, he pulled another from his bag and dropped it in a new and better place. Vinny would hit his drive in the fairway; Danny would hit his in the rough; Steve would hit his in the bunker, march into the sand, and grab the ball and toss it out, near Vinny's. It was hard to accuse him of cheating, as he didn't make the faintest attempt to disguise what he was doing. He didn't even appear to notice anything unusual in the pattern of his game. The ninth time Eisman retrieved a ball from some sand trap, or pretended his shot had not splashed into the water, he acted with the same unapologetic aplomb he had demonstrated the first time. "Because his memory is so selective, he has no scars from prior experience," said Vinny. He played the game like a child, or like someone who was bent on lampooning a sacred ritual, which amounted to the same thing. "The weird thing is," said Danny, "he's actually not bad."

After a round of golf, they headed out to a dinner at the Wynn hotel hosted by Deutsche Bank. This was the first time Eisman had ever been to a conference for bond market people and, not knowing what else to do, he had put himself in Greg Lippmann's hands. Lippmann had rented a private room in some restaurant and invited Eisman and his partners to what they assumed was something other than a free meal. "Even when he had an honest agenda, there was always something underneath the honest agenda," said Vinny. Any dinner that was Lippmann's idea must have some hidden purpose—but what?

As it turned out, Lippmann had a new problem: U.S. house prices were falling, subprime loan defaults were rising, yet subprime mortgage bonds somehow held firm, as did the price of insuring them. He was now effectively short $10 billion in subprime mortgage bonds, and it was costing him $100 million a year in premiums, with no end in sight. "He was obviously getting his nuts blown off," said Danny. Thus far Lippmann's giant bet had been subsidized by investors, like Steve Eisman, who paid him a toll when they bought and sold credit default swaps, but investors like Steve Eisman were losing heart. Some of Lippmann's former converts suspected that the subprime mortgage bond market was rigged by Wall Street to insure that credit default swaps would never pay off; others began to wonder if the investors on the other side of their bet might know something that they didn't; and some simply wearied of paying insurance premiums to bet against bonds that never seemed to move. Lippmann had staged this great game of tug-of-war, assembled a team to pull on his end of the rope, and now his teammates were in full flight. He worried that Eisman might quit, too.

The teppanyaki room inside the Okada restaurant consisted of four islands, each with a large, cast-iron hibachi and dedicated chef. Around each island Lippmann seated a single hedge fund manager whom he had persuaded to short subprime bonds, along with investors who were long those same bonds. The hedge fund people, he hoped, would *see* just how stupid the investors on the other side of those bets were, and cease to worry that the investors knew something they did not. This was shrewd of him: Danny and Vinny never stopped worrying if they were the fools at Lippmann's table. "We understood the subprime lending market and knew the loans were going bad," said Vinny. "What we didn't have any comfort in was the bond market machine. The whole reason we went to Vegas was we still felt we needed to learn how we were going to get screwed, if we were going to get screwed."

Eisman took his assigned seat between Greg Lippmann and a fellow who introduced himself as Wing Chau and said that he ran an investment firm called Harding Advisory. When Eisman asked exactly what Harding Advisory advised, Wing Chau explained that he was a CDO manager. "I had no idea there was such a thing as a CDO manager," said Eisman. "I didn't know there was anything to manage." Later Eisman would fail to recall what Wing Chau looked like, what he wore, where he'd come from, or what he ate and drank—everything but the financial idea he represented. But from his seat across the hibachi, Danny Moses watched and wondered about the man Lippmann had so carefully seated next to Eisman. He was short, with a Wall Street belly—not the bleacher bum's boiler but the discreet, necessary pouch of a squirrel just before winter. He'd graduated from the University of Rhode Island, earned a business degree at Babson College, and spent most of his career working sleepy jobs at sleepy life insurance companies—but all that was in the past. He was newly, obviously rich. "He had this smirk, like, *I know better*," said Danny. Danny didn't know Wing Chau, but when he heard that he was the end buyer of subprime CDOs, he knew exactly who he was: the sucker. "The truth is that I didn't really want to talk to him," said Danny, "because I didn't want to scare him."

When they saw that Lippmann had seated Eisman right next to the sucker, both Danny and Vinny had the same thought: *Oh no. This isn't going to end well.* Eisman couldn't contain himself. He'd figure out the guy was a fool, and let him know it, and then where would they be? They needed fools; only fools would take the other side of their trades. And they wanted to do more trades. "We didn't want people to know what we were doing," said Vinny. "We were spies, on a fact-finding mission." They watched Eisman double-dip his edamame in the communal soy sauce—dip, suck, redip, resuck—and waited for the room to explode. There was nothing to do but sit back and enjoy the show. Eisman had a curious way of listening; he didn't so much listen to what you were saying as subcontract to some remote region of his brain the task of deciding whether whatever you were saying was worth listening to, while his mind went off to play on its own. As a result, he never actually heard what you said to him the first time you said it. If his mental subcontractor detected a level of interest in what you had just said, it radioed a signal to the mother ship, which then wheeled around with the most intense focus. "Say that again," he'd say. And you would! Because now Eisman was so obviously listening to you, and, as he listened so selectively, you felt flattered. "I keep looking over at them," said Danny. "And I see Steve saying over and over, *Say that again. Say that again.*"

Later, whenever Eisman set out to explain to others the origins of the financial crisis, he'd start with his dinner with Wing Chau. Only now did he fully appreciate the central importance of the so-called mezzanine CDO—the CDO composed mainly of triple-B-rated subprime mortgage bonds—and its synthetic counterpart: the CDO composed entirely of credit default swaps on triple-B-rated subprime mortgage bonds. "You have to understand this," he'd say. "This was the engine of doom." He'd draw a picture of several towers of debt. The first tower was the original subprime loans that had been piled together. At the top of this tower was the triple-A tranche, just below it the double-A tranche, and so on down to the riskiest, triple-B tranche—the bonds Eisman had bet against. The Wall Street firms had taken these triple-B tranches—the worst of the worst—to build yet another tower of bonds: a CDO. A collateralized debt obligation. The reason they'd done this is that the rating agencies, presented with the pile of bonds backed by dubious loans, would pronounce 80 percent of the bonds in it triple-A. These bonds could then be sold to investors—pension funds, insurance companies—which were allowed to invest only in highly rated securities. It came as news to Eisman that this ship of doom was piloted by Wing Chau and people like him. The guy controlled roughly $15 billion, invested in nothing but CDOs backed by the triple-B tranche of a mortgage bond or, as Eisman put it, "the equivalent of three levels of dog shit lower than the original bonds." A year ago, the main buyer of the triple-A-rated tranche of subprime CDOs—which is to say the vast majority of CDOs—had been AIG. Now that AIG had exited the market, the main buyers were CDO managers like Wing Chau. All by himself, Chau generated vast demand for the riskiest slices of subprime mortgage bonds, for which there had previously been essentially no demand. This demand led inexorably to the supply of new home loans, as material for the bonds. The soy sauce in which Eisman double-dipped his edamame was shared by a man who had made it possible for tens of thousands of actual human beings to be handed money they could never afford to repay.

As it happened, FrontPoint Partners had spent a lot of time digging around in those loans, and knew that the default rates were already sufficient to wipe out Wing Chau's entire portfolio. "God," Eisman said to him. "You must be having a hard time."

"No," Wing Chau said. "I've sold everything out."

Say that again.

It made no sense. The CDO manager's job was to select the Wall Street firm to supply him with subprime bonds that served as the collateral for CDO investors, and then to vet the bonds themselves. The CDO manager was further charged with monitoring the hundred or so individual subprime bonds inside each CDO, and replacing the bad ones, before they went bad, with better ones. That, however, was mere theory; in practice, the sorts of investors who handed their money to Wing Chau, and thus bought the triple-A-rated tranche of CDOs—German banks, Taiwanese insurance companies, Japanese farmers' unions, European pension funds, and, in general, entities more or less required to invest in triple-A-rated bonds—did so precisely because they were meant to be foolproof, impervious to losses, and unnecessary to monitor or even think about very much. The CDO manager, in practice, didn't do much of anything, which is why all sorts of unlikely people suddenly hoped to become one. "Two guys and a Bloomberg terminal in New Jersey" was Wall Street shorthand for the typical CDO manager. The less mentally alert the two guys, and the fewer the questions they asked about the triple-B-rated subprime bonds they were absorbing into their CDOs, the more likely they were to be patronized by the big Wall Street firms. The whole point of the CDO was to launder a lot of subprime mortgage market risk that the firms had been unable to place straightforwardly. The last thing you wanted was a CDO manager who asked lots of tough questions.

The bond market had created what amounted to a double agent—a character who seemed to represent the interests of investors when he better represented the interests of Wall Street bond trading desks. To assure the big investors who had handed their billions to him that he had their deep interests at heart, the CDO manager kept ownership of what was called the "equity," or "first loss" piece, of the CDO—the piece that vanished first when the subprime loans that ultimately supplied the CDO with cash defaulted. But the CDO manager was also paid a fee of 0.1 percent off the top, before any of his investors saw a dime, and another, similar fee, off the bottom, as his investor received their money back. That doesn't sound like much, but, when you're running tens of billions of dollars with little effort and no overhead, it adds up. Just a few years earlier, Wing Chau was making $140,000 a year managing a portfolio for the New York Life Insurance Company. In one year as a CDO manager, he'd taken home $26 million, the haul from half a dozen lifetimes of working at New York Life.

Now, almost giddily, Chau explained to Eisman that he simply passed all the risk that the underlying home loans would default on to the big investors who had hired him to vet the bonds. His job was to be the CDO "expert," but he actually didn't spend a lot of time worrying about what was in CDOs. His goal, he explained, was to maximize the dollars in his care. He was now doing this so well that, from January 2007 until the market crashed in September, Harding Advisory would be the world's biggest subprime CDO manager. Among its other achievements, Harding had established itself as the go-to buyer for Merrill Lynch's awesome CDO machine, notorious not only for its rate of production (Merrill created twice as many of the things as the next biggest Wall Street firm) but also for its industrial waste (its CDOs were later proven to be easily the worst). "He 'managed' the CDOs," said Eisman, "but managed what? I was just appalled that the structured finance market could be so insane as to allow someone to manage a CDO portfolio without having any exposure to the CDOs. People would pay up to have someone 'manage' their CDOs—as if this moron was helping you. I thought, *You prick, you don't give a fuck about the investors in this thing*." Chau's real job was to serve as a new kind of front man for the Wall Street firms he "hired"; investors felt better buying a Merrill Lynch CDO if it didn't appear to be run by Merrill Lynch.

There was a reason Greg Lippmann had picked Wing Chau to sit beside Steve Eisman. If Wing Chau detected Eisman's disapproval, he didn't show it; instead, he spoke to Eisman in a tone of condescension. *I know better.* "Then he says something that blew my mind," said Eisman. "He says, 'I love guys like you who short my market. Without you I don't have anything to buy.'"

Say that again.

"He says to me, 'The more excited that you get that you're right, the more trades you'll do, and the more trades you do, the more product for me.'"

That's when Steve Eisman finally understood the madness of the machine. He and Vinny and Danny had been making these side bets with Goldman Sachs and Deutsche Bank on the fate of the triple-B tranche of subprime mortgage–backed bonds without fully understanding why those firms were so eager to accept them. Now he was face-to-face with the actual human being on the other side of his credit default swaps. Now he got it: The credit default swaps, filtered through the CDOs, were being used to replicate bonds backed by actual home loans. *There weren't enough Americans with shitty credit taking out loans to satisfy investors' appetite for the end product.* Wall Street needed his bets in order to synthesize more of them. "They weren't satisfied getting lots of unqualified borrowers to borrow money to buy a house they couldn't afford," said Eisman. "They were creating them out of whole cloth. One hundred times over! That's why the losses in the financial system are so much greater than just the subprime loans. That's when I realized they needed us to keep the machine running. I was like, *This is allowed?*"

Wing Chau didn't know he'd been handpicked by Greg Lippmann to persuade Steve Eisman that the people on the other end of his credit default swaps were either crooks or morons, but he played the role anyway. Between shots of sake he told Eisman that he would rather have $50 billion in crappy CDOs than none at all, as he was paid mainly on volume. He told Eisman that his main fear was that the U.S. economy would strengthen, and dissuade hedge funds from placing bigger bets against the subprime mortgage market. Eisman listened and tried to understand how an investor on the opposite ends of his bets could be hoping for more or less the same thing he was—and how any insurance company or pension fund could hand its capital to Wing Chau. There was only one answer: The triple-A ratings gave everyone an excuse to ignore the risks they were running.

Danny and Vinny watched them closely through the hibachi steam. As far as they could tell, Eisman and Wing Chau were getting along famously. But when the meal was over, they watched Eisman grab Greg Lippmann, point to Wing Chau, and say, "Whatever that guy is buying, I want to short it." Lippmann took it as a joke, but Eisman was completely serious: He wanted to place a bet specifically against Wing Chau. "Greg," Eisman said, "I want to short his paper. Sight unseen." Thus far Eisman had bought only credit default swaps on subprime mortgage bonds; from now on he'd buy specifically credit default swaps on Wing Chau's CDOs. "He finally met the enemy, face-to-face," said Vinny.

In what amounted to a brief attempt to live someone else's life, Charlie Ledley selected from the wall a Beretta pistol, a sawed-off shotgun, and an Uzi. Not long before he'd walked out the door for Las Vegas, he'd dashed an e-mail off to his partner Ben Hockett, who planned to meet him there, and Jamie Mai, who didn't. "Do you guys think we're screwed since we haven't preregistered for anything?" he asked. It wasn't the first time Cornwall Capital had heard about some big event in the markets to which they hadn't been formally invited and more or less invited themselves, and it wouldn't be the last. "If you just kind of show up at these things," said Jamie, "they almost always let you in." The only people Charlie knew in Vegas were a few members of the subprime mortgage machine at Bear Stearns, and he'd never actually met them in person. Nevertheless, they had sent him an e-mail telling him, after he landed in Las Vegas, to meet them not at the conference but at this indoor shooting range, a few miles from the strip. "We goin' shootin on Sunday . . . ," it began. Charlie was so taken aback, he called to ask them what it meant. "I was like, 'So you're going to go shoot . . . *guns*?'"

That Sunday afternoon of January 28, at The Gun Store in Las Vegas, it wasn't hard to spot the Bear Stearns CDO salesmen. They came dressed in khakis and polo shirts and were surrounded by burly men in tight black t-shirts who appeared to be taking the day off from hunting illegal immigrants with the local militia. Behind the cash register, the most sensational array of pistols and shotguns and automatic weapons lined the wall. To the right were the targets: a photograph of Osama bin Laden, a painting of Osama bin Laden as a zombie, various hooded al Qaeda terrorists, a young black kid attacking a pretty white woman, an Asian hoodlum waving a pistol. "They put down the Bear Stearns credit card and started buying rounds of ammunition," said Charlie. "And so I started picking my guns." It was the Uzi that made the biggest impression on him. That, and the giant photograph of Saddam Hussein he selected from the wall of targets. The shotgun kicked and bruised your shoulder, but the Uzi, with far more killing power, was almost gentle; there was a thrilling disconnect between the pain you experienced and the damage you caused. "The Beretta was fun but the Uzi was totally awesome," said Charlie, who left The Gun Store with both a lingering feeling of having broken some law of nature, and an unanswered question: Why had he been invited? The Bear Stearns guys had been great, but no one had uttered a word about subprime mortgages or CDOs. "It was totally weird, because I'd never met the guys before and I'm the only Bear Stearns customer who's there," said Charlie. "They were paying for all this ammo and so I'm like, 'Guys, I can buy a few rounds for myself if you want,' but they insisted on treating me like the customer." Of course, the safest way to expense to one's Wall Street firm a day of playing Full Metal Jacket was to invite some customer along. And, of course, the most painless customer to invite was one whose business was so trivial that his opinion of the festivities didn't actually matter. That these thoughts never occurred to Charlie told you something about him: He was not nearly as cynical as he needed to be. But that would soon change.

The next morning, Charlie and Ben wandered the halls of The Venetian. "Everyone who was trying to sell something was wearing a tie," said Ben. "Everyone who was there to buy wasn't. It was hard to find someone I wanted to talk to. We were just kind of interlopers, walking around." They knew just one person in the entire place—David Burt, the former BlackRock guy whom they were now paying $50,000 a month to evaluate the CDOs they were betting against—but they didn't think that mattered, as their plan was to go to the open sessions, the big speeches and panel discussions. "It was not entirely clear why we were there," said Ben. "We were trying to meet people. Charlie would sneak up on whoever was at the podium after speeches. We were trying to find people who could tell us why we were wrong." They were looking for some persuasive mirror image of themselves. Someone who could tell them why what the market deemed impossible was at least improbable.

Charlie's challenge was to suck unsuspecting market insiders into arguments before they thought to ask him who he was or what he did. "The consistent reaction whenever we met someone was, like, 'Wait, where did you guys come from?' They were just baffled," said Charlie. "People were like, 'Why are you here?'"

A guy from a rating agency on whom Charlie tested Cornwall's investment thesis looked at him strangely and asked, "Are you sure you guys know what you're doing?" The market insiders didn't agree with them, but they didn't offer persuasive counter-arguments. Their main argument, in defense of subprime CDOs, was that "the CDO buyer will never go away." Their main argument, in defense of the underlying loans, was that, in their short history, they had never defaulted in meaningful amounts. Above the roulette tables, screens listed the results of the most recent twenty spins of the wheel. Gamblers would see that it had come up black the past eight spins, marvel at the improbability, and feel in their bones that the tiny silver ball was now more likely to land on red. That was the reason the casino bothered to list the wheel's most recent spins: to help gamblers to delude themselves. To give people the false confidence they needed to lay their chips on a roulette table. The entire food chain of intermediaries in the subprime mortgage market was duping itself with the same trick, using the foreshortened, statistically meaningless past to predict the future.

"Usually, when you do a trade, you can find some smart people on the other side of it," said Ben. "In this instance we couldn't."

"Nobody we talked to had any credible reason to think this wasn't going to become a big problem," said Charlie. "No one was really thinking about it."

One of the Bear Stearns CDO guys, after Charlie asked him what was likely to happen to these CDOs in seven years, said, "Seven years? I don't care about seven years. I just need it to last for another two."

Three months earlier, when Cornwall bought their first $100 million in credit default swaps on the double-A-rated tranches of subprime CDOs, they believed they were making a cheap bet on an unlikely event—$500,000 a year in premium for the chance to make $100,000,000. The market, and the rating agencies, effectively had set the odds of default at 1 in 200. They thought the odds were better than that—say, 1 in 10. Still, it was, like most of their bets, a long shot. An intelligent long shot, perhaps, but a long shot nonetheless. The more they listened to the people who ran the subprime market, the more they felt the collapse of double-A-rated bonds wasn't a long shot at all, but likely. A thought crossed Ben's mind: These people believed that the collapse of the subprime mortgage market was unlikely precisely because it would be such a catastrophe. Nothing so terrible could ever actually happen.

The first morning of the conference, they'd followed a crowd of thousands out of the casino and into the vast main ballroom to attend the opening ceremony. It was meant to be a panel discussion, but of course the men on the panel had little interest in talking to each other and more interest in delivering measured, prepared remarks. They'd watch a dozen of these events over the next three days and all were tedious. This one session was different, though, because its moderator appeared to be drunk, or at least unhinged. His name was John Devaney and he ran a hedge fund that invested in subprime mortgage bonds, United Capital Markets. For a decade now, Devaney had sponsored this conference—called ASF, or the American Securitization Forum, in part because it sounded more dignified than the Association for Subprime Lending. To the extent that the market for subprime mortgage bonds had moral leaders, John Devaney was one. He was also an enthusiastic displayer of his own wealth. He owned a Renoir, a Gulfstream, a helicopter, plus, of course, a yacht. This year he'd paid some huge sum to fly in Jay Leno to serve as the entertainment.

Now, looking as if he had just rolled in from a night on the town without pausing to take a nap, John Devaney delivered what was clearly an extemporaneous rant about the state of the subprime market. "It was incredible," said Charlie. "Stream of consciousness.

He went on about how the ratings agencies were whores. How the securities were worthless. How they all knew it. He gave words to stuff we were just suspecting. It was like he was talking out of school. When he was finished there was complete silence. No one specifically attempted a defense. They just talked around him. It was like everyone pretended he hadn't said it."* On the one hand, it was exhilarating to hear a market insider say what he thought to be true; on the other, if the market became self-aware, its madness couldn't last long. Charlie and Jamie and Ben assumed they had time to think things over before they went out and bought even more credit default swaps on the double-A tranche of subprime CDOs. "That speech spooked us," said Ben. "It seemed rather than six months to get our trade on we had one week."

The trouble, as ever, was finding Wall Street firms willing to deal with them. Their one source of supply, Bear Stearns, suddenly seemed more interested in shooting than in trading with them. Every other firm treated them as a joke. *Cornhole Capital*. But here, in Las Vegas, luck found them. To their surprise, they found that the consultant they now employed to analyze CDOs for them, David Burt, enjoyed serious stature in the industry. "David Burt was like God in Vegas," said Charlie. "We started just following him around. 'Hey. That guy you're talking to. We're paying him—can we talk to you too?'" This rented God introduced Charlie to a woman from Morgan Stanley named Stacey Strauss. Her job was to find investors who wanted to buy credit default swaps as quickly as she could. Charlie never figured

* When the market cracked, Devaney went bust and was forced to sell his yacht, his plane, and his Renoir (for a nice profit) and defend himself against several nasty newspaper articles. "It takes an honest individual to admit that he was wrong," he wrote, in one of several rambling letters released over the PR Newswire. "I was long in 2007 and was wrong."

"He was incredibly cynical about the market," said Charlie. "And he lost money. I never figured that out."

out why she was willing in the extreme to bend Morgan Stanley's usual standards to do business with Cornwall. Charlie also accosted a man who analyzed the subprime mortgage bond market for Wachovia Bank, who happened to have been on the panel moderated by the shocking John Devaney. During the opening panel discussion, he, like everyone else, had pretended he hadn't heard John Devaney. When Devaney was finished, the Wachovia guy had given his little speech about the fundamental soundness of the subprime mortgage bond market. As he came off the stage, Charlie ambushed him and asked him if maybe Wachovia didn't want to put its money where its mouth was and sell him some credit default swaps.

The morning after his dinner with Wing Chau, Eisman woke up to his first glimpse of the bond market in the flesh, and a lot of sensationally phony baroque ceiling frescoes. The Venetian hotel—Palazzo Ducale on the outside, *Divine Comedy* on the inside—was overrun by thousands of white men in business casual now earning their living, one way or another, off subprime mortgages. Like all of Las Vegas, The Venetian was a jangle of seemingly random effects designed to heighten and exploit irrationality: the days that felt like nights and the nights that felt like days; the penny slots and the cash machines that spat out hundred-dollar bills; the grand hotel rooms that cost so little and made you feel so big. The point of all of it was to alter your perception of your chances and your money, and all of it depressed Eisman: He didn't even like to gamble. "I wouldn't know how to calculate odds if my life depended on it," he said. At the end of each day Vinny would head off to play low-stakes poker, Danny would join Lippmann and the other bond people at the craps tables, and Eisman would go to bed. That craps was the game of choice of the bond trader was interesting, though. Craps offered the player the illusion of control—after all, he rolled the dice—and a surface complexity that masked its deeper idiocy. "For some reason, when these people are playing it they actually believe they have the power to make the dice work," said Vinny.

Thousands and thousands of serious financial professionals, most of whom, just a few years ago, had been doing something else with their lives, were now playing craps with the money they had made off subprime mortgage bonds. The subprime mortgage industry Eisman once knew better than anyone on the planet had been a negligible corner of the capital markets. In just a few years it had somehow become the most powerful engine of profits and employment on Wall Street—and it made no economic sense. "It was like watching an unthinking machine that could not stop itself," he said. He felt as if he had moved into a new house, opened the door to what he presumed was a small closet, and discovered an entirely new wing. "I'd been to equity conferences," said Eisman. "This was totally different. At an equity conference you're lucky if you get five hundred people. There were seven thousand people at this thing. Just the fact that no one from the equity world was there told you that no one had figured it out. We knew no one. We still assumed we were the only ones who were short."

He had no interest in listening to other people's speeches. He had no interest in attending the panel discussion and hearing the potted remarks. He wanted private sessions with market insiders. Lippmann had introduced them to the people inside Deutsche Bank peddling CDOs to investors, and these helpful Deutsche Bank people had arranged for Eisman and his partners to meet the bond market's financial intermediaries: the mortgage lenders, the banks that packaged the mortgage loans into mortgage bonds, the bankers who repackaged the bonds into CDOs, and the rating agencies that blessed the process at each stage. The only interested parties missing from the conference were the ultimate borrowers, the American home buyers, but even they, in a way, were on hand, serving drinks, spinning wheels, and rolling dice. "Vegas was booming," said Danny. "The homeowners were at the fucking tables." A friend of Danny's returned from a night on the town to report he'd met a stripper with five separate home equity loans.*

The Deutsche Bank CDO salesman—a fellow named Ryan Stark—had been assigned to keep an eye on Eisman and prevent him from causing trouble. "I started getting these e-mails from him, before the conference," said Danny. "He was nervous about us. It was like, 'I just want to clarify the purpose of the meetings,' and, 'Just to be clear why we're meeting . . .' He wanted to make sure we knew we remembered that we were there to buy the bonds." Deutsche Bank had even sent along the formal handouts intended for subprime buyers, as a kind of script for them to follow. "The purpose of the conference is to convince people it's still okay to create and to buy this shit," said Danny. "It was unheard of for an equity investor looking to short the bonds to come in and scope the place out for information. The only way we got these one-on-one meetings was by saying that we weren't short. Deutsche Bank escorted us, to make sure we didn't blow up their relationships. They put a salesman in the meeting just to monitor us."

There was of course no point in trying to monitor Eisman. He saw himself as a crusader, a champion of the underdog, an enemy of sinister authority. He saw himself, roughly speaking, as Spider-Man. He was perfectly aware of how absurd it sounded when, for instance, his wife told people, "My husband thinks he and Spider-Man are living the same life." Eisman didn't go around telling strangers about the shocking number of parallels between himself and Peter Parker—when they had gone to college, what they had studied, when they'd married, and on and on—or that, by the time he was in law school, he was picking up the latest Spider-Man comic half expecting to discover

* Two years later, Las Vegas would lead the nation in its rate of home foreclosures.

in it the next turn his life would take. But Eisman was quick to see narratives, he explained the world in stories, and this was one of the stories he used to explain himself.

The first sign that Spider-Man had no interest in Deutsche Bank's dark dealings came at a speech that morning, given by the CEO of Option One, the mortgage originator owned by H&R Block. Option One had popped onto Eisman's radar screen seven months earlier, in June 2006, when the company announced a surprising loss in its portfolio of subprime mortgage loans. The loss was surprising because Option One was in the business of making loans and selling them off to Wall Street—they weren't meant to be taking risk. In these deals, however, there was a provision that allowed Wall Street to put the loans back to Option One if the borrowers failed to make their first payment. "Who takes out a home loan and doesn't make the first payment?" asked Danny Moses, putting the matter one way. "Who the fuck lends money to people who can't make the first payment?" asked Eisman, putting it another.

When the CEO of Option One got to the part of his speech about Option One's subprime loan portfolio, he claimed that the company had put its problems behind it and was now expecting a (modest) loss rate on its loans of 5 percent. Eisman raised his hand. Moses and Daniel sank in their chairs. "It wasn't a Q&A," says Moses. "The guy was giving a speech. He sees Steve's hand and says, 'Yes?'"

"Would you say that five percent is a probability or a possibility?" asked Eisman.

A probability, said the CEO, and went back to giving his speech.

Eisman had his hand up in the air again, waving it around. *Oh no*, thought Moses, and sank deeper in his chair. "The one thing Steve always says is that you must assume they are lying to you," said Daniel. "They will always lie to you." Danny and Vinny both knew what Eisman thought of these subprime lenders, but didn't see the need for him to express it here, in this manner. For Steve wasn't raising his hand to ask a question. Steve had his thumb and index finger in a big circle. Steve was using his fingers to speak on his behalf. "Zero!" they said.

"Yes?" asked the obviously irritated CEO. "Is that another question?"

"No," said Eisman. "It's a zero. There is zero probability that your default rate will be five percent." The losses on subprime loans would be far, far greater. Before the guy could reply, Eisman's cell phone rang. Rather than shut it down, Eisman reached in his pocket and answered it. "Excuse me," he said, standing up. "But I need to take this call." And with that, he walked out of the speech. The caller was his wife.

"It wasn't important at all," she says with a sigh. "I was a prop."

After that something must have come over Eisman, for he stopped looking for a fight and started looking for higher understanding. He walked around the Las Vegas casino incredulous at the spectacle before him: seven thousand people, all of whom seemed delighted with the world as they found it. A society with deep, troubling economic problems had rigged itself to disguise those problems, and the chief beneficiaries of the deceit were its financial middlemen. How could this be? Eisman actually wondered, albeit very briefly, if he was missing something. "He kept saying, 'What the hell is going on here? Who the fuck *are* all these people?'" said Danny Moses. The short answer to that second question was: the optimists. The subprime mortgage market in its current incarnation never had done anything but rise. The people in it who were regarded as successes were those who had always said "buy." Now they should really all be saying "sell," but they didn't know how to do it. "You always knew that fixed income guys thought they knew more than you did," said Eisman, "and generally that was true. I wasn't a fixed income guy, but here I'd taken this position that was a bet against their whole industry, and I wanted to know if they know something I don't. Could it really be this obvious? Could it really be this simple?" He entered private meetings with the lenders and the bankers and the rating agencies probing for an intelligence he had yet to detect. "He was in learning mode," said Vinny. "When he's fascinated about a subject, his curiosity becomes far more important than being confrontational. He'll claim it was years of therapy that enabled him to behave, but the truth is it was the first time he was connecting all the dots."

Much of Steve Eisman wanted to believe the worst, and that gave him a huge tactical advantage in the U.S. financial markets circa 2007. There was still some part of him, however, that was as credulous as the little kid who lent his new bike to a total stranger. He was still capable of being shocked. His experience with Household Finance had disabused him of any hope that the government would intercede to prevent rich corporations from doing bad things to poor people. Inside the free market, however, there might be some authority capable of checking its excess. The rating agencies, in theory, were just such an authority. As the securities became more complex, the rating agencies became more necessary. Everyone could evaluate a U.S. Treasury bond; hardly anyone could understand a subprime mortgage–backed CDO. There was a natural role for an independent arbiter to pass judgment on these opaque piles of risky loans. "In Vegas it became clear to me that this entire huge industry was just trusting in the ratings," Eisman said. "Everyone believed in the ratings, so they didn't have to think about it."

Eisman had worked on Wall Street for nearly two decades, but, like most stock market people, he'd never before sat down with anyone from Moody's or Standard & Poor's. Unless they covered insurance companies, which lost their ability to sell their product the moment their ability to meet their obligations was thrown into doubt, stock market people didn't pay much attention to the rating agencies. Now

Eisman had his first exchanges with them, and what struck him immediately—and struck Danny and Vinny, too—was the caliber of their employees. "You know how when you walk into a post office you realize there is such a difference between a government employee and other people," said Vinny. "The ratings agency people were all like government employees." Collectively they had more power than anyone in the bond markets, but individually they were nobodies. "They're underpaid," said Eisman. "The smartest ones leave for Wall Street firms so they can help manipulate the companies they used to work for. There should be no greater thing you can do as an analyst than to be the Moody's analyst. It should be, 'I can't go higher as an analyst.' Instead it's the bottom! No one gives a fuck if Goldman likes General Electric paper. If Moody's downgrades GE paper, it is a big deal. So why does the guy at Moody's want to work at Goldman Sachs? The guy who is the bank analyst at Goldman Sachs should want to go to Moody's. It should be that elite."

The entire industry had been floated on the backs of the rating agencies, but the people who worked at the rating agencies barely belonged in the industry. If they roamed the halls they might be mistaken, just, for some low-level commercial bankers at Wells Fargo, or flunkies at mortgage lenders, such as Option One: nine-to-fivers. They wore suits in Vegas, which told you half of what you needed to know about them—the other half you got from the price of those suits. Just about everyone else dressed business casual; the few guys who were actually important people wore three-thousand-dollar Italian suits. (One of the mysteries of the Wall Street male was that he was ignorant of the finer points of couture but could still tell in an instant how much another Wall Street male's suit had cost.) The rating agencies guys wore blue suits from J.C. Penney, with ties that matched too well, and shirts that were starched just a bit too stiffly. They weren't players and they didn't know the people who were, either. They got paid to rate the bonds of Lehman and Bear Stearns and Goldman Sachs, but they couldn't tell you the names of, or any of the other important facts about, the guys at Lehman and Bear Stearns and Goldman Sachs who were making a fortune exploiting loopholes in the rating agencies' models. They appeared to know enough to justify their jobs, and nothing more. They seemed timid, fearful, and risk-averse. As Danny put it, "You wouldn't see them at the craps table."

It was in Vegas that Eisman realized that "all the stuff I was worried about, the ratings agencies didn't care. I remember sitting there thinking, *Jeez, this is really pathetic.* You know when you're with someone who is intellectually powerful: You just know it. When you sit down with Richard Posner [the legal scholar], you know it's Richard Posner. When you sit down with the ratings agencies you know it's the ratings agencies." To judge from their behavior, all the rating agencies worried about was maximizing the number of deals they rated for Wall Street investment banks, and the fees they collected from them. Moody's, once a private company, had gone public in 2000. Since then its revenues had boomed, from $800 million in 2001 to $2.03 billion in 2006. Some huge percentage of the increase—more than half, certainly, but exactly how much more than half they declined to tell Eisman—flowed from the arcane end of the home finance sector, known as structured finance. The surest way to attract structured finance business was to accept the assumptions of the structured finance industry. "We asked everyone the same two questions," said Vinny. "What is your assumption about home prices, and what is your assumption about loan losses." Both rating agencies said they expected home prices to rise and loan losses to be around 5 percent—which, if true, meant that even the lowest-rated, triple-B, subprime mortgage bonds crafted from them were money-good. "It was like everyone had agreed in advance that five percent was the number," said Eisman. "They all said five percent. It was a party and there was a party line."* What shocked Eisman was that none of the people he met in Las Vegas seemed to have wrestled with anything. They were doing what they were doing without thinking very much about it.

It was in Las Vegas that Eisman and his associates' attitude toward the U.S. bond market hardened into something like its final shape. As Vinny put it, "That was the moment when we said, 'Holy shit, this isn't just credit. This is a fictitious Ponzi scheme.'" In Vegas the question lingering at the back of their minds ceased to be, Do these bond market people know something we do not? It was replaced by, Do they deserve merely to be fired, or should they be put in jail? Are they delusional, or do they know what they're doing? Danny thought that the vast majority of the people in the industry were blinded by their interests and failed to see the risks they had created. Vinny, always darker, said, "There were more morons than crooks, but the crooks were higher up." The rating agencies were about as low as you could go and still be in the industry, and the people who worked for them really did not seem to know just how badly they had been gamed by big Wall Street firms. Their meeting in Las Vegas with the third and smallest rating agency, Fitch Ratings, stuck in Vinny's mind. "I know you're sort of irrelevant," he'd said to them, as politely as he could. "There are these two big guys everyone pays attention to, and then there is you. If you want to make a statement—and get people to notice you—why don't you go your own way and be the honest one?" He expected the good people of Fitch Ratings service to see the point, and maybe even chuckle nervously. Instead they seemed almost

* In Las Vegas they also met with David Wells, who ran subprime lending for a company called Fremont Investment & Loan. Wells also said he expected losses to run 5 percent. In September, nine months later, Fremont would announce that 30 percent of its subprime loans were in default. Its pools of loans would register losses higher than 40 percent—which is to say that, even after it sold the houses it foreclosed upon, it was out nearly half the money it loaned.

offended. "They went all pure on me," said Vinny. "It was like they didn't understand what I was saying."

They had left for Las Vegas with a short position in subprime mortgage bonds of a bit less than $300 million. Upon their return they raised it to $550 million, with new bets against the CDOs created by Wing Chau. With only $500 million under management, the position now overwhelmed their portfolio. They didn't stop there, however. Their first day back in the office, they shorted the stock of Moody's Corporation, at $73.25 a share, then went searching for other companies and other people, like Wing Chau, on the other side of their trade.

CHAPTER SEVEN

The Great Treasure Hunt

Charlie Ledley and Ben Hockett returned from Las Vegas on January 30, 2007, convinced that the entire financial system had lost its mind. "I said to my mother, 'I think we might be facing something like the end of democratic capitalism,'" said Charlie. "She just said, 'Oh, Charlie,' and seriously suggested I go on lithium." They had created an investment approach that harnessed their talent for distancing themselves from other people's convictions; to find such great conviction in themselves was new and uncomfortable. Jamie penned a memo to his two partners, in which he asked them if they were making a bet on the collapse of a society—and therefore a bet that the government would never allow to succeed. "If a broad range of CDO spreads starts to widen," he wrote,* "it means that a material global financial clusterfuck is likely occurring. . . . The U.S. Fed is in

* The "spread" on any bond is simply the difference between the interest rate it pays to the investor, and some putatively risk-free rate—say, the rate paid to investors in U.S. Treasury bonds.

a position to fix the problem by intervening. . . . I guess the question is, How wide would the meltdown need to be in order to be 'too big to fail'?"

The conference in Las Vegas had been created, among other things, to boost faith in the market. The day after the subprime mortgage market insiders left Las Vegas and returned to their trading desks, the market cracked. On January 31, 2007, the ABX, a publicly traded index of triple-B-rated subprime mortgage bonds—exactly the sort of bonds used to create subprime CDOs—fell more than a point, from 93.03 to 91.98. For the past several months, it had drifted down in such tiny increments, from 100 to 93, that a full point move came as shocking—and heightened Charlie's anxiety that they'd discovered this sensational trade a moment too late to wager as much on it as they should. The woman from Morgan Stanley was, at first, true to her word: She pushed through their ISDA agreement, which would normally have taken months of negotiations, in ten days. She sent Charlie a list of double-A tranches of CDOs on which Morgan Stanley was willing to sell them credit default swaps.* Charlie stayed up nights figuring out which ones to bet against, and then called her up to find that Morgan Stanley had experienced a change of heart. She had told Charlie that he could buy insurance for around 100 basis points (1 percent of the insured amount a year), but when he called

* A brief reminder: In thinking about these towers of debt, it's handy to simplify them into three floors: a basement, called the "equity," which takes the very first losses and is not an investment-grade security; the lower floor, called the "mezzanine," with triple-B rating; and the upper floor, with triple-A rating, and generally referred to as the "senior." In practice, the towers were far more finely sliced: a CDO might have fifteen different tranches, each with a slightly different rating, from triple-B-minus all the way up to triple-A: triple-B-minus, triple-B, triple-B-plus, A-minus, A, and so on. The double-A rating of the tranche shorted by Cornwall Capital implied that the underlying bonds, though slightly more risky than supposedly gold-plated triple-As, still had a less than 0.1 percent chance of defaulting.

up the next morning to do the trade, the price had more than doubled. Charlie bitched and moaned about the unfairness of it and she and her bosses caved, a bit. On February 16, 2007, Cornwall paid Morgan Stanley 150 basis points to buy $10 million in credit default swaps on a CDO cryptically called Gulfstream, whatever that was.

Five days later, on February 21, the market began to trade an index of CDOs called the TABX. For the first time, Charlie Ledley, and everyone else in the market, was able to see on a screen the price of one of these CDOs. The price confirmed Cornwall's thesis in a way that no amount of conversation with market insiders ever could have. After the first day of trading, the tranche that took losses when the underlying bonds experienced losses of more than 15 percent of the pool—the double-A-rated tranche that Cornwall had bet against—closed at 49.25: It had lost more than half its value. There was now this huge disconnect: With one hand the Wall Street firms were selling low interest rate–bearing double-A-rated CDOs at par, or 100; with the other they were trading this index composed of those very same bonds for 49 cents on the dollar. In a flurry of e-mails, their salespeople at Morgan Stanley and Deutsche Bank tried to explain to Charlie that he should not deduce anything about the value of his bets against subprime CDOs from the prices on these new, publicly traded subprime CDOs. That it was all very complicated.

The next morning Charlie called back Morgan Stanley in hopes of buying more insurance. "She was like, 'I'm really, really sorry but we're not doing any more of this. The firm's changed its mind.'" Overnight, Morgan Stanley had gone from being wildly eager to sell insurance on the subprime mortgage market to not wanting to do it at all. "Then she puts us on the phone with her boss—because we were like, 'What the fuck is going on?'—and he's like, 'Look, I'm really sorry, but something has happened in another arm of the bank that's caused some kind of risk management decision at the very highest levels of Morgan Stanley.' And we never traded with them again." Charlie had no idea what exactly had awakened inside Morgan Stanley, and didn't think too much about it—he and Ben were too busy trying to talk the guy from Wachovia whom Charlie had pounced on in Las Vegas into dealing with Cornwall Capital. "They didn't have one hedge fund client, and they were sort of excited to see us," said Ben. "They were trying to be big-time." Wachovia, amazingly, remained willing to sell cheap insurance on subprime mortgage bonds; the risk its credit officers were unwilling to take was the risk of dealing directly with Cornwall Capital. It took a while, but Charlie arranged for his Uzi-shooting companions from Bear Stearns to sit in the middle between the two parties, for a fee. The details of a $45 million trade more or less agreed upon in February 2007 took several months to hammer out, and the trade didn't go through until early May. "Wachovia was a gift from God," said Ben. "It was like we were in a plane at thirty thousand feet, which had stalled, and Wachovia still had a few parachutes for sale. No one else was still selling parachutes, but no one really wanted to believe they were needed, either. . . . After that, the market completely shut down."

In a portfolio of less than $30 million, Cornwall Capital now owned $205 million in credit default swaps on subprime mortgage bonds, and were disturbed mainly that they didn't own more. "We were doing everything we possibly could to buy more," said Charlie. "We'd put in our bids at the offering prices. They'd call back and say, 'Oops, you almost got it!' It was very sort of Charlie Brown and Lucy. We'd go up to kick the football and they'd pull it back. We'd raise our bid and the minute we did their offer would jump up."

It made no sense: The subprime CDO market was ticking along as it had before, and yet the big Wall Street firms suddenly had no use for the investors who had been supplying the machine with raw material—the investors who wanted to buy credit default swaps. "Ostensibly other people were going long, but we were not allowed to go short," said Charlie.

He couldn't know for sure what was happening inside the big firms, but he could guess: Some of the traders on the inside had woken up to the impending disaster and were scrambling to get out of the market before it collapsed. "With the Bear guys I had this suspicion that, if there were any credit default swaps on CDOs to buy, they were buying it for themselves," said Charlie. At the end of February a Bear Stearns analyst named Gyan Sinha published a long treatise arguing that the recent declines in subprime mortgage bonds had nothing to do with the quality of the bonds and everything to do with "market sentiment." Charlie read it thinking that the person who wrote it had no idea what was actually happening in the market. According to the Bear Stearns analyst, double-A CDOs were trading at 75 basis points above the risk-free rate—that is, Charlie should have been able to buy credit default swaps for 0.75 percent in premiums a year. The Bear Stearns traders, by contrast, weren't willing to sell them to him for five times that price. "I called the guy up and said, 'What the fuck are you talking about?' He said, "Well, this is where the deals are printing.' I asked him, 'Are desks actually buying and selling at that price?' And he says, 'Gotta go,' and hung up."

Their trade now seemed to them ridiculously obvious—it was as if they had bought cheap fire insurance on a house engulfed in flames. If the subprime mortgage market had the slightest interest in being efficient, it would have shut down right there and then. For more than eighteen months, from mid-2005 until early 2007, there had been this growing disconnect between the price of subprime mortgage bonds and the value of the loans underpinning them. In late January 2007 the bonds—or rather, the ABX index made up of the bonds—began to fall in price. The bonds fell at first steadily but then rapidly—by early June, the index of triple-B-rated subprime bonds was closing in the high 60s—which is to say the bonds had lost more than 30 percent of their original value. It stood to reason that the CDOs, which were created out of these triple-B-rated subprime bonds, should collapse, too. If the oranges were rotten, the orange juice was also rotten.

Yet this did not happen. Instead, between February and June of 2007, big Wall Street firms, led by Merrill Lynch and Citigroup, created and sold $50 billion in new CDOs. "We're totally baffled," said Charlie. "Because everyone and everything just goes back to normal, even though it obviously wasn't normal. We knew the collateral for the CDOs had collapsed. And yet everything went on, as if nothing had changed."

It was as if an entire financial market had tried to change its mind—and then realized that it could not afford to change its mind. Wall Street firms—most notably Bear Stearns and Lehman Brothers—continued to publish bond market research reaffirming the strength of the market. In late April, Bear Stearns held a CDO conference, into which Charlie sneaked. On the original agenda was a presentation entitled "How to Short a CDO." It had been removed from the final conference—so, too, had been the slides that accompanied the talk that had been posted on the Bear Stearns Web site. Moody's and S&P flinched, too, but in a telling manner. In late May, the two big rating agencies announced that they were reconsidering their subprime bond ratings models. Charlie and Jamie hired a lawyer to call Moody's and ask them, if they were going to rate subprime bonds by different criteria going forward, might they also reconsider the two trillion dollars' worth or so of bonds they had already rated, badly. Moody's didn't think that was a good idea. "We were like, 'You don't have to re-rate all of them. Just the ones we're short,'" said Charlie. "They were like, 'Hmmmmmm . . . no.'"

To Charlie and Ben and Jamie it seemed perfectly clear that Wall Street was propping up the price of these CDOs so that they might either dump losses on unsuspecting customers or make a last few billion dollars from a corrupt market. In either case, they were squeezing and selling the juice from oranges that were undeniably rotten. By late March 2007, "We were pretty sure one of two things was true," said Charlie. "Either the game was totally rigged, or we had gone totally fucking crazy. The fraud was so obvious that it seemed to us it had implications for democracy. We actually got scared." They both knew reporters who worked at the *New York Times* and the *Wall Street Journal*—but the reporters they knew had no interest in their story. A friend at the *Journal* hooked them up with the enforcement division of the SEC, but the enforcement division of the SEC had no interest either. In its lower Manhattan office, the SEC met with them and listened, but politely. "It was almost like a therapy session," said Jamie. "Because we sat down and said, 'We've just had the most crazy experience.'" As they spoke, they sensed the audience's incomprehension. "We probably had like this wild-eyed we've-been-up-for-three-days-straight look in our eyes," said Charlie. "But they didn't know anything about CDOs, or asset-backed securities. We took them through our trade but I'm pretty sure they didn't understand it." The SEC never followed up.

Cornwall had a problem more immediate than the collapse of society as we know it: the collapse of Bear Stearns. On June 14, 2007, Bear Stearns Asset Management, a CDO firm, like Wing Chau's, but run by former Bear Stearns employees who had the implicit backing of the mother ship, declared that it had lost money on bets on subprime mortgage securities and that it was being forced to dump 3.8 billion dollars' worth of these bets before closing the fund. Up until this moment, Cornwall Capital had been unable to see why Bear Stearns, and no one else, had been so eager to sell them insurance on CDOs. "Bear was able to show us liquidity in the CDOs that I couldn't understand," said Ben. "They had a standing buyer on the other side. I don't know that our trades went directly into their funds, but I don't know where else they would have gone."

And therein lay a new problem: Bear Stearns had sold Cornwall 70 percent of its credit default swaps. Because Bear Stearns was big and important, and Cornwall Capital was a garage band hedge fund, Bear Stearns hadn't been required to post collateral to Cornwall. Cornwall was now totally exposed to the possibility that Bear Stearns would be unable to pay off its gambling debts. Cornwall Capital couldn't help but notice that Bear Stearns was not so much shaping the subprime mortgage bond business as being reshaped by it. "They'd turned themselves from a low-risk brokerage operation into a subprime mortgage engine," said Jamie. If the subprime mortgage market crashed, Bear Stearns was going to crash with it.

Back in March, Cornwall had bought $105 million in credit default swaps on Bear Stearns—that is, they'd made a bet on the collapse of Bear Stearns—from the British bank HSBC. If Bear Stearns failed, HSBC would owe them $105 million. Of course this only shifted their risk to HSBC. HSBC was the third largest bank in the world, and one of those places it was hard to think about going down. On February 8, 2007, however, HSBC rocked the market with the announcement that it was taking a big, surprising loss on its portfolio of subprime mortgage loans. It had entered the U.S. subprime lending business in 2003, when it had bought America's biggest consumer lending operation, Household Finance. The same Household Finance that had pushed Steve Eisman over the narrow border between Wall Street skeptic and Wall Street cynic.

From the social point of view the slow and possibly fraudulent unraveling of a multi-trillion-dollar U.S. bond market was a catastrophe. From the hedge fund trading point of view it was the opportunity of a lifetime. Steve Eisman had started out running a $60 million equity fund but was now short around 600 million dollars' worth of various subprime-related securities, and he wanted to short more. "Sometimes his ideas cannot be manifested in a trade," said Vinny. "This time they could." Eisman was enchained, however, by FrontPoint Partners and, by extension, Morgan Stanley. As FrontPoint's head trader, Danny Moses found himself caught in the middle, between Eisman and FrontPoint's risk management people, who didn't seem to completely understand what they were doing. "They'd call me and say, 'Can you get Steve to take some of this off?' I'd go to Steve and Steve would say, 'Just tell them to fuck off.' And I'd say, 'Fuck off.'" But risk management hounded them, and cramped Eisman's style. "If risk had said to us, 'We're very comfortable with this and you can do ten times this amount,'" said Danny, "Steve would have done ten times the amount." Greg Lippmann was now blasting Vinny and Danny with all sorts of negative information about the housing market, and, for the first time, Vinny and Danny began to hide the information from Eisman. "We were worried he'd come out of his office and shout, 'Do a trillion!'" said Danny.

In the spring of 2007, the subprime mortgage bond market, incredibly, had strengthened a bit. "The impact on the broader economy and the financial markets of the problems in the subprime markets seems likely to be contained," U.S. Federal Reserve chairman Ben Bernanke was quoted as saying in the newspapers on March 7. "Credit quality always gets better in March and April," said Eisman. "And the reason it always gets better in March and April is that people get their tax refunds. You would think people in the securitization world would know this. And they sort of did. But they let the credit spreads tighten. We just thought that was moronic. What are you, fucking stupid?" Amazingly, the stock market continued to soar, and the television over the FrontPoint trading desks emitted a ceaselessly bullish signal. "We turned off CNBC," said Danny Moses. "It became very frustrating that they weren't in touch with reality anymore. If something negative happened, they'd spin it positive. If something positive happened, they'd blow it out of proportion. It alters your mind. You can't be clouded with shit like that."

Upon their return from Las Vegas, they set out to pester the rating agencies, and the Wall Street people who gamed their models, for more information. "We were trying to figure out what, if anything, would make the ratings agencies downgrade," said Danny. In the process, they picked up more disturbing tidbits. They'd often wondered, for instance, why the rating agencies weren't more critical of bonds underpinned by floating-rate subprime mortgages. Subprime borrowers tended to be one broken refrigerator away from default. Few, if any, should be running the risk of their interest payment spiking up. As most of these loans were structured, however, the homeowner would pay a fixed teaser rate of, say, 8 percent for the first two years, and then, at the start of the third year, the interest rate would skyrocket to, say, 12 percent, and thereafter it would float at permanently high levels. It was easy to understand why originators like Option One and New Century preferred to make these sorts of loans: After two years the borrowers either defaulted or, if their home price had risen, refinanced. To them the default was a matter of indifference, as they kept none of the risk of the loan; the refinance was merely a chance to charge the borrower new fees. Bouncing between the rating agencies and people he knew in the subprime bond packaging business, Eisman learned that the rating agencies simply assumed that the borrower would be just as likely to make his payments when the interest rate on the loan was 12 percent as when it was 8 percent—which meant more cash flow for the bondholders. Bonds backed by floating-rate mortgages received *higher* ratings than bonds backed by fixed-rate ones—which was why the percentage of subprime mortgages with floating rates had risen, in the past five years, from 40 to 80.

A lot of these loans were now going bad, but subprime bonds weren't moving—because Moody's and S&P, disturbingly, still hadn't changed their official opinions of them. As an equity investor, FrontPoint Partners was covered by Wall Street stockbrokers. Eisman asked stock market salesmen at Goldman Sachs and Morgan Stanley and the others to bring over the bond people for a visit. "We always asked the same question," says Eisman. "'Where are the ratings agencies in all this?' And I'd always get the same reaction. It was a physical reaction because they didn't want to say it. It was a smirk." Digging deeper, he called S&P and asked what happened to default rates if real estate prices fell. The man at S&P couldn't say: Their model for home prices had no ability to accept a negative number. "They were just assuming home prices would keep going up," says Eisman.*

Eventually he'd hop onto the subway with Vinny and ride down to Wall Street to meet with a woman at S&P named Ernestine Warner. Warner worked as an analyst in the surveillance department. The surveillance department was meant to monitor subprime bonds and downgrade them if the loans that underpinned them went bad. The loans were going bad but the bonds weren't being downgraded—and so once again Eisman wondered if S&P knew something he did not. "When we shorted the bonds, all we had was the pool-level data," he said. The pool-level data gave you the general characteristics—the average FICO scores, the average loan-to-value ratios, the average number of no-doc loans, and so forth—but no view of the individual loans. The pool-level data told you, for example, that 25 percent of the home loans in some pool were insured, but not which loans—the ones likely to go bad or the ones less likely to. It was impossible to determine how badly the Wall Street firms had gamed the system. "We of course thought that the ratings agencies had more data than we had," said Eisman. "They didn't."

Ernestine Warner was working with the same rough information available to traders like Eisman. This was insane: The arbiter of the value of the bonds lacked access to relevant information about the

* A spokesman for S&P later doubted that any S&P employee would ever have said such a thing, as their model was capable of handling negative numbers.

bonds. "When we asked her why," said Vinny, "she said, 'The issuers won't give it to us.' That's when I lost it. 'You need to demand to get it!' She looked at us like, We can't do that. We were like, 'Who is in charge here? You're the grown-up. You're the cop! Tell them to fucking give it to you!!!'" Eisman concluded that "S&P was worried that if they demanded the data from Wall Street, Wall Street would just go to Moody's for their ratings."*

As an investor, Eisman was allowed to listen in on the quarterly conference calls held by Moody's, but not invited to pose questions. The people at Moody's were sympathetic to his need for more genuine interaction, however; and the CEO, Ray McDaniel, even invited Eisman and his team to his office for a visit, a gesture that forever endeared him to Eisman. "When are shorts welcome anywhere?" asked Eisman. "When you're short, the whole world is against you. The only time a company met me with complete knowledge that we were short was Moody's." After their trip to Las Vegas, Eisman and his team were so certain the world had been turned upside down that they just assumed Raymond McDaniel must know it, too. "But we're sitting there," recalls Vinny, "and he says to us, like he actually means it, 'I truly believe that our ratings will prove accurate.'" And Steve shoots up in his chair and asks, 'What did you just say?'—as if the guy had just uttered the most preposterous statement in the history

* On October 22, 2008, a former S&P subprime mortgage bond analyst named Frank Raiter would testify before the Committee on Oversight and Government Reform that the S&P managing director in charge of the surveillance of subprime mortgage bonds "did not believe loan-level data was necessary and that had the effect of quashing all requests for funds to build in-house data bases." Raiter introduced an e-mail from S&P's managing director of CDO ratings, Richard Gugliada, in which Gugliada said: "Any request for loan-level tapes is TOTALLY UNREASONABLE!! Most originators don't have it and can't provide it. Nevertheless we MUST produce a credit estimate. . . . It is your responsibility to provide those credit estimates and your responsibility to devise some method to do so."

of finance. He repeated it. And Eisman just laughed at him. "With all due respect, sir," said Vinny deferentially, as they left, "you're delusional." This wasn't Fitch or even S&P. This was Moody's. The aristocrats of the rating business, 20 percent owned by Warren Buffett. And its CEO was being told he was either a fool or a crook, by Vincent Daniel, from Queens.

By early June the subprime mortgage bond market had resumed what would become an uninterrupted decline, and the FrontPoint positions began to move—first by thousands and then by millions of dollars a day. "I know I'm making money," Eisman would often ask. "So who is losing money?" They already were short the stocks of mortgage originators and the home builders. Now they added to their short positions in the stocks of the rating agencies. "They were making ten times more rating CDOs than they were rating GM bonds," said Eisman, "and it was all going to end."

Inevitably, their attention turned to the beating heart of capitalism, the big Wall Street investment banks. "Our original thesis was that the securitization machine was Wall Street's big profit center and it was going to die," said Eisman. "And when that happened, their revenues would dry up." One of the reasons Wall Street had cooked up this new industry called structured finance was that its old-fashioned business was every day less profitable. The profits in stockbroking, along with those in the more conventional sorts of bond broking, had been squashed by Internet competition. The minute the market stopped buying subprime mortgage bonds and CDOs backed by subprime mortgage bonds, the investment banks were in trouble. Right up until the middle of 2007, Eisman had not suspected that the firms were so foolish as to invest in their own creations. He could see that their leverage had increased dramatically, in just the past few years. He could of course see that they were holding more and more risky assets with borrowed money. What he could not see was the nature of their assets. Triple-A-rated corporate bonds, or triple-A-rated subprime CDOs? "You couldn't know for sure," he said. "There was no disclosure. You didn't know what they had on their balance sheet. You naturally assumed that they got rid of this shit as soon as they created it."

A combination of new facts, and actual human contact with the people who ran the big firms and the rating agencies, had stirred his suspicion. The first new fact had been HSBC's announcement, in February 2007, that it was losing a lot of money on its subprime loans, and a second announcement, in March, that it was dumping its subprime portfolio. "HSBC were supposed to be the good guys," said Vinny. "They were supposed to have cleaned up Household. We thought, Holy crap, there are so many people worse than that." The second new fact was in Merrill Lynch's second-quarter results. In July 2007, Merrill Lynch announced yet another sensationally profitable quarter, but admitted it had suffered a decline in revenues from mortgage trading due to losses in subprime bonds. What sounded to most investors like a trivial piece of information was to Eisman the big news: Merrill Lynch owned a meaningful amount of subprime mortgage securities. Merrill's CFO, Jeff Edwards, told Bloomberg News that the market need not worry about this, as "active risk management" had allowed Merrill Lynch to reduce its exposure to the lower-rated subprime bonds. "I don't want to get too deep into exactly how we positioned ourselves at any one point in time," Edwards said, but went deep enough to say that the market was paying too much attention to whatever Merrill happened to be doing with subprime mortgage bonds. Or, as Edwards elliptically put it, "There's a disproportionate focus on a particular asset class in a particular country."

Eisman didn't think so—and two weeks later persuaded a UBS analyst named Glenn Schorr to escort him to a small meeting between Edwards and Merrill Lynch's biggest shareholders. The Merrill CFO began by explaining that this little subprime mortgage problem Merrill Lynch seemed to have was firmly under the control of Merrill Lynch's models. "We're not that far into the meeting," said someone who was there. "Jeff is still giving his prepared remarks and Steve just bursts out, 'Well, your models are wrong!' This very awkward silence comes over the room. Do you laugh? Do you try to think up some question so everyone can move on? Steve was sitting at the end of the table and he starts to put his papers in order really conspicuously—as if to say, 'If it wasn't rude, I'd walk out now.'"

Eisman, for his part, considered the event a polite exchange of views, after which he lost interest. "There was nothing more to say. I just figured, You know what? This guy doesn't get it."

On the surface, these big Wall Street firms appeared robust; below the surface, Eisman was beginning to think, their problems might not be confined to a potential loss of revenue. If they really didn't believe the subprime mortgage market was a problem for them, the subprime mortgage market might be the end of them. He and his team now set about searching for hidden subprime risk: Who was hiding what? "We called it The Great Treasure Hunt," he said. They didn't know for sure if these firms were in some way on the other side of the bets he'd been making against subprime bonds, but the more he looked, the more sure he became that they didn't know either. He'd go to meetings with Wall Street CEOs and ask them the most basic questions about their balance sheets. "They didn't know," he said. "They didn't know their own balance sheets." Once, he got himself invited to a meeting with the CEO of Bank of America, Ken Lewis. "I was sitting there listening to him. I had an epiphany. I said to myself, 'Oh my God, he's dumb!' A lightbulb went off. The guy running one of the biggest banks in the world is dumb!" They shorted Bank of America, along with UBS, Citigroup, Lehman Brothers, and a few others. They weren't allowed to short Morgan Stanley because they were owned by Morgan Stanley, but if they could have, they would have. Not long after they established their shorts against the big Wall Street banks, they had a visit from a prominent analyst who covered the firms, Brad Hintz, at Sanford C. Bernstein & Co. Hintz asked Eisman what he was up to.

"We just shorted Merrill Lynch," said Eisman.

"Why?" asked Hintz.

"We have a simple thesis," said Eisman. "There is going to be a calamity, and whenever there is a calamity, Merrill is there." When it came time to bankrupt Orange County with bad advice, Merrill was there. When the Internet went bust, Merrill was there. Way back in the 1980s, when the first bond trader was let off his leash and lost hundreds of millions of dollars, Merrill was there to take the hit. That was Eisman's logic: the logic of Wall Street's pecking order. Goldman Sachs was the big kid who ran the games in this neighborhood. Merrill Lynch was the little fat kid assigned the least pleasant roles, just happy to be a part of things. The game, as Eisman saw it, was crack the whip. He assumed Merrill Lynch had taken its assigned place at the end of the chain.

On July 17, 2007, two days before Ben Bernanke, the Fed chairman, told the U.S. Senate that he saw no more than $100 billion in losses in the subprime mortgage market, FrontPoint did something unusual: It hosted its own conference call. They'd had calls with their tiny population of investors, but this time they just opened it up. Steve Eisman had become a poorly kept secret. "Steve was one of about two investors who completely understood what was going on," said one prominent Wall Street analyst. Five hundred people called in to hear what Eisman had to say, and another five hundred logged in afterward to listen to the recording. He explained the strange alchemy of the mezzanine CDO—and said that he expected losses up to $300 billion from this sliver of the market alone. To evaluate the situation, he told his audience, "Just throw your model in the garbage can. The models are all backward-looking. The models don't have any idea of what this world has become. . . . For the first time in their *lives* people in the asset-backed securitization world are actually having to think." He explained that the rating agencies were morally bankrupt and living in fear of becoming actually bankrupt. "The ratings agencies are scared to death," he said. "They're scared to death about doing nothing because they'll look like fools if they do nothing." He expected that fully half of all U.S. home mortgage loans—many trillions of dollars' worth—would suffer losses. "We are in the midst of one of the greatest social experiments this country has ever seen," said Eisman. "It's just not going to be a fun experiment. . . . You think this is ugly. You haven't seen anything yet." When he was done, the next speaker, an Englishman who ran a separate fund at FrontPoint, was slow to respond. "Sorry," the Englishman said wryly, "I just needed to calm down from hearing Steve say the world is ending." And everyone laughed.

Later that very day, investors in the collapsed Bear Stearns hedge funds were informed that their $1.6 billion in triple-A-rated subprime-backed CDOs had not merely lost some value, they were worthless. Eisman was now convinced a lot of the biggest firms on Wall Street did not understand their own risks, and were in peril. At the bottom of his conviction lay his memory of his dinner with Wing Chau—when he grasped the central role of the mezzanine CDO and made a massive bet against those very same CDOs. This of course raised the question: What exactly is inside a CDO? "I didn't know what the fuck was in the things," said Eisman. "You couldn't do the analysis. You couldn't say, 'Give me all the ones with all California in them.' No one knew what was in them." They learned enough to know, as Danny put it, that "it was just all the pieces of shit we'd already shorted wrapped up together, into a portfolio." Beyond that they were flying blind. "Steve's nature is to put it on and figure it out later," said Vinny.

Then came news. Eisman had long subscribed to a newsletter famous in Wall Street circles and obscure outside them, *Grant's Interest Rate Observer*. Its editor, Jim Grant, had been prophesying doom ever since the great debt cycle began, in the mid-1980s. In late 2006 Grant decided to investigate these strange Wall Street creations known as CDOs. Or, rather, he had asked his young assistant, Dan Gertner, a chemical engineer with an MBA, to see if he could understand them. Gertner went off with the documents explaining CDOs to potential investors and sweated and groaned and heaved and suffered. "Then he came back," says Grant, "and said, 'I can't figure this thing out.' And I said, 'I think we have our story.'"

Gertner dug and dug and finally concluded that no matter how much digging he did he'd never be able to get to the bottom of what exactly was inside a CDO—which, to Jim Grant, meant that no investor possibly could either. In turn this suggested what Grant already knew, that far too many people were taking far too many financial statements on faith. In early 2007 Grant wrote a series of pieces suggesting that the rating agencies had abandoned their posts—that they were almost surely rating these CDOs without themselves knowing exactly what was inside them. "The readers of *Grant's* have seen for themselves how a stack of non-investment grade mortgage slices can be rearranged to form a collateral debt obligation," one piece began. "And they have stared in amazement at the improvements that this mysterious process can effect in the credit ratings of the slices . . ." For his troubles, Grant, along with his trusted assistant, was called into S&P for a dressing-down. "We were actually summoned to the rating agency and told, 'You guys just don't get it,'" says Gertner. "Jim used the term 'alchemy' and they didn't like that term."

Just a few miles north of *Grant's* Wall Street offices, an equity hedge fund manager with a darkening view of the world was wondering why he hadn't heard others voice suspicion about the bond market and its abstruse creations. In Jim Grant's essay, Steve Eisman found independent confirmation of his theory of the financial world. "When I read it," said Eisman, "I thought, *Oh my God, this is like owning a gold mine*. When I read that, I was the only guy in the equity world who almost had an orgasm."

Chapter Eight

The Long Quiet

The day Steve Eisman became the first man ever to take almost sexual pleasure in an essay in *Grant's Interest Rate Observer,* Dr. Michael Burry received from his CFO a copy of the same story, along with a jokey note: "Mike—you haven't taken a side job writing for *Grant's*, have you?"

"I haven't," Burry replied, seeing no obvious good news in the discovery that there was someone out there who thought as he did. "I'm a bit surprised we haven't been contacted by *Grant's* . . ." He was still in the financial world but apart from it, as if on the other side of a pane of glass he couldn't bring himself to tap upon. He'd been the first investor to diagnose the disorder in the American financial system in early 2003: *the extension of credit by instrument*. Complicated financial stuff was being dreamed up for the sole purpose of lending money to people who could never repay it. "I really do believe the final act in play is a crisis in our financial institutions, which are doing such dumb, dumb things," he wrote, in April 2003, to a friend who had wondered why Scion Capital's quarterly letters to its investors had turned so dark. "I have a job to do. Make money for my clients. Period. But boy it gets morbid when you start making investments that work out extra great if a tragedy occurs." Then, in the spring of 2005, he had identified, before any other investor, precisely which tragedy was most likely to occur, when he made a large, explicit bet against subprime mortgage bonds.

Now, in February 2007, subprime loans were defaulting in record numbers, financial institutions were less steady every day, and no one but him seemed to recall what he'd said and done. He had told his investors that they might need to be patient—that the bet might not pay off until the mortgages issued in 2005 reached the end of their teaser rate period. They had not been patient. Many of his investors mistrusted him, and he in turn felt betrayed by them. At the beginning he had imagined the end, but none of the parts in between. "I guess I wanted to just go to sleep and wake up in 2007," he said. To keep his bets against subprime mortgage bonds, he'd been forced to fire half his small staff, and dump billions of dollars' worth of bets he had made against the companies most closely associated with the subprime mortgage market. He was now more isolated than he'd ever been. The only thing that had changed was his explanation for it.

Not long before, his wife had dragged him to the office of a Stanford psychologist. A preschool teacher had noted certain worrying behaviors in their four-year-old son, Nicholas, and suggested he needed testing. Nicholas didn't sleep when the other kids slept. He drifted off when the teacher talked at any length. His mind seemed "very active." Michael Burry had to resist his urge to take offense. He was, after all, a doctor, and he suspected that the teacher was trying to tell them that he had failed to diagnose attention deficit disorder in his own son. "I had worked in an ADHD clinic during my residency, and had strong feelings that this was overdiagnosed," he said. "That it was a 'savior' diagnosis for too many kids whose parents wanted a medical reason to drug their children, or to explain their kids' bad behavior." He suspected his son was a bit different from the other kids, but different in a good way. "He asked a ton of questions," said Burry. "I had encouraged that, because I always had a ton of questions as a kid, and I was frustrated when I was told to be quiet." Now he watched his son more carefully, and noted that the little boy, while smart, had problems with other people. "When he did try to interact, even though he didn't do anything mean to the other kids, he'd somehow tick them off." He came home and told his wife, "Don't worry about it! He's fine!"

His wife stared at him and asked, "How would you know?"

To which Dr. Michael Burry replied, "Because he's just like me! That's how I was."

Their son's application to several kindergartens met with quick rejections, unaccompanied by explanations. Pressed, one of the schools told Burry that his son suffered from inadequate gross and fine motor skills. "He had apparently scored very low on tests involving art and scissor use," said Burry. "Big deal, I thought. I still draw like a four-year-old, and I hate art." To silence his wife, however, he agreed to have their son tested. "It would just prove he's a smart kid, an 'absentminded genius.'"

Instead, the tests administered by a child psychologist proved that their child had Asperger's syndrome. A classic case, she said, and recommended that the child be pulled from the mainstream and sent to a special school. And Dr. Michael Burry was dumbstruck: He recalled Asperger's from med school, but vaguely. His wife now handed him the stack of books she had accumulated on autism and related disorders. On top were *The Complete Guide to Asperger's Syndrome,* by a clinical psychologist named Tony Attwood, and Attwood's *Asperger's Syndrome: A Guide for Parents and Professionals.*

"Marked impairment in the use of multiple non-verbal behaviors such as eye-to-eye gaze . . ."

Check.

"Failure to develop peer relationships . . ."

Check.

"A lack of spontaneous seeking to share enjoyment, interests, or achievements with other people . . ."

Check.

"Difficulty reading the social/emotional messages in someone's eyes . . ."

Check.

"A faulty emotion regulation or control mechanism for expressing anger . . ."

Check.

". . . One of the reasons why computers are so appealing is not only that you do not have to talk or socialize with them, but that they are logical, consistent and not prone to moods. Thus they are an ideal interest for the person with Asperger's Syndrome . . ."

Check.

"Many people have a hobby. . . . The difference between the normal range and the eccentricity observed in Asperger's Syndrome is that these pursuits are often solitary, idiosyncratic and dominate the person's time and conversation."

Check . . . Check . . . Check.

After a few pages, Michael Burry realized that he was no longer reading about his son but about himself. "How many people can pick up a book and find an instruction manual for their life?" he said. "I hated reading a book telling me who I was. I thought I was different, but this was saying I was the same as other people. My wife and I were a typical Asperger's couple, and we had an Asperger's son." His glass eye no longer explained anything; the wonder is that it ever had. How did a glass eye explain, in a competitive swimmer, a pathological fear of deep water—the terror of not knowing what lurked beneath him? How did it explain a childhood passion for washing money? He'd take dollar bills and wash them, dry them off with a towel, press them between the pages of books, and then stack books on top of those books—all so he might have money that looked "new." "All of a sudden I've become this caricature," said Burry. "I've always been able to study up on something and ace something really fast. I thought it was all something special about me. Now it's like, 'Oh, a lot of Asperger's people can do that.' Now I was explained by a disorder."

He resisted the news. He had a gift for finding and analyzing information on the subjects that interested him intensely. He always had been intensely interested in himself. Now, at the age of thirty-five, he'd been handed this new piece of information about himself—and his first reaction to it was to wish he hadn't been given it. "My first thought was that a lot of people must have this and don't know it," he said. "And I wondered, Is this really a good thing for me to know at this point? Why is it good for me to know this about myself?"

He went and found his own psychologist to help him sort out the effect of his syndrome on his wife and children. His work life, however, remained uninformed by the new information. He didn't alter the way he made investment decisions, for instance, or the way he communicated with his investors. He didn't let his investors know of his disorder. "I didn't feel it was a material fact that had to be disclosed," he said. "It wasn't a change. I wasn't diagnosed with something new. It's something I'd always had." On the other hand, it explained an awful lot about what he did for a living, and how he did it: his obsessive acquisition of hard facts, his insistence on logic, his ability to plow quickly through reams of tedious financial statements. People with Asperger's couldn't control what they were interested in. It was a stroke of luck that his special interest was financial markets and not, say, collecting lawn mower catalogues. When he thought of it that way, he realized that complex modern financial markets were as good as designed to reward a person with Asperger's who took an interest in them. "Only someone who has Asperger's would read a subprime mortgage bond prospectus," he said.

By early 2007 Michael Burry found himself in a characteristically bizarre situation. He'd bought insurance on a lot of truly crappy subprime mortgage bonds, created from loans made in 2005, but they were *his* credit default swaps. They weren't traded often by others; a lot of people took the view that the loans made in 2005 were somehow sounder than the loans made in 2006; in bond market parlance, they were "off the run." That was their biggest claim: The pools of loans he had bet against were "relatively clean." To counter the assertion, he commissioned a private study, and found that the pools of loans he had shorted were nearly twice as likely to be in bankruptcy and a third more likely to have been foreclosed upon than the general run of 2005 subprime deals. The loans made in 2006 were indeed worse than those made in 2005, but the loans made in 2005 remained atrocious, and closer to the dates when their interest rates would reset. He had picked exactly the right homeowners to bet against.

All through 2006, and the first few months of 2007, Burry sent his list of credit default swaps to Goldman and Bank of America and Morgan Stanley with the idea they would show it to possible buyers, so he might get some idea of the market price. That, after all, was the dealers' stated function: middlemen. Market-makers. That is not the function they served, however. "It seemed the dealers were just sitting on my lists and bidding extremely opportunistically themselves," said Burry. The data from the mortgage servicers was worse every month—the loans underlying the bonds were going bad at faster rates—and yet the price of insuring those loans, they said, was falling. "Logic had failed me," he said. "I couldn't explain the outcomes I was seeing." At the end of each day there was meant to be a tiny reckoning: If the subprime market had fallen, they would wire money to him; if it had strengthened, he would wire money to them. The fate of Scion Capital turned on these bets, but that fate was not, in the short run, determined by an open and free market. It was determined by Goldman Sachs and Bank of America and Morgan Stanley, who decided each day whether Mike Burry's credit default swaps had made or lost money.

It was true, however, that his portfolio of credit default swaps was uncommon. They were selected by an uncommon character, with an uncommon view of the financial markets, operating alone and apart. This fact alone enabled Wall Street firms to dictate to him the market price. With no one else buying and selling exactly what Michael Burry was buying and selling, there was no hard evidence what these things were worth—so they were worth whatever Goldman Sachs and Morgan Stanley said they were worth. Burry detected a pattern in how they managed their market: All good news about the housing market, or the economy, was treated as an excuse to demand collateral from Scion Capital; all bad news was pooh-poohed as in some way irrelevant to the specific bets he had made. The firms always claimed that they had no position themselves—that they were running matched books—but their behavior told him otherwise. "Whatever the banks' net position was would determine the mark," he said. "I don't think they were looking to the market for their marks. I think they were looking to their needs." That is, the reason they refused to acknowledge that his bet was paying off was that they were on the other side of it. "When you talk to dealers," he wrote in March 2006 to his in-house lawyer, Steve Druskin, "you are getting the view from their book. Whatever they've got on their book will be their view. Goldman happens to be warehousing a lot of this risk. They'll talk as if nothing has been seen in the mortgage pools. No need to incite panic . . . and this has worked. As long as they can entice more [money] into the market, the problem is resolved. That's been the history of the last 3–4 years."

By April 2006 he'd finished buying insurance on subprime mortgage bonds. In a portfolio of $555 million, he had laid $1.9 billion of these peculiar bets—bets that should be paying off but were not. In May he adopted a new tactic: asking Wall Street traders if they would be willing to sell him even more credit default swaps at the price they claimed they were worth, knowing that they were not. "Never once has any counterparty been willing to sell me my list at my marks," he wrote in an e-mail. "Eighty to ninety per cent of the names on my list are not even available at any price." A properly functioning market would assimilate new information into the prices of securities; this multi-trillion-dollar market in subprime mortgage risk never budged. "One of the oldest adages in investing is that if you're reading about it in the paper, it's too late," he said. "Not this time." Steve Druskin was becoming more involved in the market—and couldn't believe how controlled it was. "What's amazing is that they make a market in this fantasy stuff," said Druskin. "It's not a real asset." It was as if Wall Street had decided to allow everyone to gamble on the punctuality of commercial airlines. The likelihood of United Flight 001 arriving on time obviously shifted—with the weather, mechanical issues, pilot quality, and so on. But shifting probabilities could be ignored, until the plane did or did not arrive. It didn't matter when big mortgage lenders like Ownit and ResCap failed, or some pool of subprime loans experienced higher than expected losses. All that mattered was what Goldman Sachs and Morgan Stanley decided should matter.

The world's single biggest capital market wasn't a market; it was something else—but what? "I am actually protesting to my counterparties that there must be fraud in the marketplace for credit default swaps to be at all-time lows," Burry wrote in an e-mail to an investor he trusted. "What if CDSs are a fraud? I am asking myself that question all the time, and never have I felt like I should be thinking that way more than now. No way we should be down 5% this year just in mortgage CDSs." To his Goldman Sachs saleswoman, he wrote, "I think I am short housing but am I not, because CDSs are criminal?" When, a few months later, Goldman Sachs announced it was setting aside $542,000 per employee for the 2006 bonus pool, he wrote again:

"As a former gas station attendant, parking lot attendant, medical resident and current Goldman Sachs screwee, I am offended."

In the middle of 2006, he began to hear of other money managers who wanted to make the same bet he did. A few actually called and asked for his help. "I had all these people telling me I needed to get out of this trade," he said. "And I was looking at these other people and thinking how lucky they were to be able to get into this trade." If the market had been at all rational it would have blown up long before. "Some of the biggest funds on the planet have picked my brain and copied my strategy," he wrote in an e-mail. "So it won't just be Scion that makes money if this happens. Still, it won't be everyone."

He was now undeniably miserable. "It feels like my insides are digesting themselves," he wrote to his wife in mid-September. The source of his unhappiness was, as usual, other people. The other people who bothered him the most were his own investors. When he opened his fund, in 2000, he released only his quarterly returns, and told his investors that he planned to tell them next to nothing about what he was up to. Now they were demanding monthly and even fortnightly reports, and pestered him constantly about the wisdom of his pessimism. "I almost think the better the idea, and the more iconoclastic the investor, the more likely you will get screamed at by investors," he said. He didn't worry about how screwed-up the market for some security became because he knew that eventually it would be disciplined by logic: Businesses either thrived or failed. Loans either were paid off or were defaulted upon. But these people whose money he ran were incapable of keeping their emotional distance from the market. They were now responding to the same surface stimuli as the entire screwed-up subprime mortgage market, and trying to force him to conform to its madness. "I do my best to have patience," he wrote to one investor. "But I can only be as patient as my investors." To another griping investor he wrote, "The definition of an intelligent manager in the hedge fund world is someone who has the right idea, and sees his investors abandon him just before the idea pays off." When he was making them huge sums of money, he had barely heard from them; the moment he started actually to lose a little, they peppered him with their doubts and suspicions:

> So I take it the monster dragging us out to sea is the CDS. You have created the plight of the old man and the sea.

> When do you see the end of the bleeding? (August down again 5%.) Are you running a riskier strategy now?

> You make me physically ill. . . . How dare you?

> Can you explain to me how we keep losing money on this position? If our potential losses are fixed it would seem to me based on how much we have lost that they should be a tiny part of the portfolio now.

This last question kept popping up: How could a stock picker be losing so much on this one quixotic bond market bet? And he kept trying to answer it: He was committed to paying annual premiums amounting to about 8 percent of the portfolio, every year, for as long as the underlying loans existed—likely around five years but possibly as long as thirty. Eight percent times five years came to 40 percent. If the value of the credit default swaps fell by half, Scion registered a mark-to-market loss of 20 percent.

More alarmingly, his credit default swap contracts contained a provision that allowed the big Wall Street firms to cancel their bets with Scion if Scion's assets fell below a certain level. There was suddenly a real risk that that might happen. Most of his investors had agreed to a two-year "lockup" and could not pull their money out at will.

But of the $555 million he had under management, $302 million was eligible to be withdrawn either at the end of 2006 or in the middle of 2007, and investors were lining up to ask for their money back. In October 2006, with U.S. house prices experiencing their greatest decline in thirty-five years, and just weeks before the ABX index of triple-B mortgage bonds experienced its first "credit event" (that is, loss), Michael Burry faced the likelihood of a run on his fund—a fund that was now devoted to betting against the subprime mortgage market. "We were clinically depressed," said one of the several analysts Burry employed but never figured out what to do with, as he insisted on doing all the analysis himself. "You'd go to work and you'd say, 'I don't want to be here.' The trade was moving against you and investors wanted out."

One night, as Burry was complaining to his wife about the complete absence of long-term perspective in the financial markets, a thought struck him: His agreement with his investors gave him the right to keep their money if he had invested it "in securities for which there is no public market or that are not freely tradable." It was left to the manager to decide if there was a public market for a security. If Michael Burry thought there wasn't—for instance, if he thought a market was temporarily not functioning or somehow fraudulent—he was permitted to "side-pocket" an investment. That is, he could tell his investors that they couldn't have their money back until the bet he'd made with it had run its natural course.

And so he did what seemed to him the only proper and logical thing to do: He side-pocketed his credit default swaps. The long list of investors eager to get their money back from him—a list that included his founding backer, Gotham Capital—received the news from him in a terse letter: He was locking up between 50 and 55 percent of their money. Burry followed this letter with his quarterly report, which he hoped might make everyone feel a bit better. But he had no talent for caring what others thought of him: It was almost as if he didn't know how to do it. What he wrote sounded less like an apology than an assault. "Never before have I been so optimistic about the portfolio for a reason that has nothing to do with stocks," it began, and then it went on to explain how he had established a position in the markets that should be the envy of any money manager. How he had placed a bet not on "housing Armageddon" (even though he suspected that was coming) but on "the worst 5% or so of loans made in 2005." How his investors should feel *lucky*. He wrote as if he was sitting on top of the world, when he was expected to feel as if the world was sitting on top of him. One of his biggest New York investors shot him an e-mail: "I'd be careful in the future using derogatory phrases such as 'we're short the mortgage portfolio everyone would want if they knew what they were doing' and 'sooner or later one of the big boys should really read a prospectus.'" One of his original two e-mail friends—both had stuck by him—wrote, "Nobody else except the North Korean dictator Kim Jong-Il would write a letter like that when they are down 17%."

Immediately, his partners at Gotham Capital threatened to sue him. They soon were joined by others, who began to organize themselves into a legal fighting force. What distinguished Gotham was that their leaders flew out from New York to San Jose and tried to bully Burry into giving them back the $100 million they had invested with him. In January 2006 Gotham's creator, Joel Greenblatt, had gone on television to promote a book and, when asked to name his favorite "value investors," had extolled the virtues of a rare talent named Mike Burry. Ten months later he traveled three thousand miles with his partner, John Petry, to tell Mike Burry he was a liar and to pressure him into abandoning the bet Burry viewed as the single shrewdest of his career. "If there was one moment I might have caved, that was it," said Burry. "Joel was like a godfather to me—a partner in my firm, the guy that 'discovered' me and backed me before anyone outside my family did. I respected him and looked up to him." Now, as Greenblatt told him no judge in any court of law would side with his decision to side-pocket what was clearly a tradable security, whatever feelings Mike Burry had for him vanished. When Greenblatt asked to see a list of the subprime mortgage bonds Burry had bet against, Burry refused. From Greenblatt's point of view, he had given this guy $100 million and the guy was not only refusing to give it back but to even talk to him.

And Greenblatt had a point. It was wildly unconventional to side-pocket an investment for which there was obviously a market. There was clearly some low price at which Michael Burry might bail out of his bet against the subprime mortgage bond market. To some meaningful number of his investors, it looked as if Burry simply did not want to accept the judgment of the marketplace: He'd made a bad bet and was failing to accept his loss. But to Burry, the judgment of the marketplace was fraudulent, and Joel Greenblatt didn't know what he was talking about. "It became clear to me that they still didn't understand the [credit default swap] positions," he said.

He was acutely aware that a great many of the people who had given him their money now despised him. The awareness caused him to (a) withdraw into his office and shout "Fuck" at the top of his lungs even more than usual; (b) develop a new contempt for his own investors; and (c) keep trying to explain his actions to them, even though they quite clearly were no longer listening. "I would prefer that you talk less and listen more," his lawyer, Steve Druskin, wrote to him, in late October 2006. "They are strategizing litigation."

"It was kind of interesting," said Kip Oberting, who had arranged for White Mountains to become Burry's other original investor, before leaving for other ventures. "Because he had explained exactly what he was doing. And he had made people a bunch of money. You would have thought people would stick with him." They weren't merely not sticking with him but fleeing as fast as he would allow them. They *hated* him. "I just don't understand why people just don't see that I don't mean any harm," he said. Late on the night of December 29, Michael Burry sat alone in his office and typed a quick e-mail to his wife: "So incredibly depressing; I'm trying to come home, but I'm just so mad and depressed right now."

And so in January 2007, just before Steve Eisman and Charlie Ledley headed gleefully to Las Vegas, Michael Burry sat down to explain to his investors how, in a year when the S&P had risen by more than 10 percent, he had lost 18.4 percent. A person who had had money with him from the beginning would have enjoyed gains of 186 percent over those six years, compared to 10.13 percent for the S&P 500 Index, but Burry's long-term success was no longer relevant. He was now being judged monthly. "The year just completed was one in which I underperformed nearly all my peers and friends by, variably, thirty or forty percentage points," he wrote. "A money manager does not go from being a near nobody to being nearly universally applauded to being nearly universally vilified without some effect." The effect, he went on to demonstrate, was to make him ever more certain that the entire financial world was wrong and he was right. "I have always believed that a single talented analyst, working very hard, can cover an amazing amount of investment landscape, and this belief remains unchallenged in my mind."

Then he returned, as he always did, to the not so small matter of his credit default swaps: All the important facts pointed to their eventual success. In just the last two months, three big mortgage originators had failed . . . The Center for Responsible Lending was now predicting that, in 2007, 2.2 million borrowers would lose their homes, and one in five subprime mortgages issued in 2005 and 2006 would fail . . .

Michael Burry was as good as teed up to become a Wall Street villain. His quarterly letters to his investors, which Burry considered private, were now routinely leaked to the press. A nasty piece appeared in a trade journal, suggesting that he had behaved unethically in side-pocketing his bet, and Burry felt certain it had been planted by one of his own investors. "Mike wasn't paranoid," said a New York investor who observed the behavior of other New York investors in Scion

Capital. "People really were out to get him. When he becomes a bad guy he becomes this greedy sociopath who is going to steal all the money. And he can always go back to being a neurologist. It was the first thing everyone jumped to with Mike: He was a doctor." Burry began to hear strange rumors about himself. He'd left his wife and gone into hiding. He had fled to South America. "It's an interesting life I'm leading lately," Burry wrote to one of the e-mail friends.

> With all that has gone on recently, I've had the opportunity to talk with many of our investors, which is the first time I've done so in the history of the funds. I've been shocked by what I've heard. It appears that investors only have passingly paid attention to my letters, and many have been clinging to various rumors and hearsay in place of analysis or original thought. I've variably launched a private equity fund, tried to buy a Venezuelan gold company, launched a separate hedge fund called Milton's Opus, got divorced, got blown up, never disclosed the derivatives trade, borrowed $8 billion, spent much of the last two years in Asia, accused everyone but me on Wall Street of being idiots, siphoned off the capital of the funds into my personal account, and more or less turned Scion into the next Amaranth.* None of this is made up.

He'd always been different from what one might expect a hedge fund manager to be. He wore the same shorts and t-shirts to work for days on end. He refused to wear shoes with laces. He refused to wear watches or even his wedding ring. To calm himself at work he often blared heavy metal music. "I think these personal foibles of mine were tolerated among many as long as things were going well," he said. "But when things weren't going well, they became signs of incompe-

* A Connecticut-based hedge fund that lost $6.8 billion in bets on natural gas in early 2006 and blew up in spectacular fashion.

tence or instability on my part—even among employees and business partners."

After the conference in Las Vegas the market had dropped, then recovered right through until the end of May. To Charlie Ledley at Cornwall Capital, the U.S. financial system appeared systematically corrupted by a cabal of Wall Street banks, rating agencies, and government regulators. To Steve Eisman at FrontPoint Partners, the market seemed mainly stupid or delusional: A financial culture that had experienced so many tiny panics followed by robust booms saw any sell-off as merely another buying opportunity. To Michael Burry, the subprime mortgage market looked increasingly like a fraud perpetrated by a handful of subprime bond trading desks. "Given the massive cheating on the part of our counterparties, the idea of taking the CDS[s] out of the side pocket is no longer worth considering," he wrote at the end of March 2007.

The first half of 2007 was a very strange period in financial history. The facts on the ground in the housing market diverged further and further from the prices on the bonds and the insurance on the bonds. Faced with unpleasant facts, the big Wall Street firms appeared to be choosing simply to ignore them. There were subtle changes in the market, however, and they turned up in Burry's e-mail in-box. On March 19 his salesman at Citigroup sent him, for the first time, serious analysis on a pool of mortgages. The mortgages were not subprime but Alt-A.* Still, the guy was trying to explain how much of the pool consisted of interest-only loans, what percentage was owner-occupied, and so on—the way a person might do who actually was

* The distinction had become superficial. Alt-A borrowers had FICO credit scores above 680; subprime borrowers had FICO scores below 680. Alt-A loans were poorly documented, however; the borrower would fail to provide proof of income, for instance. In practice, Alt-A mortgage loans made in the United States between 2004 and 2008 totaling $1.2 trillion were as likely to default as subprime loans totaling $1.8 trillion.

thinking about the creditworthiness of the borrowers. "When I was analyzing these back in 2005," Burry wrote in an e-mail, sounding like Stanley watching tourists march through the jungle on a path he had himself hacked, "there was nothing even remotely close to this sort of analysis coming out of brokerage houses. I glommed onto 'silent seconds'* as an indicator of a stretched buyer and made it a high-value criterion in my selection process, but at the time no one trading derivatives had any idea what I was talking about and no one thought they mattered." In the long quiet between February and June 2007, they had begun to matter. The market was on edge. In the first quarter of 2007 Scion Capital was up nearly 18 percent.

Then something changed—though at first it was hard to see what it was. On June 14, the pair of subprime mortgage bond hedge funds effectively owned by Bear Stearns went belly-up. In the ensuing two weeks, the publicly traded index of triple-B-rated subprime mortgage bonds fell by nearly 20 percent. Just then Goldman Sachs appeared to Burry to be experiencing a nervous breakdown. His biggest positions were with Goldman, and Goldman was newly unable, or unwilling, to determine the value of those positions, and so could not say how much collateral should be shifted back and forth. On Friday, June 15, Burry's Goldman Sachs saleswoman, Veronica Grinstein, vanished. He called and e-mailed her, but she didn't respond until late the following Monday—to tell him that she was "out for the day."

"This is a recurrent theme whenever the market moves our way," wrote Burry. "People get sick, people are off for unspecified reasons."

On June 20, Grinstein finally returned to tell him that Goldman Sachs had experienced "systems failure."

That was funny, Burry replied, because Morgan Stanley had said

* A silent second is a second mortgage used, in the purchase of a house, to supplement a first mortgage. It is silent only to the guy who made the first loan, and who is less likely to be repaid, as the borrower is less likely to have any financial stake at all in his own home.

more or less the same thing. And his salesman at Bank of America claimed they'd had a "power outage."

"I viewed these 'systems problems' as excuses for buying time to sort out a mess behind the scenes," he said. The Goldman saleswoman made a weak effort to claim that, even as the index of subprime mortgage bonds collapsed, the market for insuring them hadn't budged. But she did it from her cell phone, rather than the office line, on which the conversations would have been recorded.

They were caving. All of them. At the end of every month, for nearly two years, Burry had watched Wall Street traders mark his positions against him. That is, at the end of every month his bets against subprime bonds were mysteriously less valuable. The end of every month also happened to be when Wall Street traders sent their profit and loss statements to their managers and risk managers. On June 29, Burry received a note from his Morgan Stanley salesman, Art Ringness, saying that Morgan Stanley now wanted to make sure that "the marks are fair." The next day, Goldman followed suit. It was the first time in two years that Goldman Sachs had not moved the trade against him at the end of the month. "That was the *first* time they moved our marks accurately," he notes, "because they were getting in on the trade themselves." The market was finally accepting the diagnosis of its own disorder.

The moment Goldman was getting in on his trade was also the moment the market flipped. Some kind of rout was now on: Everyone at once seemed eager to talk to him. Morgan Stanley, which had been, by far, the most reluctant to acknowledge negative news in subprime, now called to say it would like to buy whatever he had "in any size." Burry heard a rumor—soon confirmed—that a fund run by Goldman, called Global Alpha, had taken huge losses in subprime and that Goldman itself had rapidly turned from betting on the subprime mortgage market to betting against it.

It was precisely the moment he had told his investors, back in the summer of 2005, that they only needed to wait for. Crappy mortgages worth three-quarters of a trillion dollars were resetting from their teaser rates to new, higher rates. A single pool of mortgages, against which Burry had laid a bet, illustrated the general point: OOMLT 2005-3. OOMLT 2005-3 was shorthand for a pool of subprime mortgage loans made by Option One—the company whose CEO had given the speech in Las Vegas that Steve Eisman had walked out of, after raising his zero in the air. Most of the loans had been made between April and July of 2005. From January to June 2007, the news from the pool—its delinquencies, its bankruptcies, its house foreclosures—had remained fairly consistent. The losses were much greater than they should have been, given the ratings of the bonds they underpinned, but the losses did not change a great deal from one month to the next. From February 25 to May 25 (the remittance data always came on the twenty-fifth of the month), the combined delinquencies, foreclosures, and bankruptcies inside OOMLT 2005-3 rose from 15.6 percent to 16.9 percent. On June 25 the total number of loans in default spiked to 18.68 percent. In July it spiked again, to 21.4 percent. In August it leapt to 25.44 percent, and by the end of the year it stood at 37.7 percent—more than a third of the pool of borrowers had defaulted on their loans. The losses were sufficient to wipe out not only the bonds Michael Burry had bet against but also a lot of the more highly rated ones in the same tower. That the panic inside Wall Street firms had begun before June 25 suggested to Michael Burry mainly that the Wall Street firms might be working with inside information about the remittance data. "The dealers often owned [mortgage] servicers," he wrote, "and might have been able to get an inside track on the deterioration in the numbers."

In the months leading up to the collapse of OOMLT 2005-3—and all of the other pools of home loans he had bought credit default swaps on—Michael Burry noted several remarks from both Ben Bernanke and the Secretary of the U.S. Treasury, Henry Paulson. Each said, repeatedly, that he saw no possibility of "contagion" in the financial markets from the losses in subprime mortgages. "When I first started shorting these mortgages in 2005," Burry wrote in an e-mail, "I knew full well that it was not likely to pay out within two years—and for a very simple reason. The vast majority of mortgages originated the last few years had a rather ominously attractive feature called the 'teaser rate period.' Those 2005 mortgages are only now reaching the end of their teaser rate periods, and it will be 2008 before the 2006 mortgages get there. What sane person on Earth would confidently conclude in early 2007, smack dab in the midst of the mother of all teaser rate scams, that the subprime fallout will not result in contagion? The bill literally has not even come due."

Across Wall Street, subprime mortgage bond traders were long and wrong, and scrambling to sell their positions—or to buy insurance on them. Michael Burry's credit default swaps were suddenly fashionable. What still shocked him, however, was that the market had been so slow to assimilate material information. "You could see that *all* these deals were sucking wind leading up to the reset date," he said, "and the reset just goosed them into another dimension of *fail*. I was in a state of perpetual disbelief. I would have thought that someone would have recognized what was coming before June 2007. If it really took that June remit data to cause a sudden realization, well, it makes me wonder what a 'Wall Street analyst' really does all day."

By the end of July his marks were moving rapidly in his favor—and he was reading about the genius of people like John Paulson, who had come to the trade a year after he had. The Bloomberg News service ran an article about the few people who appeared to have seen the catastrophe coming. Only one worked as a bond trader inside a big Wall Street firm: a formerly obscure asset-backed bond trader at Deutsche Bank named Greg Lippmann. FrontPoint and Cornwall were both missing from the piece, but the investor most conspicuously absent from the Bloomberg News article sat alone in his office, in

Cupertino, California. Michael Burry clipped the article and e-mailed it around the office with a note: "Lippmann is the guy that essentially took my idea and ran with it. To his credit." His own investors, whose money he was doubling and more, said little. There came no apologies, and no gratitude. "Nobody came back and said, 'Yeah, you were right,'" he said. "It was very quiet. It was extremely quiet. The silence infuriated me." He was left with his favored mode of communication, his letter to investors. In early July 2007, as the markets crashed, he posed an excellent question. "One rather surprising aspect of all this," he wrote, "is that there have been relatively few reports of investors actually being hurt by the subprime mortgage market troubles. . . . Why have we not yet heard of this era's Long-Term Capital?"

Chapter Nine

A Death of Interest

Howie Hubler had grown up in New Jersey and played football at Montclair State College. Everyone who met him noticed his thick football neck and his great huge head and his overbearing manner, which was interpreted as both admirably direct and a mask. He was loud and headstrong and bullying. "When confronted with some intellectual point about his trades, Howie wouldn't go to an intellectual place," said one of the people charged with supervising Hubler in his early days at Morgan Stanley. "He would go to 'Get the hell out of my face.'" Some people enjoyed Hubler, some people didn't, but, by early 2004, what others thought didn't really matter anymore, because for nearly a decade Howie Hubler had made money trading bonds for Morgan Stanley. He ran Morgan Stanley's asset-backed bond trading, which effectively put him in charge of the firm's bets on subprime mortgages. Right up to the point the subprime mortgage bond market boomed, and changed what it meant to be an asset-backed bond trader, Hubler's career had resembled Greg Lippmann's. Like every other asset-backed bond trader, he'd been playing a low-stakes poker game rigged in his favor, since nothing had ever gone seriously wrong in the market. Prices fell, but they always came back. You could either like asset-backed bonds or you could love asset-backed bonds, but there was no point in hating them, because there was no tool for betting against them.

Inside Morgan Stanley, the subprime mortgage lending boom created a who-put-chocolate-in-my peanut-butter moment. The firm had been a leader in extending into consumer loans the financial technology used to package corporate loans. Morgan Stanley's financial intellectuals—their quants—had been instrumental in teaching the rating agencies, Moody's and S&P, how to evaluate CDOs on pools of asset-backed bonds. It was only natural that someone inside Morgan Stanley should also wonder if he might invent a credit default swap on an asset-backed bond. Howie Hubler's subprime mortgage desk was creating bonds at a new and faster rate. To do so, Hubler's group had to "warehouse" loans, sometimes for months. Between the purchase of the loans and the sale of the bonds made up of those loans, his group was exposed to falling prices. "The whole reason we created the credit default swap was to protect the mortgage desk run by Howie Hubler," said one of its inventors. If Morgan Stanley could find someone to sell it insurance on its loans, Hubler could eliminate the market risk of warehousing home loans.

As originally conceived, in 2003, the subprime mortgage credit default swap was a one-off, nonstandard insurance contract, struck between Morgan Stanley and some other bank or insurance company, outside the gaze of the wider market. No ordinary human being had ever heard of these credit default swaps or, if Morgan Stanley had its way, ever would. By design they were arcane, opaque, illiquid, and thus conveniently difficult for anyone but Morgan Stanley to price. "Bespoke," in market parlance. By late 2004 Hubler had grown cynical about certain subprime mortgage bonds—and wanted to find clever ways to bet against them. The same idea had occurred to Morgan

Stanley's intellectuals. In early 2003 one of them had proposed that they cease to be intellectuals and form a little group that he, the intellectual, would manage—a fact that the traders would quickly forget. "One of the quants actually creates all this stuff and they [Hubler and his traders] stole it from him," said a Morgan Stanley bond saleswoman who observed the proceedings up close. One of Hubler's close associates, a trader named Mike Edman, became the official creator of a new idea: a credit default swap on what amounted to a timeless pool of subprime loans.

One risk of betting against subprime loans was that, as long as house prices kept rising, borrowers were able to refinance, and pay off their old loans. The pool of loans on which you've bought insurance shrinks, and the amount of your insurance shrinks with it. Edman's credit default swap solved this problem with some fine print in its contracts, which specified that Morgan Stanley was buying insurance on the last outstanding loan in the pool. Morgan Stanley was making a bet not on the entire pool of subprime home loans but on the few loans in the pool least likely to be repaid. The size of the bet, however, remained the same as if no loan in the pool was ever repaid. They had bought flood insurance that, if a drop of water so much as grazed any part of the house, paid them the value of the entire house.

Thus designed, Morgan Stanley's new bespoke credit default swap was virtually certain one day to pay off. For it to pay off in full required losses in the pool of only 4 percent, which pools of subprime mortgage loans experienced in *good times*. The only problem, from the point of view of Howie Hubler's traders, was finding a Morgan Stanley customer stupid enough to take the other side of the bet—that is, to get the customer to sell Morgan Stanley what amounted to home insurance on a house designated for demolition. "They found one client to take the long side of the triple-B tranche of some piece of shit," says one of their former colleagues, which is a complicated way of saying that they found a mark. A fool. A customer to be taken advantage of. "That's how it starts—it drives Howie's first trade."

By early 2005 Howie Hubler had found a sufficient number of fools in the market to acquire 2 billion dollars' worth of these bespoke credit default swaps. From the point of view of the fools, the credit default swaps Howie Hubler was looking to buy must have looked like free money: Morgan Stanley would pay them 2.5 percent a year over the risk-free rate to own, in effect, investment-grade (triple-B-rated) asset-backed bonds. The idea appealed especially to German institutional investors, who either failed to read the fine print or took the ratings at face value.

By the spring of 2005, Howie Hubler and his traders believed, with reason, that these diabolical insurance policies they'd created were dead certain to pay off. They wanted more of them. It was now, however, that Michael Burry began to agitate to buy standardized credit default swaps. Greg Lippmann at Deutsche Bank, a pair of traders at Goldman Sachs, and a few others came together to hammer out the details of the contract. Mike Edman at Morgan Stanley was dragged kicking and screaming into their discussion, for the moment credit default swaps on subprime mortgage bonds were openly traded and standardized, Howie Hubler's group would lose their ability to peddle their murkier, more private version.

It's now April 2006, and the subprime mortgage bond machine is roaring. Howie Hubler is Morgan Stanley's star bond trader, and his group of eight traders is generating, by their estimate, around 20 percent of Morgan Stanley's profits. Their profits have risen from roughly $400 million in 2004 to $700 million in 2005, on their way to $1 billion in 2006. Hubler will be paid $25 million at the end of the year, but he's no longer happy working as an ordinary bond trader. The best and the brightest Wall Street traders are quitting their big firms to work at hedge funds, where they can make not tens but hundreds of millions.

Collecting nickels and dimes from the trades of unthinking investors felt beneath the dignity of a big-time Wall Street bond trader. "Howie thought the customer business was stupid," says one of several traders closest to Hubler. "It was what he'd always done, but he'd lost interest in it."* Hubler could make hundreds of millions facilitating the idiocy of Morgan Stanley's customers. He could make billions by using the firm's capital to bet against them.

Morgan Stanley management, for its part, always feared that Hubler and his small team of traders might quit and create their own hedge fund. To keep them, they offered Hubler a special deal: his own proprietary trading group, with its own grandiose name: GPCG, or the Global Proprietary Credit Group. In his new arrangement, Hubler would keep for himself some of the profits this group generated. "The idea," says a member of the group, "was for us to go from making one billion dollars a year to two billion dollars a year, right away." The idea, also, was for Hubler and his small group of traders to keep for themselves a big chunk of the profits this group generated. As soon as feasible, Morgan Stanley promised, Hubler would be allowed to spin it off into a separate money management business, of which he'd own 50 percent. Among other things, this business would manage subprime-backed CDOs. They would compete, for instance, with Wing Chau's Harding Advisory.

The putative best and brightest on Morgan Stanley's bond trading floor lobbied to join him. "It was supposed to be the elite of the elite," said one of the traders. "Howie took all the smartest people with him." The chosen few moved to a separate floor in Morgan Stanley's

* Just about everyone involved in the financial crisis stands to lose money if he is caught talking about what he saw and did. Obviously those still employed at the big Wall Street firms, but even those who have moved on, as they have typically signed some nondisclosure agreement. Morgan Stanley's former employees are not quite as spooked as those who worked at Goldman Sachs, but they're close.

midtown Manhattan office, eight floors above their old trading desks. There they erected new walls around themselves, to create at least the illusion that Morgan Stanley had no conflict of interest. The traders back down on the second floor would buy and sell from customers and not pass any information about their dealings to Hubler and his group on the tenth floor. Tony Tufariello, the head of Morgan Stanley's global bond trading and thus in theory Howie Hubler's boss, was so conflicted that he built himself an office inside Howie's group, and bounced back and forth between the second floor and the tenth.* Howie Hubler didn't want only people. He wanted, badly, to take with him his group's trading positions. Their details were complicated enough that one of Morgan Stanley's own subprime mortgage bond traders said, "I don't think any of the people above Howie fully understood the trade he had on." But their gist was simple: Hubler and his group had made a massive bet that subprime loans would go bad. The crown jewel of their elaborate trading positions was still the $2 billion in bespoke credit default swaps Hubler felt certain would one day very soon yield $2 billion in pure profits. The pools of mortgage loans were just about to experience their first losses, and the moment they did, Hubler would be paid in full.

There was, however, a niggling problem: The running premiums on these insurance contracts ate into the short-term returns of Howie's group. "The group was supposed to make two billion dollars a year," said one member. "And we had this credit default swap position that

* Of all the conflicts of interests inside a Wall Street bond trading firm, here was both the most pernicious and least discussed. When a firm makes bets on stocks and bonds for its own account at the same time that it brokers them to customers, it faces great pressure to use its customers for the purposes of its own account. Wall Street firms like to say they build Chinese walls to keep information about customer trading from leaking to their own proprietary traders. Vincent Daniel of FrontPoint Partners offered the most succinct response to this pretense: "When I hear 'Chinese wall,' I think, You're a fucking liar."

was costing us two hundred million dollars." To offset the running cost, Hubler decided to sell some credit default swaps on triple-A-rated subprime CDOs, and take in some premiums of his own.* The problem was that the premiums on the supposedly far less risky triple-A-rated CDOs were only one-tenth of the premiums on the triple-Bs, and so to take in the same amount of money as he was paying out, he'd need to sell credit default swaps in roughly ten times the amount he already owned. He and his traders did this quickly, and apparently without a great deal of discussion, in half a dozen or so massive trades, with Goldman Sachs and Deutsche Bank and a few others.

By the end of January 2007, when the entire subprime mortgage bond industry headed to Las Vegas to celebrate itself, Howie Hubler had sold credit default swaps on roughly 16 billion dollars' worth of triple-A tranches of CDOs. Never had there been such a clear expression of the delusion of the elite Wall Street bond trader and, by extension, the entire subprime mortgage bond market: Between September 2006 and January 2007, the highest-status bond trader inside Morgan Stanley had, for all practical purposes, purchased $16 billion in triple-A-rated CDOs, composed entirely of triple-B-rated subprime mortgage bonds, which became valueless when the underlying pools of subprime loans experienced losses of roughly 8 percent. In effect, Howie Hubler was betting that some of the triple-B-rated subprime bonds would go bad, but not all of them. He was smart enough to be cynical about his market but not smart enough to realize how cynical he needed to be.

Inside Morgan Stanley, there was apparently never much question whether the company's elite risk takers should be allowed to buy $16 billion in subprime mortgage bonds. Howie Hubler's proprietary trading group was of course required to supply information about

* Here it's useful to remember that selling a credit default swap on a thing leaves you with the same financial risk as if you owned it. If the triple-A CDO ends up being worth zero, you lose the same amount whether you bought it outright or sold a credit default swap on it.

its trades to both upper management and risk management, but the information the traders supplied disguised the nature of their risk. The $16 billion in subprime risk Hubler had taken on showed up in Morgan Stanley's risk reports inside a bucket marked "triple A"—which is to say, they might as well have been U.S. Treasury bonds. They showed up again in a calculation known as value at risk (VaR). The tool most commonly used by Wall Street management to figure out what their traders had just done, VaR measured only the degree to which a given stock or bond had jumped around in the past, with the recent movements receiving a greater emphasis than movements in the more distant past. Having never fluctuated much in value, triple-A-rated subprime-backed CDOs registered on Morgan Stanley's internal reports as virtually riskless. In March 2007 Hubler's traders prepared a presentation, delivered by Hubler's bosses to Morgan Stanley's board of directors, that boasted of their "great structural position" in the subprime mortgage market. No one asked the obvious question: What happens to the great structural position if subprime mortgage borrowers begin to default in greater than expected numbers?

Howie Hubler was taking a huge risk, even if he failed to communicate it or, perhaps, understand it. He'd laid a massive bet on very nearly the same CDO tranches that Cornwall Capital had bet against, composed of nearly the same subprime bonds that FrontPoint Partners and Scion Capital had bet against. For more than twenty years, the bond market's complexity had helped the Wall Street bond trader to deceive the Wall Street customer. It was now leading the bond trader to deceive himself.

At issue was how highly correlated the prices of various subprime mortgage bonds inside a CDO might be. Possible answers ranged from zero percent (their prices had nothing to do with each other) to 100 percent (their prices moved in lockstep with each other). Moody's and Standard & Poor's judged the pools of triple-B-rated bonds to have a correlation of around 30 percent, which did not mean anything like what it sounds. It does not mean, for example, that if one bond goes bad, there is a 30 percent chance that the others will go bad too. It means that if one bond goes bad, the others experience very little decline at all.

The pretense that these loans were not all essentially the same, doomed to default en masse the moment house prices stopped rising, had justified the decisions by Moody's and S&P to bestow triple-A ratings on roughly 80 percent of every CDO. (And made the entire CDO business possible.) It also justified Howie Hubler's decision to buy 16 billion dollars' worth of them. Morgan Stanley had done as much as any Wall Street firm to persuade the rating agencies to treat consumer loans as they treated corporate ones—as assets whose risks could be dramatically reduced if bundled together. The people who had done the persuading saw it as a sales job: They knew there was a difference between corporate and consumer loans that the rating agencies had failed to grapple with. The difference was that there was very little history to work with in the subprime mortgage bond market, and no history at all of a collapsing national real estate market. Morgan Stanley's elite bond traders did not spend a lot of time worrying about this. Howie Hubler trusted the ratings.

The Wall Street bond traders on the other end of the phone from Howie Hubler came away with the impression that he considered these bets entirely risk-free. He'd collect a tiny bit of interest . . . for nothing. He wasn't alone in this belief, of course. Hubler and a trader at Merrill Lynch argued back and forth about a possible purchase by Morgan Stanley, from Merrill Lynch, of $2 billion in triple-A CDOs. Hubler wanted Merrill Lynch to pay him 28 basis points (0.28 percent) over the risk-free rate, while Merrill Lynch only wanted to pay 24. On a $2 billion trade—a trade that would, in the end, have transferred a $2 *billion* loss from Merrill Lynch to Morgan Stanley—the two traders were arguing over interest payments amounting to $800,000 a year. Over that sum the deal fell apart. Hubler had the same nit-picking argument with Deutsche Bank, with a difference. Inside Deutsche Bank, Greg Lippmann was now hollering at the top of his lungs that these triple-A CDOs could one day be worth zero. Deutsche Bank's CDO machine paid Hubler the 28 basis points he craved and, in December 2006 and January 2007, cut two deals, of $2 billion each. "When we did the trades, the whole time we were both like, 'We both know there is no risk in these things,'" said the Deutsche Bank CDO executive who dealt with Hubler.

In the murky and curious period from early February to June 2007, the subprime mortgage market resembled a giant helium balloon, bound to earth by a dozen or so big Wall Street firms. Each firm held its rope; one by one, they realized that no matter how strongly they pulled, the balloon would eventually lift them off their feet. In June, one by one, they silently released their grip. By edict of CEO Jamie Dimon, J.P. Morgan had abandoned the market by the late fall of 2006. Deutsche Bank, because of Lippmann, had always held on tenuously. Goldman Sachs was next, and did not merely let go, but turned and made a big bet against the subprime market—further accelerating the balloon's fatal ascent.* When its subprime hedge funds crashed in June, Bear Stearns was forcibly severed from its line—and the balloon drifted farther from the ground.

* The timing of Goldman's departure from the subprime market is interesting. Long after the fact, Goldman would claim it had made that move in December 2006. Traders at big Wall Street firms who dealt with Goldman felt certain that the firm did not reverse itself until the spring and early summer of 2007, after New Century, the nation's biggest subprime lender, filed for bankruptcy. If this is indeed when Goldman "got short," it would explain the chaos in both the subprime market and Goldman Sachs, perceived by Mike Burry and others, in late June. Goldman Sachs did not leave the house before it began to burn; it was merely the first to dash through the exit—and then it closed the door behind it.

Not long before that, in April 2007, Howie Hubler, perhaps having misgivings about the size of his gamble, had struck a deal with the guy who ran the doomed Bear Stearns hedge funds, Ralph Cioffi. On April 2, the nation's largest subprime mortgage lender, New Century, was swamped by defaults and filed for bankruptcy. Morgan Stanley would sell Cioffi $6 billion of his $16 billion in triple-A CDOs. The price had fallen a bit—Cioffi demanded a yield of 40 basis points (0.40 percent) over the risk-free rate. Hubler conferred with Morgan Stanley's president, Zoe Cruz; together they decided that they'd rather keep the subprime risk than realize a loss that amounted to a few tens of millions of dollars. It was a decision that wound up costing Morgan Stanley nearly $6 billion, and yet Morgan Stanley's CEO, John Mack, never got involved. "Mack never came and talked to Howie," says one of Hubler's closest associates. "The entire time, Howie never had a single sit-down with Mack."*

By May 2007, however, there was a growing dispute between

* There is some dispute about the conversations between Hubler and Cruz. The version of events offered by people close to Zoe Cruz is that she was worried about the legal risk of doing business with Bear Stearns's troubled hedge funds, and that Hubler never completely explained the risk of triple-A-rated CDOs to her, and led her to believe that Morgan Stanley stood no chance of suffering a huge loss—probably because Hubler himself didn't understand the risk. Hubler's friends claim that Cruz seized effective control of Hubler's trade and prevented him from ditching some large chunk of his triple-A CDOs. In my view, and in the view of Wall Street traders, Hubler's story line is far less plausible. "There's no fucking way he said, 'I have to get out now' and she said no," says one trader close to the situation. "No way Howie ever said, 'If we don't get out now we might lose ten billion dollars.' Howie presented her with a case for not getting out." The ability of Wall Street traders to see themselves in their success and their management in their failure would later be echoed, when their firms, which disdained the need for government regulation in good times, insisted on being rescued by government in bad times. Success was individual achievement; failure was a social problem.

Howie Hubler and Morgan Stanley. Amazingly, it had nothing to do with the wisdom of owning $16 billion in complex securities whose value ultimately turned on the ability of a Las Vegas stripper with five investment properties, or a Mexican strawberry picker with a single $750,000 home, to make rapidly rising interest payments. The dispute was over Morgan Stanley's failure to deliver on its promise to spin Hubler's proprietary trading group off into its own money management firm, of which he would own 50 percent. Outraged by Morgan Stanley's foot-dragging, Howie Hubler threatened to quit. To keep him, Morgan Stanley promised to pay him, and his traders, an even bigger chunk of GPCG's profits. In 2006, Hubler had been paid $25 million; in 2007, it was understood, he would make far more.

A month after Hubler and his traders improved the terms of trade between themselves and their employer, Morgan Stanley finally asked the uncomfortable question: What happened to their massive subprime mortgage market bet if lower-middle-class Americans defaulted in greater than expected numbers? How did the bet perform, for instance, using the assumption of losses generated by the most pessimistic Wall Street analyst? Up to that point, Hubler's bet had been "stress tested" for scenarios in which subprime pools experienced losses of 6 percent, the highest losses from recent history. Now Hubler's traders were asked to imagine what would become of their bet if losses reached 10 percent. The demand came directly from Morgan Stanley's chief risk officer, Tom Daula, and Hubler and his traders were angered and disturbed that he would issue it. "It was more than a little weird," says one of them. "There was a lot of angst about it. It was sort of viewed as, These folks don't know what they're talking about. If losses go to ten percent there will be, like, a million homeless people." (Losses in the pools Hubler's group had bet on would eventually reach 40 percent.) As a senior Morgan Stanley executive outside Hubler's group put it, "They didn't want to show you the results. They kept saying, *That state of the world can't happen.*"

It took Hubler's traders ten days to produce the result they really didn't want to show anyone: Losses of 10 percent turned their complicated bet in subprime mortgages from a projected profit of $1 billion into a projected loss of $2.7 billion. As one senior Morgan Stanley executive put it, "The risk officers came back from the stress test looking very upset." Hubler and his traders tried to calm him down. Relax, they said, those kinds of losses will never happen.

The risk department had trouble relaxing, however. To them it seemed as if Hubler and his traders didn't fully understand their own gamble. Hubler kept saying he was betting against the subprime bond market. But if so, why did he lose billions if it collapsed? As one senior Morgan Stanley risk manager put it, "It's one thing to bet on red or black and know that you are betting on red or black. It's another to bet on a form of red and not to know it."

In early July, Morgan Stanley received its first wake-up call. It came from Greg Lippmann and his bosses at Deutsche Bank, who, in a conference call, told Howie Hubler and his bosses that the $4 billion in credit default swaps Hubler had sold Deutsche Bank's CDO desk six months earlier had moved in Deutsche Bank's favor. Could Morgan Stanley please wire $1.2 billion to Deutsche Bank by the end of the day? Or, as Lippmann actually put it—according to someone who heard the exchange—*Dude, you owe us one point two billion.*

Triple-A-rated subprime CDOs, of which there were now hundreds of billions of dollars' worth buried inside various Wall Street firms, and which were assumed to be riskless, were now, according to Greg Lippmann, only worth 70 cents on the dollar. Howie Hubler had the same reaction. *What do you mean seventy? Our model says they are worth ninety-five*, said one of the Morgan Stanley people on the phone call.

Our model says they are worth seventy, replied one of the Deutsche Bank people.

Well, our model says they are worth ninety-five, repeated the Morgan Stanley person, and then went on about how the correlation among the thousands of triple-B-rated bonds in his CDOs was very low, and so a few bonds going bad didn't imply they were all worthless.

At which point Greg Lippmann just said, *Dude, fuck your model. I'll make you a market. They are seventy–seventy-seven. You have three choices. You can sell them back to me at seventy. You can buy some more at seventy-seven. Or you can give me my fucking one point two billion dollars.*

Morgan Stanley didn't want to buy any more subprime mortgage bonds. Howie Hubler didn't want to buy any more subprime-backed bonds: He'd released his grip on the rope that tethered him to the rising balloon. Yet he didn't want to take a loss, and insisted that, despite his unwillingness to buy more at 77, his triple-A CDOs were still worth 95 cents on the dollar. He simply handed the matter to his superiors, who conferred with their equivalents at Deutsche Bank, and finally agreed to wire over $600 million. The alternative, for Deutsche Bank, was to submit the matter to a panel of three Wall Street banks, randomly selected, to determine what these triple-A CDOs were actually worth. It was a measure of the confusion and delusion on Wall Street that Deutsche Bank didn't care to run that risk.

At any rate, from Deutsche Bank's point of view, the collateral wasn't that big a deal. "When Greg made that call," said a senior Deutsche Bank executive, "it was like last on the list of the things we needed to do to keep our business running. Morgan Stanley had seventy billion dollars in capital. We knew the money was there."

There was even some argument inside Deutsche Bank as to whether Lippmann's price was accurate. "It was such a big number," said a person involved in these discussions, "that a lot of people said it couldn't possibly be right. Morgan Stanley couldn't possibly owe us one point two billion dollars."

They did, however. It was the beginning of a slide that would end just a few months later, in a conference call between Morgan Stanley's CEO and Wall Street's analysts. The defaults mounted, the bonds universally crashed, and the CDOs composed of the bonds followed. Several times on the way down, Deutsche Bank offered Morgan Stanley the chance to exit its trade. The first time Greg Lippmann called him, Howie Hubler might have exited his $4 billion trade with Deutsche Bank at a loss of $1.2 billion; the next time Lippmann called, the price of getting out had risen to $1.5 billion. Each time, Howie Hubler, or one of his traders, argued about the price, and declined to exit. "We fought with those cocksuckers all the way down," says one Deutsche Bank trader. And, all the way down, the debt collectors at Deutsche Bank sensed the bond traders at Morgan Stanley misunderstood their own trade. They weren't lying; they genuinely failed to understand the nature of the subprime CDO. The correlation among triple-B-rated subprime bonds was not 30 percent; it was 100 percent. When one collapsed, they all collapsed, because they were all driven by the same broader economic forces. In the end, it made little sense for a CDO to fall from 100 to 95 to 77 to 70 and down to 7. The subprime bonds beneath them were either all bad or all good. The CDOs were worth either zero or 100.

At a price of 7, Greg Lippmann allowed Morgan Stanley to exit a trade it had entered into at roughly 100 cents on the dollar. On the first $4 billion of Howie Hubler's $16 billion folly, the loss came to roughly $3.7 billion. By then Lippmann was no longer speaking to Howie Hubler, because Howie Hubler was no longer employed at

Morgan Stanley. "Howie was on this vacation thing for a few weeks," says one member of his group, "and then he never came back." He'd been allowed to resign in October 2007, with many millions of dollars the firm had promised him at the end of 2006, to prevent him from quitting. The total losses he left behind him were reported to the Morgan Stanley board as a bit more than $9 billion: the single largest trading loss in the history of Wall Street. Other firms would lose more, much more; but those losses were typically associated with the generation of subprime mortgage loans. Citigroup and Merrill Lynch and others sat on huge piles of the things when the market crashed, but these were the by-product of their CDO machines. They owned subprime mortgage–backed CDOs less for their own sake than for the fees that their deals would generate once they had sold them. Howie Hubler's loss was the result of a simple bet. Hubler and his traders thought they were smart guys put on earth to exploit the market's stupid inefficiencies. Instead, they simply contributed more inefficiency.

Retiring to New Jersey, with an unlisted number, Howie Hubler took with him the comforting sense that he was not the biggest fool at the table. He might have let go of the balloon rope too late to save Morgan Stanley, but, as he fell to earth, he could look up at the balloon drifting higher in the sky and see Wall Street bodies still dangling from it. In early July, just days before Greg Lippmann had called him to ask for $1.2 billion, Hubler had found a pair of buyers for his triple-A-rated CDOs. The first was the Mizuho Financial Group, a trading arm of Japan's second biggest bank. As a people, the Japanese had been bewildered by these new American financial creations, and steered clear of them. Mizuho Financial Group, for some reason that would remain known only to itself, set itself up as a clever trader of U.S. subprime bonds, and took $1 billion in subprime-backed CDOs off Morgan Stanley's hands.

The other, bigger, buyer was UBS—which took $2 billion in Howie Hubler's triple-A CDOs, along with a couple of hundred million dollars' worth of his short position in triple-B-rated bonds. That is, in July, moments before the market crashed, UBS looked at Howie Hubler's trade and said, "We want some of that, too." Thus Howie Hubler's personal purchase of $16 billion in triple-A-rated CDOs dwindled to something like $13 billion. A few months later, seeking to explain to its shareholders the $37.4 billion it had lost in the U.S. subprime markets, UBS would publish a semi-frank report, in which it revealed that a small group of U.S. bond traders employed by UBS had lobbied hard right up until the end for the bank to buy even more of other Wall Street firms' subprime mortgage bonds. "If people had known about the trade, it would have been open revolt," said one UBS bond trader close to the action. "It was a very controversial trade in UBS. It was kept very, very secret. There were a lot of people, had they known the trade was happening, would have screamed eight ways from Sunday. We took the correlation trade off Howie's hands when everyone knew the correlation was one." (Which is to say, 100 percent.) He further explained that the traders at UBS who executed the trade were motivated mainly by their own models—which, at the moment of the trade, suggested they had turned a profit of $30 million.

On December 19, 2007, Morgan Stanley held a call for investors. The company wanted to explain how a trading loss of $9.2 billion—give or take a few billion—had more than overwhelmed the profits generated by its fifty thousand or so employees. "The results we announced today are embarrassing for me; for our firm," began John Mack. "This was a result of an error in judgment incurred on one desk in our Fixed Income area, and also a failure to manage that risk appropriately. . . .Virtually all write downs this quarter were the result of trading about [*sic*] a single desk on our mortgage business." The CEO explained that Morgan Stanley had certain "hedges" against its subprime mortgage risk and that "the hedges didn't perform adequately in extraordinary market condition of late October and November." But market conditions in October and November were not extraordinary; in October and November, for the first time, the market began accurately to price subprime mortgage risk. What was extraordinary is what had happened leading up to October and November.

After saying he wanted "to be absolutely clear [that] as head of this firm, I take responsibility for performance," Mack took questions from the bank analysts of other Wall Street firms. It took this group a while to get to the source of embarrassment, but eventually they did. Four analysts elected not to probe Mack too closely about what was almost certainly the single greatest proprietary trading loss in Wall Street history, and then William Tanona, from Goldman Sachs, spoke:

TANONA: A question on the risk again, [which] I know everybody has been dancing around. . . . Help us understand how this could happen that you could take this large of a loss. I mean, I would imagine that you guys have position limits and risk limits as such. I just—it [bewilders] me to think that you guys could have one desk that could lose $8 billion [*sic*].

JOHN MACK: That's a wrong question.

TANONA: Excuse me?

JOHN MACK: Hello. Hi. And . . .

TANONA: I missed you . . .

JOHN MACK: Bill, look, let's be clear. One, this trade was recognized and entered into our accounts. Two, it was entered into our risk management system. It's very simple. When these got, it's simple, it's very painful, so I'm not being glib. When these guys stress loss the scenario on putting on this position, they did not envision . . . that we could have this degree of default, right. It is fair to say that our risk management division did not stress those losses as well.* It's just simple as that. Those are big fat tail risks that caught us hard, right. That's what happened.

TANONA: Okay. Fair enough. I guess the other thing I would question. I am surprised that your trading VaR stayed stable in the quarter given this level of loss, and given that I would suspect that these were trading assets. So can you help me understand why your VaR didn't increase in the quarter dramatically?†

MACK: Bill, I think VaR is a very good representation of liquid trading risk. But in terms of the (inaudible) of that, I am very happy to get back to you on that when we have been out of this, because I can't answer that at the moment.

The meaningless flow of words might have left the audience with the sense that it was incapable of parsing the deep complexity of Morgan Stanley's bond trading business. What the words actually revealed was that the CEO himself didn't really understand the situation. John Mack was widely regarded among his CEO peers as relatively well informed about his bond firm's trading risks. After all, he was himself a former bond trader, and had been brought in to embolden Morgan Stanley's risk-taking culture. Yet not only had he failed to grasp what his traders were up to, back when they were still

* It's too much to expect the people who run big Wall Street firms to speak plain English, since so much of their livelihood depends on people believing that what they do cannot be translated into plain English. What John Mack's trying to say, without coming right out and saying that no one else at Morgan Stanley had a clue what risks Howie Hubler was running, is that no one else at Morgan Stanley had a clue what risks Howie Hubler was running—and neither did Howie Hubler.

† Another way to put the same question: How could Howie Hubler's bonds plunge from 100 to 7 and the reports you received still suggest that they were incapable of dramatic movement?

up to it; he couldn't even fully explain what they had done after they had lost $9 billion.

At length the moment had come: The last buyer of subprime mortgage risk had stopped buying. On August 1, 2007, shareholders brought their first lawsuit against Bear Stearns in connection with the collapse of its subprime-backed hedge funds. Among its less visible effects was to alarm greatly the three young men at Cornwall Capital who sat on what was for them an enormous pile of credit default swaps purchased mostly from Bear Stearns. Ever since Las Vegas, Charlie Ledley had been unable to shake his sense of the enormity of the events they were living through. Ben Hockett, the only one of the three who had worked inside a big Wall Street firm, also tended to travel very quickly in his mind to some catastrophic endgame. And Jamie Mai just thought a lot of people on Wall Street were scumbags. All three were worried that Bear Stearns might fail and be unable to make good on its gambling debts. "There can come a moment when you can't trade with a Wall Street firm anymore," said Ben, "and it can come like *that*."

That first week in August, they kicked around and tried to get a feel for the prices of double-A-rated CDOs, which just a few months earlier had been trading at prices that suggested they were essentially riskless. "The underlying bonds were collapsing and all the people we'd dealt with were saying we'll give you two points," said Charlie. Right up through late July, Bear Stearns and Morgan Stanley were saying, in effect, that double-A CDOs were worth 98 cents on the dollar. The argument between Howie Hubler and Greg Lippmann was replaying itself throughout the market.

Cornwall Capital owned credit default swaps on twenty crappy CDOs, but each was crappy in its own special way, and so it was hard to get a read on exactly where they stood. One thing was clear: Their long-shot bet was no longer a long shot. Their Wall Street dealers had always told them that they'd never be able to get out of these obscure credit default swaps on double-A tranches of CDOs, but the market was panicking, and seemed eager to buy insurance on anything related to subprime mortgage bonds. The calculation had changed: For the first time, Cornwall stood to lose quite a bit of money if something happened that caused the market to rebound—if, say, the U.S. government stepped in and guaranteed all the subprime mortgages. And of course if Bear Stearns went down, they'd lose it all. Oddly alert to the possibility of catastrophe, they now felt oddly exposed to one. They rushed to cover themselves—to find some buyer of these strange and newly relevant insurance policies they had accumulated.

The job fell to Ben Hockett. Charlie Ledley had tried a few times to act as their trader and failed miserably. "There are all these little rules," said Charlie. "You have to know exactly what to say, and if you don't, everyone gets pissed off at you. I'd think I'd be saying, like, 'Sell!' and it turned out I was saying, like, 'Buy!' I sort of stumbled into the realization that I should not be doing trades." Ben had traded for a living and was the only one of the three who knew what to say and how to say it. Ben, however, was in the south of England, on vacation with his wife's family.

And so it was that Ben Hockett found himself sitting in a pub called The Powder Monkey, in the city of Exmouth, in the county of Devon, England, seeking a buyer of $205 million in credit default swaps on the double-A tranches of mezzanine subprime CDOs. The Powder Monkey had the town's lone reliable wireless Internet connection, and none of the enthusiastic British drinkers seemed to mind, or even notice, the American in the corner table bashing on his Bloomberg machine and talking into his cell phone from two in the afternoon until eleven at night. Up to that point, only three Wall Street firms had proved willing to deal with Cornwall Capital and give them the ISDA agreements necessary for dealing in credit default swaps: Bear

Stearns, Deutsche Bank, and Morgan Stanley. "Ben had always told us that it's *possible* to do a trade without an ISDA, but it was really not typical," said Charlie. This was not a typical moment. On Friday, August 3, Ben called every major Wall Street firm and said, *You don't know me and I know you won't give us an ISDA agreement, but I've got insurance on subprime mortgage–backed CDOs I'm willing to sell. Would you be willing to deal with me without an ISDA agreement?* "The stock answer was no," said Ben. "And I'd say, 'Call your head of credit trading and call your head of risk management and see if they feel differently.'" That Friday only one bank seemed eager to deal with him: UBS. And they were very eager. The last man clinging to the helium balloon had just let go of his rope.

On Monday, August 6, Ben returned to The Powder Monkey and began to trade. For insurance policies costing half of 1 percent, UBS was now offering him 30 points up front—that is, Cornwall's $205 million in credit default swaps, which cost about a million bucks to buy, were suddenly worth a bit more than $60 million (30 percent of $205 million). UBS was no longer alone in their interest, however; the people at Citigroup and Merrill Lynch and Lehman Brothers, so dismissive on Friday, were eager on Monday. All of them were sweating and moaning to price the risks of these CDOs their firms had created. "It was easier for me because they had to look at every single deal," said Ben. "And I just wanted money." Cornwall had twenty separate positions to sell. Ben's Internet connection came and went, as did his cell phone reception. Only the ardor of the Wall Street firms, desperate to buy fire insurance on their burning home, remained undimmed. "It's the first time we're seeing any prices that reflect anything close to like what they're really worth," said Charlie. "We had positions that were being valued by Bear Stearns at six hundred grand that went to six million *the next day*."

By eleven o clock Thursday night Ben was finished. It was August 9, the same day that the French bank BNP announced that investors in their money market funds would be prevented from withdrawing their savings because of problems with U.S. subprime mortgages. Ben, Charlie, and Jamie were not clear on why three-quarters of their bets had been bought by a Swiss bank. The letters *U B S* had scarcely been mentioned inside Cornwall Capital until the bank had started begging them to sell them what was now very high-priced subprime insurance. "I had no particular reason to think UBS was even in the subprime business," said Charlie. "In retrospect, I can't believe we didn't turn around and get short UBS." In taking Cornwall's credit default swaps off its hands, neither UBS nor any of their other Wall Street buyers expressed the faintest reservations that they were now assuming the risk that Bear Stearns might fail: That thought, inside big Wall Street firms, was still unthinkable. Cornwall Capital, started four and a half years earlier with $110,000, had just netted, from a million-dollar bet, more than $80 million. "There was a relief that we had not been the chumps at the table," said Jamie. They had not been the chumps at the table. The long shot had paid 80:1. And no one at The Powder Monkey ever asked Ben what he was up to.

His wife's extended English family of course wondered where he had been, and he tried to explain. He thought what was happening was critically important. The banking system was insolvent, he assumed, and that implied some grave upheaval. When banking stops, credit stops, and when credit stops, trade stops, and when trade stops—well, the city of Chicago had only eight days of chlorine on hand for its water supply. Hospitals ran out of medicine. The entire modern world was premised on the ability to buy now and pay later. "I'd come home at midnight and try to talk to my brother-in-law about our children's future," said Ben. "I asked everyone in the house to make sure their accounts at HSBC were insured. I told them to keep some cash on hand, as we might face some disruptions. But it was hard to explain." How do you explain to an innocent citizen of the free world the importance of a credit default swap on a double-A tranche of a subprime-backed collateralized debt obligation? He tried, but his English in-laws just looked at him strangely. They understood that someone else had just lost a great deal of money and Ben had just made a great deal of money, but never got much past that. "I can't really talk to them about it," he says. "They're English."

Twenty-two days later, on August 31, 2007, Michael Burry lifted the side pocket and began to unload his own credit default swaps in earnest. His investors could have their money back. There was now more than twice as much of it as they had given him. Just a few months earlier, Burry was being offered 200 basis points—or 2 percent of the principal—for his credit default swaps, which peaked at $1.9 billion. Now he was being offered 75, 80, and 85 *percent* by Wall Street firms desperate to cushion their fall. At the end of the quarter, he'd report that the fund was up more than 100 percent. By the end of the year, in a portfolio of less than $550 million, he would have realized profits of more than $720 million. Still he heard not a peep from his investors. "Even when it was clear it was a big year and I was proven right, there was no triumph in it," he said. "Making money was nothing like I thought it would be." To his founding investor, Gotham Capital, he shot off an unsolicited e-mail that said only, "You're welcome." He'd already decided to kick them out of the fund, and insist that they sell their stake in his business. When they asked him to suggest a price, he replied, "How about you keep the tens of millions you nearly prevented me from earning for you last year and we call it even?"

When he'd started out, he'd decided not to charge his investors the usual 2 percent or so management fee for his services. In the one year in which he had not turned his investors' money into more money, the absence of a fee had meant having to fire employees. He now wrote his investors a letter letting them know he'd changed his policy—which enabled his investors to be angry with him all over again, even as he was making them rich. "I just wonder where you come up with the ways you find to piss people off," one of his e-mail friends wrote to him. "You have a gift."

One of the things he'd learned about Asperger's, since he'd discovered that he had it, was the role that his interests served. They were a safe place to which he could retreat from a hostile world. That was why people with Asperger's experienced them so intensely. That was also, oddly, why they couldn't control them. "The therapist I see helped me figure it out," he wrote in an e-mail, "and it makes a lot of sense when I look back at my own life:

> Let me see if I can get it right—it always sounds better when the therapist says it. Well, if you start with a person who has tremendous difficulty integrating himself into the social workings of society, and often feels misunderstood, slighted, and lonely as a result, you will see where an intense interest can be something that builds up the ego in the classical sense. Asperger's kids can apply tremendous focus and ramp up knowledge of a subject in which they have an interest very quickly, often well beyond the level of any peers. That ego-reinforcement is very soothing, providing something that Asperger's kids just do not experience often, if at all. As long as the interest provides that reinforcement, there is little danger of a change. But when the interest encounters a rocky patch, or the person experiences failure in the interest, the negativity can be felt very intensely, especially when it comes from other people. The interest in such a case can simply start to mimic all that the Asperger's person was trying to escape—the apparent persecution, the misunderstanding, the exclusion by others. And the person with Asperger's would have to find another interest to build up and maintain the ego.

Most of 2006 and early 2007 Dr. Michael Burry had experienced as a private nightmare. In an e-mail, he wrote, "The partners closest to me tend to ultimately hate me. . . . This business kills a part of life that is pretty essential. The thing is, I haven't identified what it kills. But it is something vital that is dead inside of me. I can feel it." As his interest in financial markets seeped out of him, he bought his first guitar. It was strange: He couldn't play the guitar and had no talent for it. He didn't even *want* to play the guitar. He just needed to learn all about the sorts of wood used to make guitars, and to buy guitars and tubes and amps. He just needed to . . . know everything there was to know about guitars.

He'd picked an intelligent moment for the death of his interest. It was the moment at which the end was written: the moment at which there was nothing left to prevent. Six months from that moment, the International Monetary Fund would put losses on U.S.-originated subprime-related assets at a trillion dollars. One trillion dollars in losses had been created by American financiers, out of whole cloth, and embedded in the American financial system. Each Wall Street firm held some share of those losses, and could do nothing to avoid them. No Wall Street firm would be able to extricate itself, as there were no longer any buyers. It was as if bombs of differing sizes had been placed in virtually every major Western financial institution. The fuses had been lit and could not be extinguished. All that remained was to observe the speed of the spark, and the size of the explosions.

CHAPTER TEN

Two Men in a Boat

Virtually no one—be they homeowners, financial institutions, rating agencies, regulators, or investors—anticipated what is occurring.

—Deven Sharma, president of S&P
Testimony before U.S. House of Representatives
October 22, 2008

Pope Benedict XVI was the first to predict the crisis in the global financial system . . . Italian Finance Minister Giulio Tremonti said. "The prediction that an undisciplined economy would collapse by its own rules can be found" in an article written by Cardinal Joseph Ratzinger [in 1985], Tremonti said yesterday at Milan's Cattolica University.

—Bloomberg News, November 20, 2008

Greg Lippmann had imagined the subprime mortgage market as a great financial tug-of-war: On one side pulled the Wall Street machine making the loans, packaging the bonds, and repackaging the worst of the bonds into CDOs and then, when they ran out of loans, creating fake ones out of thin air; on the other side, his noble army of short sellers betting against the loans. The optimists versus the pessimists. The fantasists versus the realists. The sellers of credit default swaps versus the buyers. The wrong versus the right. The metaphor was apt, up to a point: this point. Now the metaphor was two men in a boat, tied together by a rope, fighting to the death. One man kills the other, hurls his inert body over the side—only to discover himself being yanked over the side. "Being short in 2007 and making money from it was fun, because we were short *bad guys,*" said Steve Eisman. "In 2008 it was the entire financial system that was at risk. We were still short. But you don't want the system to crash. It's sort of like the flood's about to happen and you're Noah. You're on the ark. Yeah, you're okay. But you are not happy looking out at the flood. That's not a *happy* moment for Noah."

By the end of 2007 FrontPoint's bets against subprime mortgages had paid off so spectacularly that they had doubled the size of their fund, from a bit over $700 million to $1.5 billion. The moment it was clear they had made a fantastic pile of money, both Danny and Vinny wanted to cash in their bets. Neither one of them had ever come around to completely trusting Greg Lippmann, and their mistrust extended even to this fantastic gift he had given them. "I'd never buy a car from Lippmann," said Danny. "But I bought five hundred million dollars' worth of credit default swaps from him." Vinny had an almost karmic concern about making so much money so quickly. "It was the trade of a lifetime," he said. "If we gave up the trade of a lifetime for greed, I'd have killed myself."

All of them, including Eisman, thought Eisman was temperamentally less than perfectly suited to making short-term trading judgments. He was emotional, and he acted on his emotions. His bets against subprime mortgage bonds were to him more than just bets; he intended them almost as insults. Whenever Wall Street people tried to argue—as they often did—that the subprime lending problem was caused by the mendacity and financial irresponsibility of ordinary Americans, he'd say, "What—the entire American population woke up one morning and said, 'Yeah, I'm going to lie on my loan application'? Yeah, people lied. They lied because they were told to lie." The outrage that fueled his gamble was aimed not at the entire financial system but at the people at the top of it, who knew better, or should have: the people inside the big Wall Street firms. "It was more than an argument," Eisman said. "It was a moral crusade. The world was upside down." The subprime loans at the bottom of their gamble were worthless, he argued, and if the loans were worthless, the insurance they owned on those loans should go nowhere but up. And so they held on to their credit default swaps, and waited for more loans to default. "Vinny and I would have done fifty million dollars and made twenty-five million dollars," said Danny. "Steve did five hundred and fifty million and made four hundred million."

The Great Treasure Hunt had yielded a long list of companies exposed to subprime loans. By March 14, 2008, they had sold short the stocks of virtually every financial firm in any way connected to the doomsday machine. "We were positioned for Armageddon," said Eisman, "but always at the back of our minds was, What if Armageddon doesn't happen?"

On March 14, the question became moot. From the time Bear Stearns's subprime hedge funds had collapsed, in June 2007, the market was asking questions about the rest of Bear Stearns. Over the past decade, like every other Wall Street firm, Bear Stearns had increased the size of the bets it made with every dollar of its capital. In just the past five years, Bear Stearns's leverage had gone from 20:1 to 40:1. Merrill Lynch's had gone from 16:1 in 2001 to 32:1 in 2007. Morgan Stanley and Citigroup were now at 33:1, Goldman Sachs looked conservative at 25:1, but then Goldman had a gift for disguising how leveraged it actually was. To bankrupt any of these firms, all that was required was a very slight decline in the value of their assets.

The trillion-dollar question was, What were those assets? Until March 14, the stock market had given the big Wall Street firms the benefit of the doubt. No one knew what was going on inside Bear Stearns or Merrill Lynch or Citigroup, but these places had always been the smart money, ergo their bets must be the smart bets. On March 14, the market changed its opinion.

That morning, Eisman had been invited on short notice by Deutsche Bank's prominent bank analyst Mike Mayo to address a roomful of big investors. In an auditorium at Deutsche Bank's Wall Street headquarters, Eisman was scheduled to precede the retired chairman of the Federal Reserve, Alan Greenspan, and be paired with a famous investor named Bill Miller—who also happened to own more than $200 million of Bear Stearns stock. Eisman obviously thought it insane that anyone would sink huge sums of money into any Wall Street firm. Greenspan he viewed as almost beneath his contempt, which was saying something. "I think Alan Greenspan will go down as the worst chairman of the Federal Reserve in history," he'd say, when given the slightest chance. "That he kept interest rates too low for too long is the least of it. I'm convinced that he knew what was happening in subprime, and he ignored it, because the consumer getting screwed was not his problem. I sort of feel sorry for him because he's a guy who is really smart who was basically wrong about everything."

There was now hardly an important figure on Wall Street whom Eisman had not insulted, or tried to. At a public event in Hong Kong, after the chairman of HSBC had claimed that his bank's subprime losses were "contained," Eisman had raised his hand and said, "You don't actually believe that, do you? Because your whole book is fucked." Eisman had invited the bullish-on-subprime Bear Stearns analyst Gyan Sinha to his office and grilled him so mercilessly that a Bear Stearns salesman had called afterward and complained.

"Gyan is upset," he said.

"Tell him not to be," said Eisman. "We enjoyed it!"

At the end of 2007, Bear Stearns had nevertheless invited Eisman to a warm and fuzzy meet and greet with their new CEO, Alan Schwartz. *Christmas with Bear*, they called it. Schwartz told his audience how "crazy" the subprime bond market was, as no one in it seemed to be able to agree on the price of any given bond.

"And whose fault is that?" Eisman had blurted out. "This is how you guys *wanted* it. So you could rip off your customers."

To which the new CEO replied, "I don't want to cast blame."

Which Wall Street big shots Eisman had insulted was a matter of which Wall Street big shots' presence Eisman was allowed into. On March 14, 2008, he was invited into the presence of one of the biggest and most famous bullish investors in Wall Street banks, plus that of the illustrious former chairman of the Federal Reserve. It was a busy day in the markets—there were rumors that Bear Stearns might be having troubles—but, given a choice between watching the markets and watching Eisman, Danny Moses and Vincent Daniel and Porter Collins didn't think twice. "Let's be honest," said Vinny. "We went for the entertainment. It's like Ali–Frazier. Why would you *not* want to be there?" They drove to the fight with Ali, but took seats in the back row, and prepared to hide.

Eisman sat at a long table with the legendary Bill Miller. Miller spoke for maybe three minutes, and explained the wisdom of his investment in Bear Stearns. "And now for our bear," said Mike Mayo. "Steve Eisman."

"I got to stand up for this," said Eisman.

Miller had given his little talk sitting down. The event was meant to be more of a panel discussion than a speech, but Eisman made for the podium. Noting the presence of his mother in the third row, but ignoring his partners in the back, along with the crowd of twenty his partners had alerted (free tickets to Ali–Frazier!), Eisman launched a ruthlessly reasonable dissection of the U.S. financial system. "Why

This Time Is Different" was the title of his speech—even though it still wasn't clear he was meant to be giving anything so formal as a speech. "We are going through the greatest deleveraging in the history of financial services and it's going to go on and on and on," he said. "There is no solution other than time. Time to take the pain . . ."

As Eisman had risen, Danny had sunk in his chair, instinctively. "There is always the possibility of embarrassment," Danny said. "But it's like watching a car crash. You can't *not* watch." All around him men hunched over their BlackBerrys. They wanted to hear what Eisman had to say, clearly, but the stock market was distracting them from the show. At 9:13, as Eisman was finding his place at the front of the room, Bear Stearns had announced that it had gotten a loan from J.P. Morgan. Nine minutes later, as Bill Miller explained why it was such a good idea to own stock in Bear Stearns, Alan Schwartz had issued a press release. "Bear Stearns has been the subject of a multitude of rumors concerning our liquidity," it began. *Liquidity*. When an executive said his bank had plenty of liquidity it *always* meant that it didn't.

At 9:41, or roughly the time Eisman made his bid for the podium, Danny sold some Bear Stearns shares that Eisman, oddly enough, had bought the night before, at $53 a share. They'd made a few bucks, but it was still mystifying that Eisman had bought them, over everyone else's objections. Every now and then, Eisman made some short-term trade of trivial size that totally contradicted everything they believed. Danny and Vinny both thought the problem in this case was Eisman's affinity for Bear Stearns. The most hated firm on Wall Street, famous mainly for its total indifference to the good opinion of its competitors, Eisman identified with the place! "He'd always say Bear Stearns could never be acquired by anyone because the culture of the firm could never be assimilated into anything else," said Vinny. "I think he saw some of himself in them." Eisman's wife, Valerie, had her own theory. "It's this weird antidote he has to his 'the world is going to blow up' theory," she said. "Every now and then he would show up at home with this totally bizarre long."

Whatever the psychological origins of Eisman's sudden urge, the previous afternoon, to buy a few shares in Bear Stearns, Danny was just glad to be done with the matter. Eisman was now explaining why the world was going to blow up, but his partners were only half-listening . . . because the financial world was blowing up. "The minute Steve starts to speak," said Vinny, "the stock starts to fall." As Eisman explained why no one in his right mind would own the very shares he had bought sixteen hours earlier, Danny dashed off text messages to his partners.

9:49. Oh my—Bear at 47

"If [the U.S. financial system] sounds like a circular Ponzi scheme it's because it is."

9:55. Bear is 43 last OMG

"The banks in the United States are only beginning to come to grips with their massive loan problems. For instance, I wouldn't own a single bank in the State of Florida because I think they might all be gone."

10:02. Bear 29 last!!!!

"The upper classes of this country raped this country. You fucked people. You built a castle to rip people off. Not once in all these years have I come across a person inside a big Wall Street firm who was having a crisis of conscience. Nobody ever said, 'This is wrong.' And no one ever gave a shit about what I had to say."

Actually, Eisman didn't speak those final sentences that morning; he merely thought them. And he didn't actually know what was happening in the stock market; the one time he couldn't check his BlackBerry was when he was speaking. But *as he spoke* a Wall Street investment bank was failing, for a reason other than fraud. And the obvious question was, Why?

The collapse of Bear Stearns would later be classified as a run on the bank, and in a sense that was correct—other banks were refusing to do business with it, hedge funds were pulling their accounts. It raised a question, however, that would be raised again six months later: Why did the market suddenly distrust a giant Wall Street firm whose permanence it not so very long before took for granted? The demise of Bear Stearns had been so unthinkable in March of 2007 that Cornwall Capital had bought insurance against its collapse for less than three-tenths of 1 percent. They'd put down $300,000 to make $105 million.

"Leverage" was Eisman's answer, on this day. To generate profits, Bear Stearns, like every other Wall Street firm, was perching more and more speculative bets on top of each dollar of its capital. But the problem was obviously more complicated than that. The problem was also the nature of those speculative bets.

The subprime mortgage market had experienced at least two distinct phases. The first, in which AIG had taken most of the risk of a market collapse, lasted until the end of 2005. When AIG abruptly changed its mind, traders inside AIG FP assumed their decision might completely shut down the subprime mortgage market.* That's not

* It's interesting to imagine how the disaster might have played out if AIG FP had simply continued to take all the risk. If Wall Street, following Goldman Sachs's lead, had dumped all of the risk of subprime mortgage bonds into AIG FP, the problem might well have been classified as having nothing to do with Wall Street and as being the sole responsibility of this bizarre insurance company.

what happened, of course. Wall Street was already making too much money using CDOs to turn crappy triple-B-rated subprime bonds into putatively riskless triple-A ones to simply stop doing it. The people who ran the CDO machine at the various firms had acquired too much authority. From the end of 2005 until the middle of 2007, Wall Street firms created somewhere between $200 and $400 billion in subprime-backed CDOs: No one was exactly sure how many there were. Call it $300 billion, of which roughly $240 billion would have been triple-A-rated and thus treated, for accounting purposes, as riskless, and therefore unnecessary to disclose. Much, if not all, of it was held off balance sheets.

By March 2008 the stock market had finally grasped what every mortgage bond salesman had long known: Someone had lost at least $240 billion. But who? Morgan Stanley still owned $13 billion or so in CDOs, courtesy of Howie Hubler. The idiots in Germany owned some, Wing Chau and CDO managers like him owned some more, though whose money they were using to buy the bonds was a bit murky. Ambac Financial Group and MBIA Inc., which had long made their living insuring municipal bonds, had taken over where AIG had left off, and owned maybe 10 billion dollars' worth each. The truth is it was impossible to know how big the losses were, or who had them. All that anyone knew was that any Wall Street firm deep in the subprime market was probably on the hook for a lot more of them than they had confessed. Bear Stearns was deep in the subprime market. It had $40 in bets on its subprime mortgage bonds for every dollar of capital it held against those bets. The question wasn't how Bear Stearns could possibly fail but how it could possibly survive.

Finishing his little speech and heading back to his chair, Steve Eisman passed Bill Miller and patted him on the back, almost sympathetically. In the brief question-and-answer session that followed, Miller pointed out how unlikely it was that Bear Stearns might fail, because thus far, big Wall Street investment banks had failed only after they were caught in criminal activities. Eisman blurted out, "It's only five past ten. Give it time." Apart from that, he'd been almost polite. In the back of the room, Vinny and Danny felt the curious combination of relief and disappointment that followed a tornado that narrowly missed the big city.

It wasn't Eisman who upset the tone in the room, but some kid in the back. He looked to be in his early twenties, and he was, like everyone else, punching on his BlackBerry the whole time Miller and Eisman spoke. "Mr. Miller," he said. "From the time you started talking, Bear Stearns stock has fallen more than twenty points. Would you buy more now?"

Miller looked stunned. "He clearly had no idea what had happened," said Vinny. "He just said, 'Yeah, sure, I'd buy more here.' "

After that, the men in the room rushed for the exits, apparently to sell their shares in Bear Stearns. By the time Alan Greenspan arrived to speak, there was hardly anyone who cared to hear what he had to say. The audience was gone. By Monday, Bear Stearns was of course gone, too, sold to J.P. Morgan for $2 a share.*

The people rising out of the hole in the ground on the northeast corner of Madison Avenue and Forty-seventh Street at 6:40 in the morning revealed a great deal about themselves, if you knew what to look for. Anyone in that place at that time probably worked on Wall Street, for instance. The people emerging from the holes surrounding Penn Station, where Vincent Daniel's train arrived at exactly the same time, weren't so easy to predict. "Vinny's morning train is only fifty-five percent financial, because that's where the construction workers come in," said Danny Moses. "Mine's ninety-five." To the untrained eye, the Wall Street people who rode from the Connecticut suburbs to

* Later revised to about $10 a share.

Grand Central were an undifferentiated mass, but within that mass Danny noted many small and important distinctions. If they were on their BlackBerrys, they were probably hedge fund guys, checking their profits and losses in the Asian markets. If they slept on the train they were probably sell-side people—brokers, who had no skin in the game. Anyone carrying a briefcase or a bag was probably not employed on the sell side, as the only reason you'd carry a bag was to haul around brokerage research, and the brokers didn't read their own reports—at least not in their spare time. Anyone carrying a copy of the *New York Times* was probably a lawyer or a back-office person or someone who worked in the financial markets without actually being *in* the markets.

Their clothes told you a lot, too. The guys who ran money dressed as if they were going to a Yankees game. Their financial performance was supposed to be all that mattered about them, and so it caused suspicion if they dressed too well. If you saw a buy-side guy in a suit, it usually meant that he was in trouble, or scheduled to meet with someone who had given him money, or both. Beyond that, it was hard to tell much about a buy-side person from what he was wearing. The sell side, on the other hand, might as well have been wearing their business cards: The guy in the blazer and khakis was a broker at a second-tier firm; the guy in the three-thousand-dollar suit and the hair just so was an investment banker at J.P. Morgan or someplace like that. Danny could guess where people worked by where they sat on the train. The Goldman Sachs, Deutsche Bank, and Merrill Lynch people, who were headed downtown, edged to the front—though when Danny thought about it, few Goldman people actually rode the train anymore. They all had private cars. Hedge fund guys such as himself worked uptown and so exited Grand Central to the north, where taxis appeared haphazardly and out of nowhere to meet them, like farm trout rising to corn kernels. The Lehman and Bear Stearns people used to head for the same exit as he did, but they were done.

One reason why, on September 18, 2008, there weren't nearly as many people on the northeast corner of Forty-seventh Street and Madison Avenue at 6:40 in the morning as there had been on September 18, 2007.

Danny noticed many little things about his fellow financial man—that was his job, in a way. To notice the little things. Eisman was the big-picture guy. Vinny was the analyst. Danny, the head trader, was their eyes and ears on the market. Their source for the sort of information that never gets broadcast or written down: rumors, the behavior of the sell-side brokers, the patterns on the screens. His job was to be alive to detail, quick with numbers—and to avoid getting fucked.

To that end he kept five computer screens on his desk. One scrolled newswires, another showed moment-to-moment movements inside their portfolio, the other three scrolled Danny's conversations with maybe forty Wall Street brokers and fellow investors. His e-mail in-box for the month contained 33,000 messages. To an outsider, this torrent of picayune detail about the financial markets would have been disorienting. To him it all made sense, as long as he didn't really need to make sense of it. Danny was the small-picture guy.

By Thursday, September 18, 2008, however, the big picture had grown so unstable that the small picture had become nearly incoherent to him. On Monday, Lehman Brothers had filed for bankruptcy, and Merrill Lynch, having announced $55.2 billion in losses on subprime bond–backed CDOs, had sold itself to Bank of America. The U.S. stock market had fallen by more than it had since the first day of trading after the attack on the World Trade Center. On Tuesday the U.S. Federal Reserve announced that it had lent $85 billion to the insurance company AIG, to pay off the losses on the subprime credit default swaps AIG had sold to Wall Street banks—the biggest of which was the $13.9 billion AIG owed to Goldman Sachs. When you added in the $8.4 billion in cash AIG had already forked over to Goldman in collateral, you saw that Goldman had transferred more than $20 billion in subprime mortgage bond risk into the insurance company, which was in one way or another being covered by the U.S. taxpayer. That fact alone was enough to make everyone wonder at once how much more of this stuff was out there, and who owned it.

The Fed and the Treasury were doing their best to calm investors, but on Wednesday no one was obviously calm. A money market fund called the Reserve Primary Fund announced that it had lost enough on short-term loans to Lehman Brothers that its investors were not likely to get all their money back, and froze redemptions. Money markets weren't cash—they paid interest, and thus bore risk—but, until that moment, people thought of them as cash. *You couldn't even trust your own cash.* All over the world corporations began to yank their money out of money market funds, and short-term interest rates spiked as they had never before spiked. The Dow Jones Industrial Average had fallen 449 points, to its lowest level in four years, and most of the market-moving news was coming not from the private sector but from government officials. At 6:50 on Thursday morning, when Danny arrived, he learned that the chief British financial regulator was considering banning short selling—an act that, among other things, would put the hedge fund industry out of business—but that didn't begin to explain what now happened. "All hell was breaking loose in a way I had never seen in my career," said Danny.

FrontPoint was positioned perfectly for exactly this moment. By agreement with their investors, their fund could be 25 percent net short or 50 percent net long the stock market, and the gross positions could never exceed 200 percent. For example, for every $100 million they had to invest, they could be net short $25 million, or net long $50 million—and all of their bets combined could never exceed $200 million. There was nothing in the agreement about credit default swaps, but that no longer mattered. ("We never figured out how to put it in," said Eisman.) They'd sold their last one back to Greg Lippmann two months earlier, in early July. They were now back to being, exclusively, stock market investors.

At that moment they were short nearly as much as they were allowed to be short, and all of their bets were against banks, the very companies collapsing the fastest: Minutes after the market opened they were up $10 million. The shorts were falling, the longs—mainly smaller banks removed from the subprime market—were falling less. Danny should have been elated: Everything they had thought might happen was now happening. He wasn't elated, however; he was anxious. At 10:30, an hour into trading, every financial stock went into a free fall, whether it deserved to or not. "All this information goes through me," he said. "I'm supposed to know how to transmit information. Prices were moving so quickly I couldn't get a fix. It felt like a black hole. The abyss."

It had been four days since Lehman Brothers had been allowed to fail, but the most powerful effects of the collapse were being felt right now. The stocks of Morgan Stanley and Goldman Sachs were tanking, and it was clear that nothing short of the U.S. government could save them. "It was the equivalent of the earthquake going off," he said, "and then, much later, the tsunami arrives." Danny's trading life was man versus man, but this felt more like man versus nature: The synthetic CDO had become a synthetic natural disaster. "Usually, you feel you have the ability to control your environment," said Danny. "You're good because you know what's going on. Now it didn't matter what I knew. Feel went out the window."

FrontPoint had maybe seventy different bets on, in various stock markets around the world. All of them were on financial institutions. He scrambled to keep a handle on them all, but couldn't. They owned shares in KeyBank and were short the shares of Bank of America, both of which were doing things they'd never done before. "There were no bids in the market for anything," said Danny. "There was no market. It was really only then that I realized there was a bigger issue than just our portfolio. Fundamentals didn't matter. Stocks were going to move up or down on pure emotion and speculation of what the government would do." The most unsettling loose thought rattling around his mind was that Morgan Stanley was about to go under. Their fund was owned by Morgan Stanley. They had almost nothing to do with Morgan Stanley, and felt little kinship with the place. They did not act or feel like Morgan Stanley employees—Eisman often said how much he wished he was allowed to short Morgan Stanley stock. They acted and felt like the managers of their own fund. If Morgan Stanley failed, however, its share in their fund wound up as an asset in a bankruptcy proceeding. "I'm thinking, *We've got the world by the fucking balls and the company we work for is going bankrupt?*"

Then Danny sensed something seriously wrong—with himself. Just before eleven in the morning, wavy black lines appeared in the space between his eyes and his computer screen. The screen appeared to be fading in and out. "I felt this shooting pain in my head," he said. "I don't get headaches. I thought I was having an aneurysm." Now he became aware of his heart—he looked down and he could actually see it banging against his chest. "I spend my morning trying to control all this energy and all this information," he said, "and I lost control."

He'd had this experience only once before. On September 11, 2001, at 8:46 a.m., he'd been at his desk on the top floor of the World Financial Center. "You know when you're in the city and one of those garbage trucks passes and you're like, 'What the fuck was that?'" Until someone told him it was a commuter plane hitting the North Tower, he assumed the first plane was one of those trucks. He walked to the window to look up at the building across the street. A small commuter plane wouldn't have been big or strong enough to do all that much damage, to his way of thinking, and he expected to see it poking out of the side of the building. All he could see was the black hole, and smoke. "My first thought was, *That was not an accident. No fucking way.*" He was still working at Oppenheimer and Co.—Steve and Vinny had already left—and some authoritative-sounding voice came over the loudspeaker to announce that no one was to leave the building. Danny remained at the window. "That's when people started jumping," he said. "Bodies are falling." The rumble of another garbage truck. "When the second plane hit I was like, 'Bye, everybody.'" By the time he reached the elevator, he found himself escorting two pregnant women. He walked them uptown, left one at her apartment on Fourteenth Street and the other at the Plaza Hotel, and then walked home to his pregnant wife on Seventy-second Street.

Four days later he was leaving, or rather fleeing, New York City with his wife and small son. They were on the highway at night in the middle of a storm when he was overcome by the certainty that a tree would fall and crush the car. He began to shake and sweat with sheer terror. The trees were fifty yards away: They could never reach the car. "You need to see someone," his wife said, and he had. He had thought he might have something wrong with his heart, and had spent half a day hooked up to an EKG machine. The loss of self-control embarrassed him—he preferred not to talk about it—and he was deeply relieved when the attacks became less frequent and less severe. Finally, a few months after the terrorist attack, they vanished completely.

On September 18, 2008, he failed to make the connection between how he'd felt then and how he felt now. He rose from his desk and looked for someone. Eisman normally sat across from him, but Eisman was out at some conference trying to raise money—which showed you how unprepared they all were at the arrival of the moment for which they thought themselves perfectly prepared. Danny turned to the colleague beside him. "Porter, I think I'm having a heart attack," he said.

Porter Collins laughed and said, "No, you're not." An Olympic rowing career had left Porter Collins a bit inured to the pain of others, as he assumed they usually didn't know what pain was.

"No," said Danny. "I need to go to the hospital." His face had gone pale but he was still able to stand on his own two feet. How bad could it be? Danny was always a little jumpy.

"That's why he's good at his job," said Porter. "I kept saying, 'You're not having a heart attack.' Then he stopped talking. And I said, 'All right, maybe you are.'" This actually wasn't all that helpful. Unsteadily, Danny turned to Vinny, who had been watching everything from the far end of the long trading desk and was thinking about calling an ambulance.

"I got to get out of here. Now," he said.

Cornwall Capital's bet against subprime mortgage bonds had quadrupled its capital, from a bit more than $30 million to $135 million, but its three founders never had a Champagne moment. "We were focused on, Where do we put our money that's safe?" said Ben Hockett. Before, they had no money. Now, they were rich; but they feared they had no ability to preserve their wealth. By nature a bit tortured, they were now, by nurture, even more so. They actually spent time wondering how people who had been so sensationally right (i.e., they themselves) could preserve the capacity for diffidence and doubt and uncertainty that had enabled them to be right. The more sure you were of yourself and your judgment, the harder it was to find opportunities premised on the notion that you were, in the end, probably wrong.

The long-shot bet, in some strange way, was a young man's game. Charlie Ledley and Jamie Mai no longer felt, or acted, quite so young. Charlie now suffered from migraines, and was consumed with what might happen next. "I think there is something fundamentally scary about our democracy," said Charlie. "Because I think people have a sense that the system is rigged, and it's hard to argue that it isn't." He and Jamie spent a surprising amount of their time and energy thinking up ways to attack what they viewed as a deeply corrupt financial system. They cooked up a plan to seek revenge upon the rating agencies, for instance. They'd form a not-for-profit legal entity whose sole purpose was to sue Moody's and S&P, and donate the proceeds to investors who lost money investing in triple-A-rated securities.

As Jamie put it, "Our plan was to go around to investors and say, 'You guys don't know how badly you got fucked. You guys should really sue.'" They'd had so many bad experiences with big Wall Street firms, and the people who depended on them for their living, that they feared sharing the idea with New York lawyers. They drove up to Portland, Maine, and found a law firm who would listen to them. "They were just like, 'You guys are nuts,'" said Charlie. Suing the rating agencies for the inaccuracy of their ratings, the Maine lawyers told them, would be like suing *Motor Trend* magazine for plugging a car that wound up crashing.

Charlie knew a prominent historian of financial crises, a former professor of his, and took to calling him. "These calls often came late at night," says the historian, who preferred to remain anonymous. "And they would go on for a pretty long time. I remember he started out by asking, 'Do you know what a mezzanine CDO is?' And he started to explain to me how it all worked": how Wall Street investment banks somehow had conned the rating agencies into blessing piles of crappy loans; how this had enabled the lending of trillions of dollars to ordinary Americans; how the ordinary Americans had happily complied and told the lies they needed to tell to obtain the loans; how the machinery that turned the loans into supposedly riskless securities was so complicated that investors had ceased to evaluate risks; how the problem had grown so big that the end was bound to be cataclysmic and have big social and political consequences. "He wanted to talk through his reasoning," said the historian, "and see if I thought he was nuts. He asked if the Fed would ever buy mortgages, and I said I thought that was pretty unlikely. It would have to be a calamity of colossal proportions for the Fed to ever consider doing something like that." What struck the distinguished financial historian, apart from the alarming facts of the case, was that . . . he was hearing them for the first time from Charlie Ledley. "Would I have ever predicted that Charlie Ledley would have anticipated the greatest financial crisis since the Depression?" he said. "No." It wasn't that Charlie was stupid; far from it. It was that Charlie wasn't a money person. "He's not materialistic in any obvious way," said the professor. "He's not driven by money in any obvious way. He would get angry. He took it personally."

Even so, on the morning of September 18, 2008, Charlie Ledley was still capable of being surprised. He and Jamie did not normally sit in front of their Bloomberg screens and watch the news scroll by, but by Wednesday, the seventeenth, that's what they were doing. The losses announced by the big Wall Street firms on subprime mortgage bonds had started huge and kept growing. Merrill Lynch, which had begun by saying they had $7 billion in losses, now admitted the number was over $50 billion. Citigroup appeared to have about $60 billion. Morgan Stanley had its own $9-plus billion hit, and who knew what behind it. "We'd been wrong in our interpretation of what was going on," said Charlie. "We had always assumed that they sold the triple-A CDOs to, like, the Korean Farmers Corporation. The way they were all blowing up implied they hadn't. They'd kept it themselves."

The big Wall Street firms, seemingly so shrewd and self-interested, had somehow become the dumb money. The people who ran them did not understand their own businesses, and their regulators obviously knew even less. Charlie and Jamie had always sort of assumed that there was some grown-up in charge of the financial system whom they had never met; now, they saw there was not. "We were never inside the belly of the beast," said Charlie. "We saw the bodies being carried out. But we were never inside." A Bloomberg News headline that caught Jamie's eye, and stuck in his mind: "Senate Majority Leader on Crisis: No One Knows What to Do."

Early on, long before others came around to his view of the world, Michael Burry had noted how morbid it felt to turn his investment portfolio into what amounted to a bet on the collapse of the financial system. It wasn't until after he'd made a fortune from that collapse that he began to wonder about the social dimensions of his financial strategy—and wonder if other people's view of him might one day be as distorted as their view of the financial system had been. On June 19, 2008, three months after the death of Bear Stearns, Ralph Cioffi and Matthew Tannin, the two men who had run Bear Stearns's bankrupt subprime hedge funds, were arrested by the FBI, and led away in handcuffs from their own homes.* Late that night, Burry dashed off an e-mail to his in-house lawyer, Steve Druskin. "Confidentially, this case is a pretty big stress for me. I'm worried that I'm volatile enough to send out e-mails that can be taken out of context in ways that could get me in trouble, even if my actions and my ultimate outcomes are entirely correct. . . . I can't imagine how I'd ever tolerate ending up in prison having done nothing wrong but be a bit careless with having no filter between my random thoughts during tough times and what I put in an e-mail. In fact I'm so over worried about this that tonight I started to think I should shut the funds down."

He was now looking for reasons to abandon money management. His investors were helping him to find them: He had made them a great deal of money, but they did not appear to feel compensated for

* The case brought by the U.S. Department of Justice against Cioffi and Tannin sought to prove that the two men had knowingly deceived their investors, overlooking the possibility that they simply had no idea what they were doing, and failed to grasp the real risk of a triple-A-rated subprime-backed CDO. The case was weak, and turned on a couple of e-mails obviously ripped from context. A member of the jury that voted to acquit the Bear Stearns subprime bond traders told Bloomberg News afterward not only that she thought they were innocent as charged but that she would happily invest money with them.

the ride he had taken them on over the past three years. By June 30, 2008, any investor who had stuck with Scion Capital from its beginning, on November 1, 2000, had a gain, after fees and expenses, of 489.34 percent. (The gross gain of the fund had been 726 percent.) Over the same period, the S&P 500 returned just a bit more than 2 percent. In 2007 alone Burry had made his investors $750 million—and yet now he had only $600 million under management. His investors' requests for their money back came in hard and fast. No new investors called—not a single one. Nobody called him to solicit his views of the world, or his predictions for the future, either. So far as he could see, no one even seemed to want to know how he had done what he had done. "We have not been terribly popular," he wrote.

It outraged him that the people who got credit for higher understanding were those who spent the most time currying favor with the media. No business could be more objective than money management, and yet even in this business, facts and logic were overwhelmed by the nebulous social dimension of things. "I must say that I have been astonished by how many people now say they saw the subprime meltdown, the commodities boom, and the fading economy coming," Burry wrote, in April 2008, to his remaining investors. "And if they don't always say it in so many words, they do it by appearing on TV or extending interviews to journalists, stridently projecting their own confidence in what will happen next. And surely, these people would never have the nerve to tell you what's happening next, if they were so horribly wrong on what happened last, right? Yet I simply don't recall too many people agreeing with me back then." It was almost as if it counted against him to have been exactly right—his presence made a lot of people uncomfortable. A trade magazine published the top seventy-five hedge funds of 2007, and Scion was nowhere on it—even though its returns put it at or near the very top. "It was as if they took one swimmer in the Olympics and made him swim in a separate pool," Burry said. "His time won the gold. But he got no medal. I honestly think that's what killed it for me. I was looking for some recognition. There was none. I trained for the Olympics, and then they told me to go and swim in the retard pool." A few of his remaining investors asked why he hadn't been more aggressive on the public relations—as if that were a part of the business!

In early October 2008, after the U.S. government had stepped in to say it would, in effect, absorb all the losses in the financial system and prevent any big Wall Street firm from failing, Burry had started to buy stocks with enthusiasm, for the first time in years. The stimulus would lead inevitably to inflation, he thought, but also to a boom in stock prices. He might be early, of course, and stocks might fall some before they rose, but that didn't matter to him: The value was now there, and the bet would work out in the long run. Immediately, his biggest remaining investor, who had $150 million in the fund, questioned his judgment and threatened to pull his money out.

On October 27, Burry wrote to one of his two e-mail friends: "I'm selling off the positions tonight. I think I hit a breaking point. I haven't eaten today, I'm not sleeping, I'm not talking with my kids, not talking with my wife, I'm broken. Asperger's has given me some great gifts, but life's been too hard for too long because of it as well." On a Friday afternoon in early November, he felt chest pains and went to an emergency room. His blood pressure had spiked. "I felt like I am heading towards a short life," he wrote. A week later, on November 12, he sent his final letter to investors. "I have been pushed repeatedly to the brink by my own actions, the Fund's investors, business partners, and even former employees," he wrote. "I have always been able to pull back and carry on my often overly intense affair with this business. Now, however, I am facing personal matters that have carried me irrefutably over the threshold, and I have come to the sullen realization that I must close down the Fund." With that, he vanished, leaving a lot of people wondering what had happened.

What had happened was that he had been right, the world had

been wrong, and the world hated him for it. And so Michael Burry ended where he began—alone, and comforted by his solitude. He remained inside his office in Cupertino, California, big enough for a staff of twenty-five people, but the fund was shuttered and the office was empty. The last man out was Steve Druskin, and among Druskin's last acts was to figure out what to do about Michael Burry's credit default swaps on subprime mortgage bonds. "Mike kept a couple of them, just for fun," he said. "Just a couple. To see if we could get paid off in full." And he had, though it wasn't for fun but vindication: to prove to the world that the investment-grade bonds he had bet against were indeed entirely without value. The two bets he had saved were against subprime bonds created back in 2005 by Lehman Brothers. They'd gone to zero at roughly the same time as their creator. Burry had wagered $100,000 or so on each, and made $5 million.

The problem, from the point of view of a lawyer closing an investment fund, was that these strange contracts did not expire until 2035. The brokers had long since paid them in full: 100 cents on the dollar. No Wall Street firm even bothered to send them quotes on the things anymore. "I don't get a statement from a broker saying we have an open position with them," says Druskin. "But we do. It's like no one wants to talk about this anymore. It's like, 'All right, you've got your ten million dollars. Don't keep haranguing me about it.' "

On Wall Street, the lawyers play the same role as medics in war: They come in after the shooting is over to clean up the mess. Thirty-year contracts that had some remote technical risk of repayment—exactly what that risk was he was still trying to determine—was the last of Michael Burry's mess. "It's possible the brokers have thrown the contracts away," Druskin said. "No one three years ago expected this to happen on the brokerage side. So no one's been trained to deal with this. We've pretty much said, 'We're going out of business.' And they said, 'Okay.'"

By the time Eisman got the call from Danny Moses saying that he might be having a heart attack, and that he and Vinny and Porter were sitting on the steps of St. Patrick's Cathedral, he was in the midst of a slow, almost menopausal, change. He'd been unprepared for his first hot flash, in the late fall of 2007. By then it was clear to many that he had been right and they had been wrong and that he had gotten rich to boot. He'd gone to a conference put on by Merrill Lynch, right after they'd fired their CEO, Stan O'Neal, and disclosed $20 billion or so of their $52 billion in subprime-related losses. There he had sidled up to Merrill's chief financial officer, Jeff Edwards, the same Jeff Edwards Eisman had taunted, some months earlier, about Merrill Lynch's risk models. "You remember what I said about those risk models of yours?" Eisman now said. "I guess I was right, huh?" Instantly, and amazingly, he regretted having said it. "I felt bad about it," said Eisman. "It was obnoxious. He was a lovely guy. He was just wrong. I was no longer the underdog. And I had to conduct myself in a different way."

Valerie Feigen watched in near bewilderment as her husband acquired, haltingly, in fits and starts, a trait resembling tact. "There was a void after everything happened," she said. "Once he was proved right, all this anxiety and anger and energy went away. And it left this big void. He went on an ego thing for a while. He was really kind of full of himself." Eisman had been so vocal about the inevitable doom that all sorts of unlikely people wanted to hear what he now had to say. After the conference in Las Vegas, he had come down with a parasite. He'd told the doctor who treated him that the financial world as we knew it was about to end. A year later, he went back to the same doctor for a colonoscopy. Stretched out on the table, he hears the doctor say, "Here's the guy who predicted the crisis! Come on in and listen to this." And in the middle of Eisman's colonoscopy, a roomful of doctors and nurses retold the story of Eisman's genius.

The story of Eisman's genius quickly grew old to his wife. Long ago she had established a sort of Eisman social emergency task force with her husband's therapist. "We beat him up and said, 'You really just have to knock this shit off.' And he got it. And he started being nice. And he liked being nice! It was a new experience for him." All around, she and others found circumstantial evidence of a changed man. At the Christmas party at the building next door, for example. She wasn't planning to even let Eisman know about it, as she never knew what he might do or say. "I was just kind of trying to sneak out of our apartment," she said. "And he stops me and says, 'How will it look if I don't go?'" The sincerity of his concern shocked her into giving him a chance. "You can go, but you have to behave," she said. To which Eisman replied, "Well, I know how to behave now." And so she took him to the Christmas party, and he was as sweet as he could be. "He's become a pleasure," said Valerie. "Go figure."

That afternoon of September 18, 2008, the new and possibly improving Eisman ambled toward his partners on the steps of St. Patrick's Cathedral. Getting places on foot always took him too long. "Steve's such a fucking slow walker," said Danny. "He walks like an elephant would walk if an elephant could only take human-size steps." The weather was gorgeous—one of those rare days where the blue sky reaches down through the forest of tall buildings and warms the soul. "We just sat there," says Danny, "watching the people pass."

They sat together on the cathedral steps for an hour or so. "As we sat there we were weirdly calm," said Danny. "We felt insulated from the whole market reality. It was an out-of-body experience. We just sat and watched the people pass and talked about what might happen next. How many of these people were going to lose their jobs? Who was going to rent these buildings, after all the Wall Street firms had collapsed?"

Porter Collins thought that "it was like the world stopped. We're looking at all these people and saying, 'These people are either ruined or about to be ruined.'" Apart from that, there wasn't a whole lot of hand-wringing inside FrontPoint. This was what they had been waiting for: total collapse.

"The investment banking industry is fucked," Eisman had said six weeks earlier. "These guys are only beginning to understand how fucked they are. It's like being a scholastic, prior to Newton. Newton comes along and one morning you wake up: 'Holy shit, I'm wrong!'" Lehman Brothers had vanished, Merrill had surrendered, and Goldman Sachs and Morgan Stanley were just a week away from ceasing to be investment banks. Investment bankers were not just fucked: They were extinct. "That Wall Street has gone down because of this is *justice*," Eisman said. The only one among them who wrestled a bit with their role—as the guys who had made a fortune betting against their own society—was Vincent Daniel. "Vinny, being from Queens, needs to see the dark side of everything," said Eisman.

To which Vinny replied, "The way we thought about it, which we didn't like, was, 'By shorting this market we're creating the liquidity to keep the market going.'"

"It was like feeding the monster," said Eisman. "We fed the monster until it blew up."

The monster was exploding. Yet on the streets of Manhattan there was no sign anything important had just happened. The force that would affect all of their lives was hidden from their view. That was the problem with money: What people did with it had consequences, but they were so remote from the original action that the mind never connected the one with the other. The teaser-rate loans you make to people who will never be able to repay them will go bad not immediately but in two years, when their interest rates rise. The various bonds you make from those loans will go bad not as the loans go bad but months later, after a lot of tedious foreclosures and bankruptcies and forced sales. The various CDOs you make from the bonds will go bad not right then but after some trustee sorts out whether there will ever be enough cash to pay them off. Whereupon the end owner of the CDO receives a little note, *Dear Sir, We regret to inform you that your bond no longer exists* . . . But the biggest lag of all was right here, on the streets. How long would it take before the people walking back and forth in front of St. Patrick's Cathedral figured out what had just happened to them?

EPILOGUE

Everything Is Correlated

Around the time Eisman and his partners sat on the steps of the midtown cathedral, I sat on a banquette on the east side, waiting for John Gutfreund, my old boss, to arrive for lunch, and wondering, among other things, why any restaurant would seat, side by side, two men without the slightest interest in touching each other.

When I published my book about the financial 1980s, the financial 1980s were supposed to be ending. I received a lot of undeserved credit for my timing. The social disruption caused by the collapse of the savings and loan industry and the rise of hostile takeovers and leveraged buyouts had given way to a brief period of recriminations. Just as most students at Ohio State University read *Liar's Poker* as a how-to manual, most TV and radio interviewers read me as a whistle-blower. (Geraldo Rivera was the big exception. He included me in a show, along with some child actors who'd gone on to become drug addicts, called "People Who Succeed Too Early in Life.") Anti–Wall Street feelings then ran high enough for Rudolph Giuliani to float a political career upon them, but the result felt more like a witch hunt than an honest reappraisal of the financial order. The public lynching of Michael Milken, and then of Salomon Brothers CEO Gutfreund, were excuses for not dealing with the disturbing forces underpinning their rise. Ditto the cleaning up of Wall Street trading culture. Wall Street firms would soon be frowning upon profanity, forcing their male employees to treat women almost as equals, and firing traders for so much as glancing at a lap dancer. Bear Stearns and Lehman Brothers in 2008 more closely resembled normal corporations with solid, Middle American values than did any Wall Street firm circa 1985.

The changes were camouflage. They helped to distract outsiders from the truly profane event: the growing misalignment of interests between the people who trafficked in financial risk and the wider culture. The surface rippled, but down below, in the depths, the bonus pool remained undisturbed.

The reason that American financial culture was so difficult to change—the reason the political process would prove so slow to force change upon it, even after the subprime mortgage catastrophe—was that it had taken so long to create, and its assumptions had become so deeply embedded. There was an umbilical cord running from the belly of the exploded beast back to the financial 1980s. The crisis of 2008 had its roots not just in the subprime loans made in 2005 but in ideas that had hatched in 1985. A friend of mine in my Salomon Brothers training program created the first mortgage derivative in 1986, the year after we left the program. ("Derivatives are like guns," he still likes to say. "The problem isn't the tools. It's who is using the tools.") The mezzanine CDO was invented by Michael Milken's junk bond department at Drexel Burnham in 1987. The first mortgage-backed CDO was created at Credit Suisse in 2000 by a trader who had spent his formative years, in the 1980s and early 1990s, in the Salomon Brothers mortgage department. His name was Andy Stone, and along with his intellectual connection to the subprime crisis came a personal one: He was Greg Lippmann's first boss on Wall Street.

I'd not seen Gutfreund since I quit Wall Street. I'd met him, nervously, a couple of times on the trading floor. A few months before I quit, my bosses asked me to explain to our CEO what at the time seemed like exotic trades in derivatives I'd done with a European hedge fund, and I'd tried. He claimed not to be smart enough to understand any of it, and I assumed that was how a Wall Street CEO showed he was the boss, by rising above the details. There was no reason for him to remember any of these encounters, and he didn't: When my book came out, and became a public relations nuisance to him, he'd told reporters we'd never met. Over the years, I'd heard bits and pieces about him. I knew that after he'd been forced to resign from Salomon Brothers, he'd fallen on harder times. I heard, later, that a few years before our lunch, he'd sat on a panel about Wall Street at the Columbia Business School. When his turn came to speak, he advised the students to find some more meaningful thing to do with their lives than go to work on Wall Street. As he began to describe his career, he'd broken down and wept.

When I e-mailed Gutfreund to invite him to lunch, he could not have been more polite, or more gracious. That attitude persisted as he was escorted to the table, made chitchat with the owner, and ordered his food. He'd lost a half-step, and was more deliberate in his movements, but otherwise he was completely recognizable. The same veneer of courtliness masked the same animal impulse to see the world as it is, rather than as it should be.

We spent twenty minutes or so determining that our presence at the same lunch table was not going to cause the earth to explode. We discovered a mutual friend. We agreed that the Wall Street CEO had no real ability to keep track of the frantic innovation occurring inside his firm. ("I didn't understand all the product lines and they don't either.") We agreed, further, that the CEO of the Wall Street investment bank had shockingly little control over his subordinates. ("They're buttering you up and then doing whatever the fuck they want to do.") He thought the cause of the financial crisis was "simple. Greed on both sides—greed of investors and the greed of the bankers." I thought it was more complicated. Greed on Wall Street was a given—almost an obligation. The problem was the system of incentives that channeled the greed.

The line between gambling and investing is artificial and thin. The soundest investment has the defining trait of a bet (you losing all of your money in hopes of making a bit more), and the wildest speculation has the salient characteristic of an investment (you might get your money back with interest). Maybe the best definition of "investing" is "gambling with the odds in your favor." The people on the short side of the subprime mortgage market had gambled with the odds in their favor. The people on the other side—the entire financial system, essentially—had gambled with the odds against them. Up to this point, the story of the big short could not be simpler. What's strange and complicated about it, however, is that pretty much all the important people on both sides of the gamble left the table rich. Steve Eisman and Michael Burry and the young men at Cornwall Capital each made tens of millions of dollars for themselves, of course. Greg Lippmann was paid $47 million in 2007, although $24 million of it was in restricted stock that he could not collect unless he hung around Deutsche Bank for a few more years. But all of these people had been right; they'd been on the winning end of the bet. Wing Chau's CDO managing business went bust, but he, too, left with tens of millions of dollars—and had the nerve to attempt to create a business that would buy up, cheaply, the very same subprime mortgage bonds in which he had lost billions of dollars' worth of other people's money. Howie Hubler lost more money than any single trader in the history of Wall Street—and yet he was permitted to keep the tens of millions of dollars he had made. The CEOs of every major Wall Street firm were also on the wrong end of the gamble. All of them, without exception, either ran their public corporations into bankruptcy or were saved from bankruptcy by the United States government. They all got rich, too.

What are the odds that people will make smart decisions about money if they don't need to make smart decisions—if they can get rich making dumb decisions? The incentives on Wall Street were all wrong; they're still all wrong. But I didn't argue with John Gutfreund. Just as you revert to being about nine years old when you go home to visit your parents, you revert to total subordination when you are in the presence of your former CEO. John Gutfreund was still the King of Wall Street and I was still a geek. He spoke in declarative statements, I spoke in questions. But as he spoke, my eyes kept drifting to his hands. His alarmingly thick and meaty hands. They weren't the hands of a soft Wall Street banker but of a boxer. I looked up. The boxer was smiling—though it was less a smile than a placeholder expression. And he was saying, very deliberately, "Your . . . fucking . . . book."

I smiled back, though it wasn't quite a smile.

"Why did you ask me to lunch?" he asked, though pleasantly. He was genuinely curious.

You can't really tell someone that you asked him to lunch to let him know that you didn't think of him as evil. Nor can you tell him that you asked him to lunch because you thought you could trace the biggest financial crisis in the history of the world back to a decision he had made. John Gutfreund had done violence to the Wall Street social order—and got himself dubbed the King of Wall Street—when, in 1981, he'd turned Salomon Brothers from a private partnership into Wall Street's first public corporation. He'd ignored the outrage of Salomon's retired partners. ("I was disgusted by his materialism," William Salomon, the son of one of the firm's founders, who had made Gutfreund CEO only after he'd promised never to sell the firm, had told me.) He'd lifted a giant middle finger in the direction of the moral disapproval of his fellow Wall Street CEOs. And he'd seized the day. He and the other partners not only made a quick killing; they transferred the ultimate financial risk from themselves to their shareholders. It didn't, in the end, make a great deal of sense for the shareholders. (One share of Salomon Brothers, purchased when I arrived on the trading floor, in 1986, at a then market price of $42, would be worth 2.26 shares of Citigroup today, which, on the first day of trading in 2010, had a combined market value of $7.48.) But it made fantastic sense for the bond traders.

But from that moment, the Wall Street firm became a black box. The shareholders who financed the risk taking had no real understanding of what the risk takers were doing, and, as the risk taking grew ever more complex, their understanding diminished. All that was clear was that the profits to be had from smart people making complicated bets overwhelmed anything that could be had from servicing customers, or allocating capital to productive enterprise. The customers became, oddly, beside the point. (Is it any wonder that mistrust of the sellers by the buyers in the bond market had reached the point where the buyers could not see a get-rich-quick scheme when a seller, Greg Lippmann, offered it to them?) In the late 1980s and early 1990s Salomon Brothers had entire years—great years!—in which five proprietary traders, the intellectual forefathers of Howie Hubler, generated more than the firm's annual profits. Which is to say that the firm's ten thousand or so other employees, as a group, lost money.

The moment Salomon Brothers demonstrated the potential gains to be had from turning an investment bank into a public corporation and leveraging its balance sheet with exotic risks, the psychological foundations of Wall Street shifted, from trust to blind faith. No investment bank owned by its employees would have leveraged itself 35:1, or bought and held $50 billion in mezzanine CDOs. I doubt any partnership would have sought to game the rating agencies, or leapt into bed with loan sharks, or even allowed mezzanine CDOs to be sold to its customers. The short-term expected gain would not have justified the long-term expected loss.

No partnership, for that matter, would have hired me, or anyone remotely like me. Was there ever any correlation between an ability to get into, and out of, Princeton, and a talent for taking financial risk?

At the top of Charlie Ledley's list of concerns, after Cornwall Capital had laid its bets against subprime loans, was that the powers that be might step in at any time to prevent individual American subprime mortgage borrowers from failing. The powers that be never did that, of course. Instead they stepped in to prevent the failure of the big Wall Street firms that had contrived to bankrupt themselves by making a lot of dumb bets on subprime borrowers.

After Bear Stearns failed, the government encouraged J.P. Morgan to buy it by offering a knockdown price and guaranteeing Bear Stearns's shakiest assets. Bear Stearns bondholders were made whole and its stockholders lost most of their money. Then came the collapse of the government-sponsored entities, Fannie Mae and Freddie Mac, both promptly nationalized. Management was replaced, shareholders badly diluted, and creditors left intact but with some uncertainty. Next came Lehman Brothers, which was simply allowed to go bankrupt—whereupon things became even more complicated. At first, the Treasury and the Federal Reserve claimed they allowed Lehman to fail to send the signal that recklessly managed Wall Street firms did not all come with government guarantees; but then, when all hell broke loose, and the market froze, and people started saying that letting Lehman fail was a dumb thing to have done, they changed their story and claimed they lacked the legal authority to rescue Lehman. But then AIG failed a few days later, or tried to, before the Federal Reserve extended it a loan of $85 billion—soon increased to $180 billion—to cover the losses from its bets on subprime mortgage bonds. This time the Treasury charged a lot for the loans and took most of the equity. Washington Mutual followed, and was unceremoniously seized by the Treasury, wiping out both its creditors and its shareholders entirely. And then Wachovia failed, and the Treasury and FDIC encouraged Citigroup to buy it—again at a knockdown price and with a guarantee of the bad assets.

The people in a position to resolve the financial crisis were, of course, the very same people who had failed to foresee it: Treasury Secretary Henry Paulson, future Treasury Secretary Timothy Geithner, Fed Chairman Ben Bernanke, Goldman Sachs CEO Lloyd Blankfein, Morgan Stanley CEO John Mack, Citigroup CEO Vikram Pandit, and so on. A few Wall Street CEOs had been fired for their roles in the subprime mortgage catastrophe, but most remained in their jobs, and they, of all people, became important characters operating behind the closed doors, trying to figure out what to do next. With them were a handful of government officials—the same government officials who should have known a lot more about what Wall Street firms were doing, back when they were doing it. All shared a distinction: They had proven far less capable of grasping basic truths in the heart of the U.S. financial system than a one-eyed money manager with Asperger's syndrome.

By late September 2008 the nation's highest financial official, U.S. Treasury Secretary Henry Paulson, persuaded the U.S. Congress that he needed $700 billion to buy subprime mortgage assets from banks. Thus was born TARP, which stood for Troubled Asset Relief Program. Once handed the money, Paulson abandoned his promised strategy and instead essentially began giving away billions of dollars to Citigroup, Morgan Stanley, Goldman Sachs, and a few others unnaturally selected for survival. For instance, the $13 billion AIG owed to Goldman Sachs, as a result of its bet on subprime mortgage loans, was paid off in full by the U.S. government: 100 cents on the dollar.

These fantastic handouts—plus the implicit government guarantee that came with them—not only prevented Wall Street firms from failing but spared them from recognizing the losses in their subprime mortgage portfolios. Even so, just weeks after receiving its first $25 billion taxpayer investment, Citigroup returned to the Treasury to confess that—lo!—the markets still didn't trust Citigroup to survive. In response, on November 24, the Treasury granted another $20 billion from TARP and simply guaranteed $306 billion of Citigroup's assets. Treasury didn't ask for a piece of the action, or management changes, or for that matter anything at all except for a teaspoon of out-of-the-money warrants and preferred stock. The $306 billion guarantee—nearly 2 percent of U.S. gross domestic product, and roughly the combined budgets of the departments of Agriculture, Education, Energy, Homeland Security, Housing and Urban Development, and Transportation—was presented undisguised, as a gift. The Treasury didn't ever actually get around to explaining what the crisis was, just that the action was taken in response to Citigroup's "declining stock price."

By then it was clear that $700 billion was a sum insufficient to grapple with the troubled assets acquired over the previous few years by Wall Street bond traders. That's when the U.S. Federal Reserve took the shocking and unprecedented step of buying bad subprime mortgage bonds directly from the banks. By early 2009 the risks and losses associated with more than a trillion dollars' worth of bad investments were transferred from big Wall Street firms to the U.S. taxpayer. Henry Paulson and Timothy Geithner both claimed that the chaos and panic caused by the failure of Lehman Brothers proved to them that the system could not tolerate the chaotic failure of another big financial firm. They further claimed, albeit not until months after the fact, that they had lacked the legal authority to wind down giant financial firms in an orderly manner—that is, to put a bankrupt bank out of business. Yet even a year later they would have done very little to acquire that power. This was curious, as they obviously weren't shy about asking for power.

The events on Wall Street in 2008 were soon reframed, not just by Wall Street leaders but also by both the U.S. Treasury and the Federal Reserve, as a "crisis in confidence." A simple, old-fashioned financial panic, triggered by the failure of Lehman Brothers. By August 2009 the president of Goldman Sachs, Gary Cohn, even claimed, publicly, that Goldman Sachs had never actually needed government help, as Goldman had been strong enough to withstand any temporary panic. But there's a difference between an old-fashioned financial panic and what had happened on Wall Street in 2008. In an old-fashioned panic, perception creates its own reality: Someone shouts "Fire!" in a crowded theater and the audience crushes each other to death in its rush for the exits. On Wall Street in 2008 the reality finally overwhelmed perceptions: A crowded theater burned down with a lot of people still in their seats. Every major firm on Wall Street was either bankrupt or fatally intertwined with a bankrupt system. The problem wasn't that Lehman Brothers had been allowed to fail. The problem was that Lehman Brothers had been allowed to succeed.

This new regime—free money for capitalists, free markets for everyone else—plus the more or less instant rewriting of financial history vexed all sorts of people, but few were as enthusiastically vexed as Steve Eisman. The world's most powerful and most highly paid financiers had been entirely discredited; without government intervention every single one of them would have lost his job; and yet those same financiers were using the government to enrich themselves. "I can understand why Goldman Sachs would want to be included in the conversation about what to do about Wall Street," he said. "What I can't understand is why anyone would listen to them." In Eisman's view, the unwillingness of the U.S. government to allow the bankers to fail was less a solution than a symptom of a still deeply dysfunctional financial system. The problem wasn't that the banks were, in and of themselves, critical to the success of the U.S. economy. The problem, he felt certain, was that some gargantuan, unknown dollar amount of credit default swaps had been bought and sold on every one of them. "There's no limit to the risk in the market," he said. "A bank with a market capitalization of one billion dollars might have one trillion dollars' worth of credit default swaps outstanding. No one knows how many there are! And no one knows where they are!" The failure of, say, Citigroup might be economically tolerable. It would trigger losses to Citigroup's shareholders, bondholders, and employees—but the sums involved were known to all. Citigroup's failure, however, would also trigger the payoff of a massive bet of unknown dimensions: from people who had sold credit default swaps on Citigroup to those who had bought them.

This was yet another consequence of turning Wall Street partnerships into public corporations: It turned them into objects of speculation. It was no longer the social and economic relevance of a bank that rendered it too big to fail, but the number of side bets that had been made upon it.

At some point I could not help but ask John Gutfreund about his biggest and most fateful act: Combing through the rubble of the avalanche, the decision to turn the Wall Street partnership into a public corporation looked a lot like the first pebble kicked off the top of the hill. "Yes," he said. "They—the heads of the other Wall Street firms—all said what an awful thing it was to go public and how could you do such a thing. But when the temptation rose, they all gave in to it." He agreed, though: The main effect of turning a partnership into a corporation was to transfer the financial risk to the shareholders. "When things go wrong it's their problem," he said—and obviously not theirs alone. When the Wall Street investment bank screwed up badly enough, its risks became the problem of the United States government. "It's laissez-faire until you get in deep shit," he said, with a half chuckle. He was out of the game. It was now all someone else's fault.

He watched me curiously as I scribbled down his words. "What's this for?" he asked.

I told him that I thought it might be worth revisiting the world I'd described in *Liar's Poker*, now that it was finally dying. Maybe bring out a twentieth anniversary edition.

"That's nauseating," he said.

Hard as it was for him to enjoy my company, it was harder for me not to enjoy his: He was still tough, straight, and blunt as a butcher. He'd helped to create a monster but he still had in him a lot of the old Wall Street, where people said things like "a man's word is his bond." On that Wall Street people didn't walk out of their firms and cause trouble for their former bosses by writing a book about them. "No," he said, "I think we can agree about this: Your fucking book destroyed my career and it made yours." With that, the former king of a former Wall Street lifted the plate that held his appetizer and asked, sweetly, "Would you like a deviled egg?"

Until that moment I hadn't paid much attention to what he'd been eating. Now I saw he'd ordered the best thing in the house, this gorgeous, frothy confection of an earlier age. Who ever dreamed up the deviled egg? Who knew that a simple egg could be made so complicated, and yet so appealing? I reached over and took one. Something for nothing. It never loses its charm.

Afterword

Writing this book I bumped up early and often against a new discomfort: the material would not allow me to do what I naturally would like to do with it. It was as if I'd been asked to play basketball using only my right hand, or write a sonnet using only sight rhymes. It took me a while to understand the problem: I was accustomed to writing stories that were, at heart, comic. The story of the investors who made their fortunes from the collapse of the U.S. financial system had lots of funny bits to it, but it was, at heart, a tragedy.

The story was also "serious" in the sense that important people felt they needed to know about it. The instant the book was published it brought with it another experience new to me: the interest of politicians. In the space of a few months I was asked to address one large room filled with Republican congressmen and another large room filled with Democratic congressmen. Half a dozen U.S. senators phoned to chat, and one even tried to persuade me to testify before his subcommittee. The central bankers of decent-sized foreign countries took an interest in the book, and one even got in touch to discuss it. The Financial Crisis Inquiry Commission, which had been created by Congress to investigate the causes of the collapse, became a kind of pestilence in my life. By the fourth time they called I was closing my eyes and thinking of America. It's not that their work is not important; it is, extremely. It's that I had nothing to add to it outside the pages of this story—and yet they refused to believe me. A book I had thought of mainly as a real-life story so good that its author could only screw it up had somehow become a policy paper on the roots of the financial crisis. The transformation was as mysterious as the journey of the apple from forbidden fruit to daily medicine.

I still find it bewildering. Most of what I knew about the financial crisis I knew from the characters of my book. Yet important people who read it felt the need to talk to me rather than to these people who had firsthand knowledge of events. I became something I naturally am not, an authority. My book had wandered by chance into a vacuum. The U.S. government was finally faced with having to reform Wall Street, or at least to understand it. But Wall Street had grown so complicated that it was virtually impossible for an outsider to understand it without help. After an ordinary financial crisis political leaders typically would turn to the people on Wall Street whom they trusted for advice and education. After this financial crisis there was no one on Wall Street whom they could trust. The sort of people who had once formed the American financial elite had so discredited themselves that U.S. senators no longer believed these people were capable of giving honest advice to their country in its time of need. And so the senators began to read up on the subject for themselves. . . .

The absurdity of the relationship between author and government finally became clear on the sixth call from the Financial Inquiry Commission. It came from a man assigned to formally depose witnesses. It quickly became clear that he knew more than I did about the U.S. financial crisis—that if we were forced to take a test on the subject he would score the higher grade. He was polite about it, though, and kept on asking his questions. An hour or so into the conversation he asked me who else in the U.S. government I had spoken to about the financial crisis. I rattled off the long list of dignitaries I had met in the last few months.

"So what did they tell you?" he asked. (Roughly, I'm doing this from memory.)

"What did *they* tell *me*?"

"Yes, any insights into what happened. Anything that we might pursue."

"No, no, no," I said, "you don't understand: *they* called *me* to ask what happened."

With that, he began to laugh. The air went out of the balloon. The interview with the Financial Inquiry Commission was over. I haven't heard from them since.

In the meantime I have heard from several others. One of the problems with books, from the point of view of people described in them, is how difficult it is to file a formal complaint about them. There are no letters to the editors, at least none that find their way to the reading public. If they existed this book would have elicited at least three worth printing. The first came from Deutsche Bank analyst Eugene Xu, who wrote to me, in English, to express his dismay that readers of Greg Lippmann's description of him ("How can a guy who can't speak English lie?") might put down the book thinking he spoke no English at all. The second came from the founder of Gotham Partners, Joel Greenblatt, who felt that readers might come away thinking ill of him for his treatment of Michael Burry, and wanted the reader to know that (a) he never wanted a fight with Michael Burry, (b) he only asked for his money back from Michael Burry because his own investors were asking for their money back and he needed to get it from somewhere, and (c) Burry did not communicate in a straightforward manner with him or his other investors. The reasons for that are plain from the story.

The third letter came from Ace Greenberg, the eighty-three-year-old former CEO of Bear Stearns and, more importantly, former broker to Cornwall Capital, who didn't like the idea that his former clients thought of him as a remote, almost spectral presence. "I can tell you that I have never been criticized of the way I care, feed, and coddle clients," he wrote. "Hope this negative impression of me is corrected in your next book. I do not intend to sue." To which, in a postscript, he added, "My book comes out on June 1, 2010. I come out fine."

Acknowledgments

My editor at the now deceased *Portfolio*, Kyle Pope, encouraged me at the start, as I set off to retrace my steps back to Wall Street. Brandon Adams generously offered his help digging out strange facts and figures and proved to be so smart about the subject that I half-wondered if perhaps he, instead of I, should be writing the book. Among other treasures he unearthed was A. K. Barnett-Hart, a Harvard undergraduate who had just written a thesis about the market for subprime mortgage–backed CDOs that remains more interesting than any single piece of Wall Street research on the subject. Marc Rosenthal served as my jungle guide in the netherworld of subprime lending, and the inner workings of the rating agencies' models, and could not have been more generous with his time or his insight. Al Zuckerman, at Writers House, represented this book ably, as he has my others. Several people read all or part of this manuscript and offered useful advice: John Seo, Doug Stumpf, my father, Tom Lewis, and my wife, Tabitha Soren. Janet Byrne performed an almost startlingly thorough, energetic, and intelligent job copyediting the manuscript, and also proved to be an ideal reader. Starling Lawrence at W. W. Norton, who has edited all but one of my books, and who edited *Liar's Poker*, was his usual wise and wonderful self.

I've found it impossible to write a decent nonfiction narrative without unusually deep cooperation from my subjects. Steve Eisman, Michael Burry, Charlie Ledley, Jamie Mai, Vincent Daniel, Danny Moses, Porter Collins, and Ben Hockett allowed me to enter their lives. At some unquantifiable risk to themselves, they shared with me their thoughts and feelings. For that I'm eternally grateful.

Index